I0010019

Hands-On Natural Language Processing with Python

A practical guide to applying deep learning architectures to your NLP applications

Rajesh Arumugam
Rajalingappaa Shanmugamani

BIRMINGHAM - MUMBAI

Hands-On Natural Language Processing with Python

Commissioning Editor: Pravin Dhandre
Acquisition Editor: Aman Singh
Content Development Editor: Snehal Kolte
Technical Editor: Sayli Nikalje
Copy Editor: Safis Editing
Project Coordinator: Manthan Patel
Proofreader: Safis Editing
Indexer: Pratik Shirodkar
Graphics: Jisha Chirayil
Production Coordinator: Nilesh Mohite

First published: July 2018

Production reference: 1160718

Published by Packt Publishing Ltd.
Livery Place
35 Livery Street
Birmingham
B3 2PB, UK.

ISBN 978-1-78913-949-5

www.packtpub.com

`mapt.io`

Mapt is an online digital library that gives you full access to over 5,000 books and videos, as well as industry leading tools to help you plan your personal development and advance your career. For more information, please visit our website.

Why subscribe?

- Spend less time learning and more time coding with practical eBooks and Videos from over 4,000 industry professionals

- Improve your learning with Skill Plans built especially for you

- Get a free eBook or video every month

- Mapt is fully searchable

- Copy and paste, print, and bookmark content

PacktPub.com

Did you know that Packt offers eBook versions of every book published, with PDF and ePub files available? You can upgrade to the eBook version at `www.PacktPub.com` and as a print book customer, you are entitled to a discount on the eBook copy. Get in touch with us at `service@packtpub.com` for more details.

At `www.PacktPub.com`, you can also read a collection of free technical articles, sign up for a range of free newsletters, and receive exclusive discounts and offers on Packt books and eBooks.

Foreword

Intelligent digital assistants in form of voice transcription, machine translation, conversational agents, and sentiment analysis are ubiquitously applied across various domains to facilitate human-computer interactions. Chatbot's are becoming an integrated part of any website; while virtual assistants are gaining more popularity in homes and office spaces. Consequently, given numerous existing resources that contain these topics under the notion of **natural language processing (NLP)**, a contribution that covers a comprehensive guide to the fundamentals and the state-of-the-art, and on top of that includes practical examples with most popular frameworks and tool kits, is a rare find.

When I was first asked to write the foreword for this book, I was very delighted to convey the level of passion that drove the authors to write it, and yet was uncertain on how to best present an excellent source of up-to-date knowledge and a practical handbook of **machine learning (ML)** for NLP that truly stands out from the crowd.

The leading authors' reputation in ML needs no further explanation. With both equipped with academic education in world-class universities and many years of leadership in ML development, Rajesh and Rajalingappa's qualification to lead the authorship of this book is confirmed. I have come to know them not only as knowledgeable individuals but also as passionate educators who convey the most sophisticated concepts in the simplest words. Raja's passion to help start-ups get off the ground and to offer his expertise to young companies with an open heart is admirable. I'm sure that, even as readers of this book, you can approach him for questions and be sure of a convincing response.

The book itself is very well organized and written to serve the purpose. From concrete examples to explain the fundamentals to code snippets for guiding readers with different levels of deep learning backgrounds, the chapters are structured to retain full attention of the reader all throughout. You will discover an exciting combination of the most popular techniques and state-of-the-art approaches to text processing and classification.

By reading this book, you can expect to learn how to perform common NLP tasks, such as preprocessing and exploratory analysis of text using the Python's Natural Language Toolkit. You will understand deep neural networks, Google's TensorFlow framework, and the building blocks of **recurrent neural networks (RNNs)**, including Long Short-Term Memory. And you will grasp the notion of word embeddings to allow for semantics in context.

Having taught the basics, the book further takes you through the development of architectures and deep neural network models for a variety of applications, including text classification, text generation and summarization, question-answering, language translation, speech recognition, and text-to-speech.

The book concludes by presenting various methods to deploy a trained model for NLP tasks, on a variety of platforms. By the end of your experience with the book, you will have learned the data science paradigm in NLP and can hopefully deploy deep learning models in commercial applications in a production environment as the authors envisioned.

Maryam Azh, PhD
Founder of Overlay Technologies

Contributors

About the authors

Rajesh Arumugam is an ML developer at SAP, Singapore. Previously, he developed ML solutions for smart city development in areas such as passenger flow analysis in public transit systems and optimization of energy consumption in buildings when working with Centre for Social Innovation at Hitachi Asia, Singapore. He has published papers in conferences and has pending patents in storage and ML. He holds a PhD in computer engineering from Nanyang Technological University, Singapore.

> *I would like to thank my wife Priya and my wonderful children: Akash and Akila for their support and understanding while writing this book. Special thanks to Raja for providing the opportunity to co-write this book.*

Rajalingappaa Shanmugamani is a deep learning lead at SAP, Singapore. Previously, he worked and consulted at various start-ups for developing computer vision products. He has a masters from IIT Madras, where his thesis was based on applications of computer vision in manufacturing. He has published articles in peer-reviewed journals and conferences and applied for a few patents in ML. In his spare time, he teaches programming and machine learning to school students and engineers.

> *I thank my spouse, Ezhil, my family, and friends for their immense support. I thank all the teachers, colleagues, managers, and mentors from whom I have learned a lot.*

Karthik Muthusamy works for SAP, Singapore, as an ML researcher. He has designed and developed ML solutions for problems ranging from algorithms that guide autonomous vehicles to understanding semantic meanings of sentences in documents. He is currently a Google Developer Expert in ML. He gives talks and conducts workshops on ML for the developer community with an aim of reducing the entry barriers to developing ML applications. He graduated from Nanyang Technological University, Singapore, with a PhD in computer engineering.

Chaitanya Joshi is working towards obtaining a bachelor's in Computer Science from Nanyang Technological University in 2019. He has experience in building deep learning solutions for automatic accounting at SAP, Singapore, and conversational chatbots at Evie.ai. He is also a research assistant with the dialog systems group at Laboratory of Artificial Intelligence, Swiss Federal Institute of Technology, Lausanne (EPFL). His research at EPFL was recently published the Conference on Neural Information Processing Systems (NIPS 2017) in Los Angeles.

I would like to thank all my mentors and colleagues over the years for guiding me in my endeavors and patiently answering my questions.

Auguste Byiringiro is an ML developer at SAP, Singapore, in the cash application team. Previously, he mainly worked in healthcare. At GE Healthcare, he built deep learning models to detect diseases in CT images. Then at Fibronostics, a start-up focused on non-invasive medical diagnosis, he heavily contributed to two products: LiverFASt, an ML-based tool to diagnose fatty liver disease, and HealthFACTR, a data-driven algorithm used by Gravity-Fitness First in Singapore to optimize the fitness, diet, and long-term health of its members.

I would like to thank Raja Shanmugamani, who gave me the opportunity to contribute to this book, as well as all the people who supported me while I was co-writing the book.

About the reviewer

Chintan Gajjar is an associate senior consultant in KNOWARTH Technologies. He has played dynamic roles during his career in developing ERP, search engines with Python, **Single-Page Applications (SPA)**, and mobile apps with Node.js, MongoDB, and AngularJS.

He received multiple awards in recognition of his valuable contributions to the team and the company. He has also contributed to the books *Hadoop Backup and Recovery Solutions*, *MySQL 8 for Big Data*, and *MySQL 8 Administrator's Guide*. He has a master's in computer applications from Ganpat University.

> *It's a great experience reviewing this book with the Packt team. I would like to thank the wonderful team at Packt for this effort. I would also like to thank Chintan Mehta, my office colleagues, and my family, who invested their time directly or indirectly to support me throughout the reviewing of this book. I also want to thank all the authors of this book.*

Packt is searching for authors like you

If you're interested in becoming an author for Packt, please visit `authors.packtpub.com` and apply today. We have worked with thousands of developers and tech professionals, just like you, to help them share their insight with the global tech community. You can make a general application, apply for a specific hot topic that we are recruiting an author for, or submit your own idea.

Table of Contents

Preface

Before the advent of deep learning, traditional **natural language processing** (**NLP**) approaches had been widely used in tasks such as spam filtering, sentiment classification, and **part of speech** (**POS**) tagging. These classic approaches utilized statistical characteristics of sequences such as word count and co-occurrence, as well as simple linguistic features. However, the main disadvantage of these techniques was that they could not capture complex linguistic characteristics, such as context and intra-word dependencies.

Recent developments in neural networks and deep learning have given us powerful new tools to match human-level performance on NLP tasks and build products that deal with natural language. Deep learning for NLP is centered around the concept of word embeddings or vectors, also known as Word2vec, which encapsulate the meanings of words and phrases as dense vector representations. Word vectors, which are able to capture semantic information about words better than traditional one-hot representations, allow us to handle the temporal nature of language in an intuitive way when used in combination with a class of neural networks known as **recurrent neural networks** (**RNNs**). While RNNs can capture only local word dependencies, recently proposed vector-based operations for attention and alignment over word vector sequences allow neural networks to model global intra-word dependencies, including context. Due to their capability to model the syntax and semantics of language, strong empirical performance, and ability to generalize to new data, neural networks have become the go-to model for building highly sophisticated commercial products, such as search engines, translation services, and dialog systems.

This book introduces the basic building blocks of deep learning models for NLP and explores cutting-edge techniques from recent literature. We take a problem-based approach, where we introduce new models as solutions to various NLP tasks. Our focus is on providing practical code implementations in Python that can be applied to your use cases to bring human capabilities into your applications.

Who this book is for

This book is intended for developers who want to leverage NLP techniques to develop intelligent applications with rich human-centric interfaces. The book assumes introductory knowledge of **machine learning** (**ML**) or deep learning and intermediate Python programming skills. Our aim is to introduce cutting-edge techniques for NLP tasks, such as sentiment detection, conversational systems, language translation, speech-to-text, and much more, using the TensorFlow framework and Python.

The reader will go from the basic concepts of deep learning to state-of-the-art algorithms and best practices for dealing with natural language. Our focus is on implementing applications using real-world data and deploying deep learning models to add human capabilities to commercial applications in a production environment.

What this book covers

Chapter 1, *Getting Started*, explores the basic concepts of NLP and the various problems it tries to solve. We also look at some of the real-world applications to give the reader the feeling of the wide range of applications that leverage NLP.

Chapter 2, *Text Classification and POS Tagging Using NLTK*, introduces the popular NLTK Python library. We will be using NLTK to describe basic NLP tasks, such as tokenizing, stemming, tagging, and classic text classification. We also explore POS tagging with NLTK. We provide the reader with the tools and techniques necessary to prepare data for input into deep learning models.

Chapter 3, *Deep Learning and TensorFlow*, introduces the basic concepts of deep learning. This chapter will also help the reader to set up the environment and tools such as TensorFlow. At the end of the chapter, the reader will get an understanding of basic deep learning concepts, such as CNN, RNN, LSTM, attention-based models, and problems in NLP.

Chapter 4, *Semantic Embedding Using Shallow Models*, explores how to identify semantic relationships between words in a document, and in the process, we obtain a vector representation for words in a corpus. The chapter describes developing word embedding models, such as CBOW using neural networks. It also describes techniques for developing neural network models to obtain document vectors. At the end of this chapter, the reader will get familiar with training embeddings for word, sentence, and document; and visualize simple networks.

Chapter 5, *Text Classification Using LSTM*, discusses various approaches for classifying text, a specific application of which is to classify sentiments of words or phrases in a document. The chapter introduces the problem of text classification. Following this, we describe techniques for developing deep learning models using CNNs and LSTMs. The chapter also explains transfer learning for text classification using pretrained word embeddings. At the end, the reader will get familiar with implementing deep learning models for sentiment classification, spam detection, and using pretrained word embeddings for his/her classification task.

Chapter 6, *Searching and Deduplicating Using CNNs*, covers the problems of searching, matching and deduplicating documents and approaches used in solving them. The chapter describes developing deep learning models for searching text in a corpus. At the end of this chapter, you will learn to implement a CNN-based deep learning model for searching and deduplicating text.

Chapter 7, *Named Entity Recognition Using Character LSTM*, describes methods and approaches to perform **Named Entity Recognition** (**NER**), a sub-task of information extraction, to locate and classify entities in text of a document. The chapter introduces the problem of NER and the applications where it can be used. We then explain the implementation of a deep learning model using character-based LSTM for identifying named entities trained using labeled datasets.

Chapter 8, *Text Generation and Summarization Using GRUs*, covers the methods used for the task of generating text, an extension of which can be used to create summaries from text data. We then explain the implementation of a deep learning model for generating text. This is followed by a description of implementing GRU-based deep learning models to summarize text. At the end of this chapter, the reader will learn the techniques of implementing deep learning models for text generation and summarization.

Chapter 9, *Question-Answering and Chatbots Using Memory Networks*, describes how to train a deep learning model to answer questions and extend it to build a chatbot. The chapter introduces the problem of question answering and the approaches used in building an answering engine using deep learning models. We then describe how to leverage a question-answering engine to build a chatbot capable of answering questions like a conversation. At the end of this chapter, you will be able to implement an interactive chatbot.

Chapter 10, *Machine Translation Using Attention-Based Models*, covers various methods for translating text from one language to another, without the need to learn the grammar structure of either language. The chapter introduces traditional machine translation approaches, such as **Hidden Markov Model** (**HMM**) based methods. We then explain the implementation of an encoder-decoder model with attention for translating text from French to the English language. At the end of this chapter, the reader will be able to implement deep learning models for translating text.

Chapter 11, *Speech Recognition Using Deep Speech*, describes the problem of converting voice to text, as a beginning of a conversational interface. The chapter begins with feature extraction from speech data. This is followed by a brief introduction of the deep speech architecture. We then explain the detailed implementation of the Deep Speech architecture to transcribe speech to text. At the end of this chapter, the reader will be equipped with the knowledge to implement a speech-to-text deep learning model.

Chapter 12, *Text to Speech Using Tacotron*, describes the problem of converting text to speech. The chapter describes the implementation of the Tacotron model to convert text to voice. At the end, the reader will get familiar with the implementation of a text-to-speech model based on the Tacotron architecture.

Chapter 13, *Deploying Trained Models*, is the concluding chapter and describes model deployments in various cloud and mobile platforms.

To get the most out of this book

The prerequisites for the book are basic knowledge of ML or deep learning and intermediate Python skills, although both are not mandatory. We have given a brief introduction to deep learning, touching upon topics such as multi-layer perceptrons, **Convolutional Neural Networks** (**CNNs**), and RNNs in Chapter 1, *Getting Started*. It would be helpful if the reader knows general ML concepts, such as overfitting and model regularization, and classical models, such as linear regression and random forest. In more advanced chapters, the reader might encounter in-depth code walkthroughs that expect at least a basic level of Python programming experience.

All the code examples in the book can be downloaded from the code book repository as described in the next section. The examples mainly utilize open source tools and open data repositories, and were written for Python 3.5 or higher. The major libraries that are extensively used throughout the book are TensorFlow and NLTK. Detailed installation instructions for these packages can be found in Chapter 1, *Getting Started*, and Chapter 2, *Text Classification and POS Tagging Using NLTK*, respectively. Though a GPU is not required for the examples to run, it is advisable to have a system that has one. We recommend training models from the second half of the book on a GPU, as more complicated tasks involve bigger models and larger datasets.

Download the example code files

You can download the example code files for this book from your account at www.packtpub.com. If you purchased this book elsewhere, you can visit www.packtpub.com/support and register to have the files emailed directly to you.

You can download the code files by following these steps:

1. Log in or register at www.packtpub.com.
2. Select the **SUPPORT** tab.
3. Click on **Code Downloads & Errata**.
4. Enter the name of the book in the **Search** box and follow the onscreen instructions.

Once the file is downloaded, please make sure that you unzip or extract the folder using the latest version of:

- WinRAR/7-Zip for Windows
- Zipeg/iZip/UnRarX for Mac
- 7-Zip/PeaZip for Linux

The code bundle for the book is also hosted on GitHub at https://github.com/PacktPublishing/Hands-On-Natural-Language-Processing-with-Python. In case there's an update to the code, it will be updated on the existing GitHub repository.

We also have other code bundles from our rich catalog of books and videos available at https://github.com/PacktPublishing/. Check them out!

Download the color images

We also provide a PDF file that has color images of the screenshots/diagrams used in this book. You can download it here: https://www.packtpub.com/sites/default/files/downloads/HandsOnNaturalLanguageProcessingwithPython_ColorImages.pdf.

Conventions used

There are a number of text conventions used throughout this book.

`CodeInText`: Indicates code words in text, database table names, folder names, filenames, file extensions, pathnames, dummy URLs, user input, and Twitter handles. Here is an example: "The `pip` installer can be used to install NLTK, with an optional installation of `numpy`."

A block of code is set as follows:

```
>>> large_words = dict([(k,v) for k,v in frequency_dist.items() if
len(k)>3])
>>> frequency_dist = nltk.FreqDist(large_words)
>>> frequency_dist.plot(50,cumulative=False)
```

Any command-line input or output is written as follows:

```
import nltk
nltk.download()
```

Bold: Indicates a new term, an important word, or words that you see onscreen. For example, words in menus or dialog boxes appear in the text like this. Here is an example: "Navigate to **stopwords** and install it for future use."

Warnings or important notes appear like this.

Tips and tricks appear like this.

Get in touch

Feedback from our readers is always welcome.

General feedback: Email feedback@packtpub.com and mention the book title in the subject of your message. If you have questions about any aspect of this book, please email us at questions@packtpub.com.

Errata: Although we have taken every care to ensure the accuracy of our content, mistakes do happen. If you have found a mistake in this book, we would be grateful if you would report this to us. Please visit www.packtpub.com/submit-errata, selecting your book, clicking on the Errata Submission Form link, and entering the details.

Piracy: If you come across any illegal copies of our works in any form on the Internet, we would be grateful if you would provide us with the location address or website name. Please contact us at copyright@packtpub.com with a link to the material.

If you are interested in becoming an author: If there is a topic that you have expertise in and you are interested in either writing or contributing to a book, please visit authors.packtpub.com.

Reviews

Please leave a review. Once you have read and used this book, why not leave a review on the site that you purchased it from? Potential readers can then see and use your unbiased opinion to make purchase decisions, we at Packt can understand what you think about our products, and our authors can see your feedback on their book. Thank you!

For more information about Packt, please visit packtpub.com.

Getting Started 1

Natural language processing (**NLP**) is the field of understanding human language using computers. It involves the analysis and of large volumes of natural language data using computers to glean meaning and value for consumption in real-world applications. While NLP has been around since the 1950s, there has been tremendous growth in practical applications in the area, due to recent advances in **machine learning** (**ML**) and deep learning. The majority of this book will focus on various real-world applications of NLP, such as **text classification**, and sub-tasks of NLP, such as **Named Entity Recognition** (**NER**), with a particular emphasis on deep learning approaches. In this chapter, we will first introduce the basic concepts and terms in NLP. Following this, we will discuss some of the currently used applications that leverage NLP.

Basic concepts and terminologies in NLP

The following are some of the important terminologies and concepts in NLP mostly related to the language data. Getting familiar with these terms and concepts will help the reader in getting up to speed in understanding the contents in later chapters of the book:

- Text corpus or corpora
- Paragraph
- Sentences
- Phrases and words
- N-grams
- Bag-of-words

We will explain these in the following sections.

Text corpus or corpora

The language data that all NLP tasks depend upon is called the text corpus or simply corpus. A corpus is a large set of text data that can be in one of the languages like English, French, and so on. The corpus can consist of a single document or a bunch of documents. The source of the text corpus can be social network sites like Twitter, blog sites, open discussion forums like Stack Overflow, books, and several others. In some of the tasks like machine translation, we would require a multilingual corpus. For example we might need both the English and French translations of the same document content for developing a machine translation model. For speech tasks, we would also need human voice recordings and the corresponding transcribed corpus.

In most of the later chapters, we will be using text corpus and speech recordings available from the internet or open source data repositories. For many of the NLP task, the corpus is split into chunks for further analysis. These chunks could be at the paragraph, sentence, or word level. We will touch upon these in the following sections.

Paragraph

A paragraph is the largest unit of text handled by an NLP task. Paragraph level boundaries by itself may not be much use unless broken down into sentences. Though sometimes the paragraph may be considered as context boundaries. Tokenizers that can split a document into paragraphs are available in some of the Python libraries. We will look at such tokenizers in later chapters.

Sentences

Sentences are the next level of lexical unit of language data. A sentence encapsulates a complete meaning or thought and context. It is usually extracted from a paragraph based on boundaries determined by punctuations like period. The sentence may also convey opinion or sentiment expressed in it. In general, sentences consists of **parts of speech** (POS) entities like nouns, verbs, adjectives, and so on. There are tokenizers available to split paragraphs to sentences based on punctuations.

Phrases and words

Phrases are a group of consecutive words within a sentence that can convey a specific meaning. For example, in the sentence *Tomorrow is going to be a rainy day* the part *going to be a rainy day* expresses a specific thought. Some of the NLP tasks extract key phrases from sentences for search and retrieval applications. The next smallest unit of text is the word. The common tokenizers split sentences into text based on punctuations like spaces and comma. One of the problems with NLP is ambiguity in the meaning of same words used in different context. We will later see how this is handled well when we discuss word embeddings.

N-grams

A sequence of characters or words forms an N-gram. For example, character unigram consists of a single character, a bigram consists of a sequence of two characters and so on. Similarly word N-grams consists of a sequence of *n* words. In NLP, N-grams are used as features for tasks like text classification.

Bag-of-words

Bag-of-words in contrast to N-grams does not consider word order or sequence. It captures the word occurrence frequencies in the text corpus. Bag-of-words is also used as features in tasks like sentiment analysis and topic identification.

In the following sections, we will look at an overview of the following applications of NLP:

- Analyzing sentiment
- Recognizing named entities
- Linking entities
- Translating text
- Natural language interfaces
- Semantic Role Labeling
- Relation extraction
- SQL query generation, or semantic parsing
- Machine Comprehension
- Textual entailment
- Coreference resolution
- Searching

- Question answering and chatbots
- Converting text to voice
- Converting voice to text
- Speaker identification
- Spoken dialog systems
- Other applications

Applications of NLP

In this section, we will provide an overview of the major applications of NLP. While the topics listed here are not quite exhaustive, they will give the reader a sense of the wide range of applications where NLP is used.

Analyzing sentiment

The sentiment in a sentence or text reflects the overall positive, negative, or neutral opinion or thought of the person who produces or consumes it. It indicates whether a person is happy, unhappy, or neutral about the subject or context that describes the text. It can be quantified as a discrete value, such as 1 for happy, -1 for unhappy, and 0 for neutral, or it can be quantified on a continuous scale of values, from 0-1. Sentiment analysis, therefore, is the process of deriving this value from a piece of text that can be obtained from different data sources, such as social networks, product reviews, news articles, and so on. One real-world application of sentiment analysis is in social network data to derive actionable insights, such as customer satisfaction, product or brand popularity, fashion trends, and so on. The screenshot that follows shows one of the applications of sentiment analysis, in capturing the overall opinion of a particular news article about Google. The reader may refer to the application, or API, from Google Cloud at `https://cloud.google.com/natural-language/`:

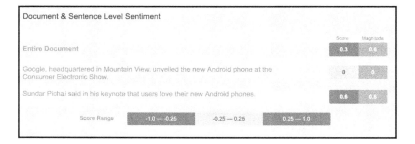

The preceding screenshot indicates that sentiment data is captured for the whole document, as well as at the individual sentence level.

Recognizing named entities

NER is a type of text annotation task. In NER, words or tokens in a piece of text are labeled or annotated into categories, such as organizations, locations, people, and so on. In effect, NER converts unstructured text data into structured data that can later be used for further analysis. The following screenshot is a visualization from the Google Cloud API. The reader can try out the API with the link provided in the preceding subsection:

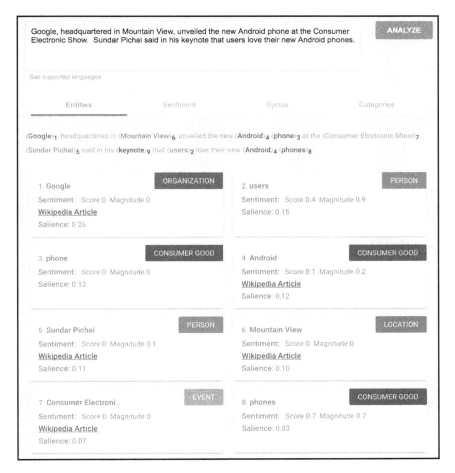

The output result in the preceding screenshot shows how the different entities, such as **ORGANISATION (Google)**, **PERSON (Sundar Pitchai)**, **EVENT (CONSUMER ELECTRONICS SHOW)**, and so on, are automatically extracted from the unstructured raw text by NER. The output also gives the sentiment for each label or category, based on sentiment analysis. The reader can experiment with different text using the link provided earlier. When we click on the **Categories** tab, we can see the following:

Entities	Sentiment	Syntax	Categories
/Computers & Electronics		/Internet & Telecom/Mobile & Wireless	
Confidence: 0.61		Confidence: 0.53	
/News			
Confidence: 0.53			

The preceding screenshot shows how the system also classifies a particular piece of text into **Computer & Electronics**, **News**, and so on, using the recognized named entities in the text. Such a categorization, called **topic modeling,** is another important NLP task, used to identify the main theme or topic of a sentence or document.

Linking entities

Another practical application is **entity linking**. One good example of it can be found in the Microsoft Azure Text Analytics API, at `https://azure.microsoft.com/is-is/services/cognitive-services/text-analytics/`. The following screenshot shows output from a sample text:

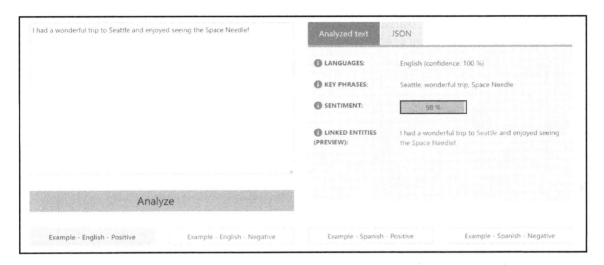

The preceding screenshot shows how the system has automatically extracted the entity **Seattle** as a place. Interestingly, it has also correctly extracted **the Space Needle** as a landmark place, by linking it with **Seattle**. This shows how powerful named entity linking can be when extracting useful relationships between entities.

Translating text

Machine translation is the task of translating a given piece of text from one language to another target language. The language of the task is first identified, and then translated into the target language. The translation app from Google has proven very useful for traveling and has taken down language barriers. The latest techniques have improved the translation accuracy by a large margin.

Following is an example of translation from **Chinese** to **English**, using Google Translate at `https://cloud.google.com/translate/`:

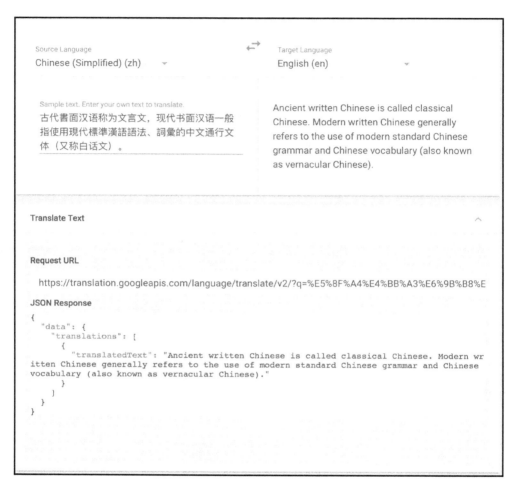

The preceding screenshot also shows the JSON response of the translated text, when we use the Translation API service from Google (`https://cdn-images-1.medium.com/max/1600/1*3f414lrLFFhgvVsvjhNzAQ.jpeg`).

Natural Language Inference

Natural Language Inference (**NLI**) tasks classify the relationship between a premise and hypothesis. During inference, a premise and hypothesis are given as input to output whether a hypothesis is true based on a given premise.

Semantic Role Labeling

Semantic Role Labeling (**SRL**) determines the relationship between a given sentence and a predicate, such as a verb. Sometimes, the inference is provided as a question. An example of a role might be: where or when did something happen? The following is a visualization from `http://demo.allennlp.org/semantic-role-labeling`:

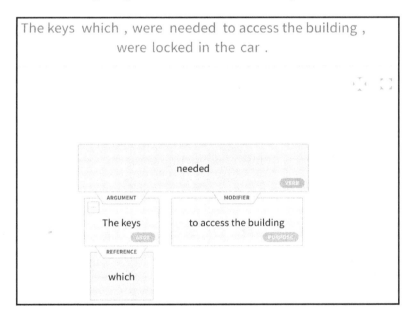

The preceding visualization shows semantic labeling, which created semantic associations between the different pieces of text, such as **The keys** being **needed** for the purpose **to access the building**. The reader may experiment with different examples using the URL link provided earlier.

Relation extraction

Relation extraction predicts a relationship when a text and type of relation are provided. There may be cases where the relationships can't be extracted. The following screenshot shows an example of relation extraction, based on predicates and objects:

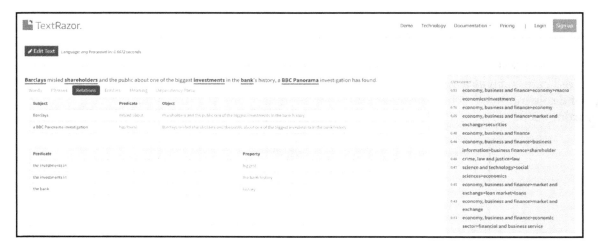

Example of relation extraction

The preceding example shows relationship extraction from the sample text to a subject, a predicate, and objects.

SQL query generation, or semantic parsing

Semantic parsing helps to convert a natural language into SQL queries in order to query a database. The following screenshot shows an example of converting a free text query to a DBpedia database SPARQL query, which is quite similar to SQL:

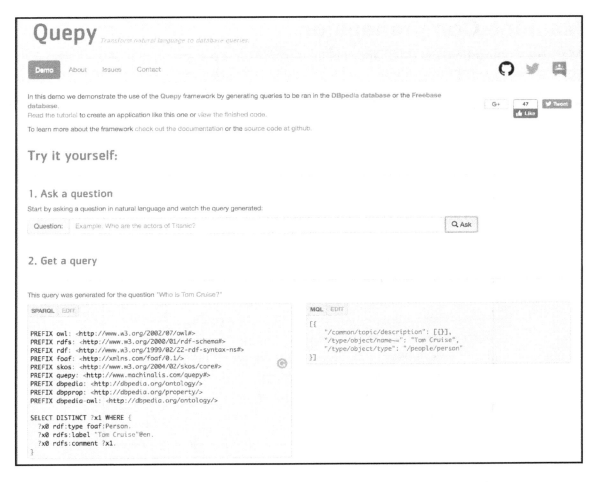

The preceding visualization shows the query **Who is Tom Cruise**, converted into a SPARQL query at the bottom. You can experiment with other queries at `http://quepy.machinalis.com/`.

Machine Comprehension

Machine Comprehension (MC) answers questions from a paragraph. It is akin to school children doing comprehension tests. The following screenshot is a visualization from `http://demo.allennlp.org/machine-comprehension`, for the question **Who stars in The Matrix?** The answer is shown in the screenshot, along with the paragraph:

Answer

Keanu Reeves, Laurence Fishburne, Carrie-Anne Moss, Hugo Weaving, and Joe Pantoliano

Passage Context

The Matrix is a 1999 science fiction action film written and directed by The Wachowskis, starring Keanu Reeves, Laurence Fishburne, Carrie-Anne Moss, Hugo Weaving, and Joe Pantoliano . It depicts a dystopian future in which reality as perceived by most humans is actually a simulated reality called "the Matrix", created by sentient machines to subdue the human population, while their bodies' heat and electrical activity are used as an energy source. Computer programmer "Neo" learns this truth and is drawn into a rebellion against the machines, which involves other people who have been freed from the "dream world."

We can also see a visualization of how the model works, by highlighting certain words:

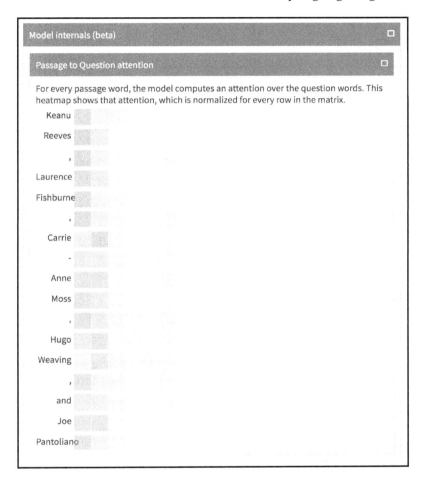

Textual Entailment

Textual Entailment (**TE**) predicts whether the facts in different texts are the same. The following is a visualization from `http://demo.allennlp.org/textual-entailment`:

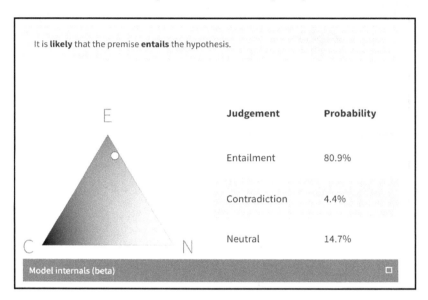

The premise is: **If you help the needy, God will reward you.** The hypothesis is: **Giving money to the poor has good consequences**. The probabilities of **Entailment**, **Contradiction**, and **Neutral** are presented.

Coreference resolution

Pronoun resolution resolves the pronouns in a text when there are several people interacting. The following is a visualization from `http://demo.allennlp.org/coreference-resolution`:

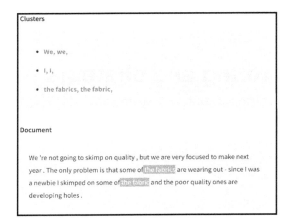

Searching

Searching websites for information is an integral part of accessing the internet, and is an application of NLP. The search services are provided by Bing API, from `https://azure.` `microsoft.com/en-us/services/cognitive-services/bing-web-search-api/`:

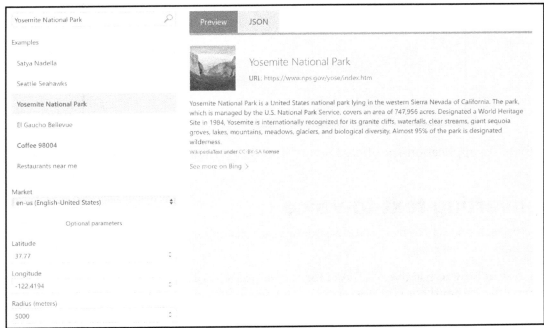

Search results displaying Yosemite National Park

Search APIs can be integrated with applications for a better user experience.

Question answering and chatbots

For question answering systems, a context is supplied with a question in order to generate an answer. The schema of a chatbot is shown in the following screenshot from `https://aws.amazon.com/lex/details/`:

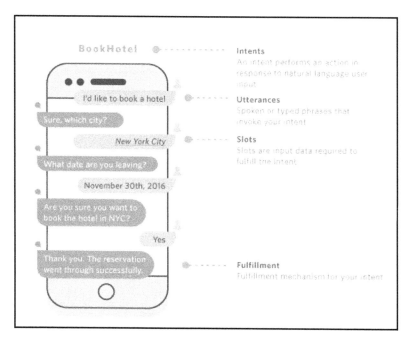

Chatbots are application-specific, as integration varies among applications.

Converting text-to-voice

Sometimes, a text has to be converted into a voice. It can be useful for a personal bot to speak back to a user.

Let's look at how to use the AWS API for text-to-speech Amazon Polly. With the API, you can pass the text and convert it to speech. The audio file can be either streamed or downloaded.

The voice should be natural sounding, to connect with the user. Google can provide this in 30 different voices, in 12 different languages. The speed and pitch can be adjusted. Go to `https://cloud.google.com/text-to-speech/` and try out a demo. The following screenshot shows an example; all of the parameters can be tuned:

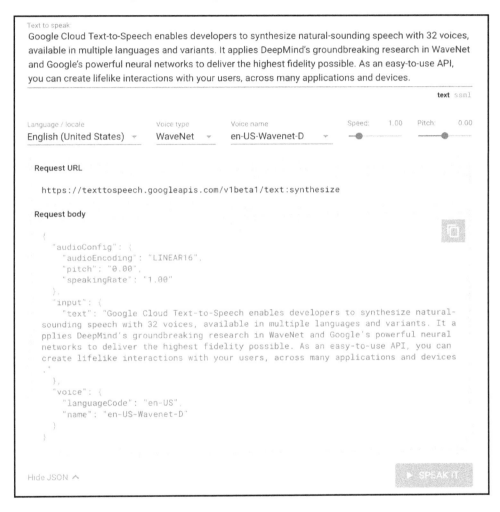

Tuning of parameters

The requests can be sent from any connected device, such as a mobile, car, TV, and so on. It can be used for customer service, presenting educational text, or for animation content.

Converting voice-to-text

Sometimes, a voice has to be converted to text. This is a speech recognition problem. The Google speech recognition system works in 120 languages. The audio can be streamed, or a prerecorded video can be sent. Formatting can be done for different categories, such as proper nouns and punctuation. The following example is from `https://cloud.google.com/speech-to-text/`:

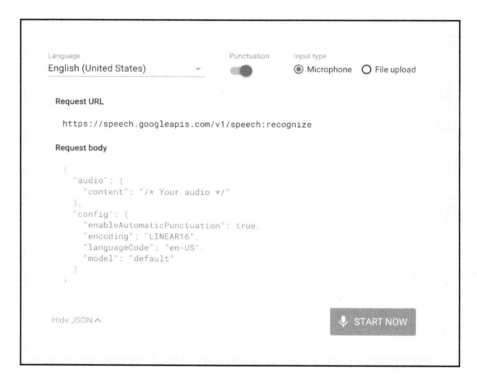

There are different models provided, for videos, phone calls, and search-based audio. This works even when there is background noise, and the system can filter inappropriate content.

Speaker identification

Speaker identification is the task of finding the name of the person that is speaking. Check out a demo at `https://azure.microsoft.com/en-us/services/cognitive-services/speaker-recognition/#identification`:

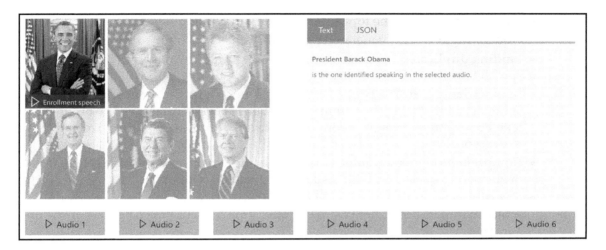

The voices of several people can be identified with audio clips.

Spoken dialog systems

Home assistants, such as Google Voice, Apple's Siri, and Amazon's Alexa, are examples of spoken dialog systems. All of the applications, such as chatbots, voice-to-text, text-to-voice, speaker identification, and searching, can be combined to form the experience of spoken dialog systems.

Other applications

There are several other applications of NLP; the following is a list of some of them:

- **Detecting spam**: The emails that we receive can be classified as spam or not spam.
- **News classification**: It can be useful to classify a news item based on several categories.
- **Identifying the speakers, gender, or age**: From a piece of text, the writer's gender and age can be detected. Similar attributes can be marked with voice data.

- **Discovering topics**: The topics of an article can be identified.
- **Generating text**: Text generated by machines has a lot of interesting applications.
- **Finding duplicates**: Skype has launched a live translation feature that involves speech to text, machine translation, and text-to-speech.
- **Summarizing text**: The summarization task takes a text as input and outputs a summary of that text. The summary is usually much shorter than the original text. For example, after a meeting, the transcript text can be summarized and sent to everyone.
- **Comprehending paragraphs**: Paragraph comprehension is the high school task of answering questions, with respect to a given piece of prose.
- **Constituency parsing**: Constituency parsing predicts a tree composition of a sentence into its constituents http://demo.allennlp.org/constituency-parsing.

Summary

In this chapter, you learned the basics of NLP and saw several applications where it can be useful. You saw some APIs provided by cloud providers that are used to access NLP applications. Having seen the cloud products, you will learn the science behind the applications in future chapters.

In the next chapter, we will look at the basics of the NLTK library. We will cover basic feature engineering and will program a simple task for text classification.

2
Text Classification and POS Tagging Using NLTK

The **Natural Language Toolkit** (**NLTK**) is a Python library for handling **natural language processing** (**NLP**) tasks, ranging from segmenting words or sentences to performing advanced tasks, such as parsing grammar and classifying text. NLTK provides several modules and interfaces to work on natural language, useful for tasks such as document topic identification, **parts of speech** (**POS**) tagging, sentiment analysis, and so on. For experimentation with various NLP tasks, NLTK also includes modules for a wide range of text corpora, from basic text collections to tagged and structured texts, such as **WordNet**. While the NLTK library provides a vast set of APIs, we will only cover the most important aspects that are commonly used in practical NLP applications.

We will cover the following topics in this chapter:

- Installing NLTK and its modules
- Text preprocessing and exploratory analysis
- Exploratory analysis of text
- POS tagging
- Training a sentiment classifier for movie reviews
- Training a bag-of-words classifier

Installing NLTK and its modules

Before getting started with the examples, we will set the system up with NLTK and other dependent Python libraries. The `pip` installer can be used to install NLTK, with an optional installation of `numpy`, as follows:

```
sudo pip install -U nltk
sudo pip install -U numpy
```

The NLTK corpora and various modules can be installed by using the common NLTK downloader in the Python interactive shell or a Jupyter Notebook, shown as follows:

```
import nltk
nltk.download()
```

The preceding command will open an **NLTK Downloader**, as follows. Select the packages or collections that are required:

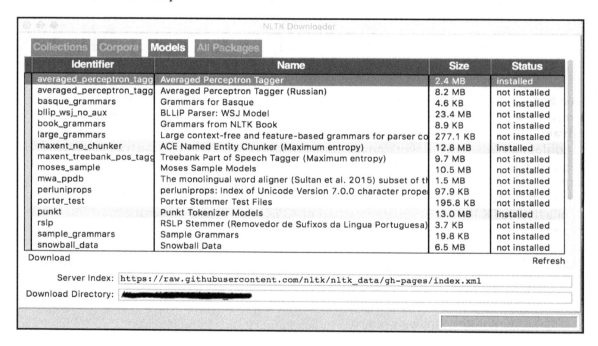

As shown in the preceding screenshot, specific collections, text corpora, NLTK models, or packages, can be selected and installed. Navigate to **stopwords** and install it for future use. The following is a list of modules that are required for this chapter's examples:

No	Package Name	Description
1	brown	Brown text corpus
2	gutenberg	Gutenberg text corpus
3	max_ne_chunker	Module for text chunking
4	movie_reviews	Movie review sentiment polarity data
5	product_reviews_1	Basic product reviews corpus
6	punkt	Word and sentence tokenizer modules

7	treebank	Penn Treebank dataset sample
8	twitter_samples	Twitter messages sample
9	universal_tagset	Universal POS tag mapping
10	webtext	Web text corpus
11	wordnet	WordNet corpus
12	words	Word list

Text preprocessing and exploratory analysis

First, we will provide a hands-on overview of NLTK by working on some basic NLP tasks, such as text preprocessing and exploratory analysis. The text preprocessing step involves tasks such as **tokenization**, **stemming**, and **stop word removal**. An exploratory analysis of prepared text data can be performed to understand its main characteristics, such as the main topic of the text and word frequency distributions.

Tokenization

Word tokens are the basic units of text involved in any NLP task. The first step, when processing text, is to split it into tokens. NLTK provides different types of **tokenizers** for doing this. We will look at how to tokenize Twitter comments from the Twitter samples corpora, available in NLTK. From now on, all of the illustrated code can be run by using the standard Python interpreter on the command line:

```
>>> import nltk
>>> from nltk.corpus import twitter_samples as ts
>>> ts.fileids()
['negative_tweets.json', 'positive_tweets.json', 'tweets.20150430-
223406.json']
>>> samples_tw = ts.strings('tweets.20150430-223406.json')
>>> samples_tw[20]
"@BOMBSKARE the anti-Scottish feeling is largely a product of Tory press
scaremongering. In practice most people won't give a toss!"
>>> from nltk.tokenize import word_tokenize as wtoken
>>> wtoken(samples_tw[20])
['@', 'BOMBSKARE', 'the', 'anti-Scottish', 'feeling', 'is', 'largely', 'a',
'product', 'of', 'Tory', 'press', 'scaremongering', '.', 'In', 'practice',
'most', 'people', 'wo', "n't", 'give', 'a', 'toss', '!']
```

To split text based on punctuation and white spaces, NLTK provides the `wordpunct_tokenize` tokenizer. This will also tokenize the punctuation characters. This step is illustrated in the following code:

```
>>> samples_tw[20]
"@BOMBSKARE the anti-Scottish feeling is largely a product of Tory press
scaremongering. In practice most people won't give a toss!"
>>> wordpunct_tokenize(samples_tw[20])
['@', 'BOMBSKARE', 'the', 'anti', '-', 'Scottish', 'feeling', 'is',
'largely', 'a', 'product', 'of', 'Tory', 'press', 'scaremongering', '.',
'In', 'practice', 'most', 'people', 'won', "'", 't', 'give', 'a', 'toss',
'!']
```

As you can see, some of the words between hyphens are also tokenized as well as other punctuations mark, compared to the `word_tokenize`. We can build custom tokenizers using NLTK's regular expression tokenizer, as shown in the following code:

```
>>> from nltk import regexp_tokenize
>>> patn = '\w+'
>>> regexp_tokenize(samples_tw[20],patn)
['BOMBSKARE', 'the', 'anti', 'Scottish', 'feeling', 'is', 'largely', 'a',
'product', 'of', 'Tory', 'press', 'scaremongering', 'In', 'practice',
'most', 'people', 'won', 't', 'give', 'a', 'toss']
```

In the preceding code, we used a simple regular expression (`regexp`) to detect a word containing only alphanumeric characters. As another example, we will use a regular expression that detects words along with a few punctuation characters:

```
>>> patn = '\w+|[!,\-,]'
>>> regexp_tokenize(samples_tw[20],patn)
['BOMBSKARE', 'the', 'anti', '-', 'Scottish', 'feeling', 'is', 'largely',
'a', 'product', 'of', 'Tory', 'press', 'scaremongering', 'In', 'practice',
'most', 'people', 'won', 't', 'give', 'a', 'toss', '!']
```

By changing the `regexp` pattern to include punctuation marks, we were able to tokenize the characters in the result, which is apparent through the tokens ! and – being present in the resulting Python list.

Stemming

Stemming is a text preprocessing task for transforming related or similar variants of a word (such as walking) to its base form (to walk), as they share the same meaning. One of the basic transformation stemming actions is to reduce a plural word to its singular form: *apples* is reduced to *apple*, for example. While this is a very simple transformation, more complex ones do exist. We will use the popular **Porter stemmer**, by Martin Porter, to illustrate this, as shown in the following code:

```
>>> import nltk
>>> from nltk.stem import PorterStemmer
>>> stemming = PorterStemmer()
>>> stemming.stem("enjoying")
'enjoy'
>>> stemming.stem("enjoys")
'enjoy'
>>> stemming.stem("enjoyable")
'enjoy'
```

In this case, stemming has reduced the different verb (enjoying, enjoy) and adjective (enjoyable) forms of a word to its base form, enjoy. The Porter algorithm used by the stemmer utilizes various language-specific rules (in this case, English) to arrive at the stem words. One of these rules is removing suffixes such as ing from the word, as seen in the aforementioned example code. Stemming does not always produce a stem that is a word by itself, as shown in the following example:

```
>>> stemmer.stem("variation")
'variat'
>>> stemmer.stem("variate")
'variat'
```

Here, variat itself is not an English word. The nltk.stem.snowball module includes the snowball stemmers for other different languages, such as French, Spanish, German, and so on. Snowball is a stemming language that can be used to create standard rules for stemming in different languages. Just such as with tokenizers, we can create custom stemmers, using the following regular expressions:

```
>>> regexp_stemmer = RegexpStemmer("able$|ing$",min=4)
>>> regexp_stemmer.stem("flyable")
'fly'
>>> regexp_stemmer.stem("flying")
'fly'
```

The regex pattern, `able$|ing$` ,removes the suffixes `able` and `ing`, if present in a word, and `min` specifies the minimum length of the stemmed word.

Removing stop words

Commonly used words in English such as *the, is, he*, and so on, are generally called **stop words**. Other languages have similar commonly used words that fall under the same category. **Stop word removal** is another common preprocessing step for an NLP application. In this step, we remove words that do not signify any importance to the document, such as grammar articles and pronouns. Some examples of such words are *a, an, he*, and *her*. By themselves, these words may not have an impact on NLP tasks, such as text categorization or search, as they are frequently used throughout the text. Let us look at a sample of stop words in the English language, in the following code:

```
>>> from nltk.corpus import stopwords
>>> sw_l = stopwords.words('english')
>>> sw_l[20:40]
['himself', 'she', "she's", 'her', 'hers', 'herself', 'it', "it's", 'its',
'itself', 'they', 'them', 'their', 'theirs', 'themselves', 'what', 'which',
'who', 'whom', 'this']
```

The preceding code output only shows some of the sample stop words in English, as we have printed only the first `20` items. We will look at how these words can be removed from the text in the following code:

```
>> example_text = "This is an example sentence to test stopwords"
>>> example_text_without_stopwords=[word for word in example_text.split()
if word not in sw_l]
>>> example_text_without_stopwords
['This', 'example', 'sentence', 'test', 'stopwords']
```

As you can see, some of the articles, such as *an*, `is`, and `to`, are removed. NLTK provides stop word corpora for 21 languages, in addition to those for the English language, described in the examples here. As another example, we can also look at the percentage of stop words in a specific text corpus, using the following code:

```
>> from nltk.corpus import gutenberg
>>> words_in_hamlet = gutenberg.words('shakespeare-hamlet.txt')
>>> words_in_hamlet_without_sw = [word for word in words_in_hamlet if word
not in sw_l]
>>> len(words_in_hamlet_without_sw)*100.0/len(words_in_hamlet)
69.26124197002142
```

The preceding example shows that a significant percentage (approximately 30%) of the text in Shakespeare's *Hamlet* is formed of stop words. In many of the NLP tasks, these stop words do not have much significance, and therefore, they can be removed during the preprocessing.

Exploratory analysis of text

Once we have the tokenized data, one of the basic analyses that is commonly performed is counting words or tokens and their distributions in the document. This will enable us to know more about the main topics in the document. Let's start by analyzing the web text data that comes with NLTK:

```
>>> import nltk
>>> from nltk.corpus import webtext
>>> webtext_sentences = webtext.sents('firefox.txt')
>>> webtext_words = webtext.words('firefox.txt')
>>> len(webtext_sentences)
1142
>>> len(webtext_words)
102457
```

Note that we have only loaded the text related to the Firefox discussion forum (`firefox.txt`), though the web text data has other data, as well (like advertisements and movie script text). The preceding code output gives the number of sentences and words, respectively, in the entire text corpus. We can also get the size of the vocabulary by passing it through a set, as shown in the following code:

```
>>> vocabulary = set(webtext_words)
>>> len(vocabulary)
8296
```

To get the frequency distribution of the words in the text, we can utilize the `nltk.FreqDist()` function, which obtains the top words used in the text, providing a rough idea? of the main topic in the text data, as shown in the following code:

```
>>> frequency_dist = nltk.FreqDist(webtext_words)
>>> sorted(frequency_dist,key=frequency_dist.__getitem__,
reverse=True)[0:30]
['.', 'in', 'to', '"', 'the', "'", 'not', '-', 'when', 'on', 'a', 'is',
't', 'and', 'of', '(', 'page', 'for', 'with', ')', 'window', 'Firefox',
'does', 'from', 'open', ':', 'menu', 'should', 'bar', 'tab']
```

This gives the top 30 words used in the text, though it is obvious that some of the stop words, such as `the`, frequently occur in the English language. However, we can also see that words such as `Firefox` appear because the text we used for analysis comes from a discussion forum about the Firefox browser. We can also look at the frequency distribution of words with a length greater than 3, which will exclude words such as `the` and `is`, by using the following code:

```
>>> large_words = dict([(k,v) for k,v in frequency_dist.items() if
len(k)>3])
>>> frequency_dist = nltk.FreqDist(large_words)
>>> frequency_dist.plot(50,cumulative=False)
```

Here, we filtered all words with a length greater than 3, and we created a dictionary of word-frequency tuples. This will be passed to the NLTK frequency distribution plot. We will now take a look at the plot that follows, which shows the frequency distribution of the words:

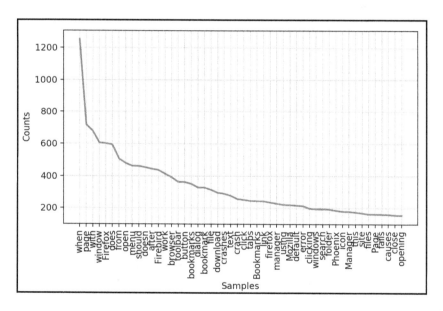

This shows the distribution of frequency counts for the top 50 words. From the frequency distribution, we can generate a word cloud, to get an intuitive visualization of the words used in the text. For this, we have to install the `wordcloud` Python package, as follows:

```
pip install wordcloud
```

This will install the `wordcloud` package, which can generate word clouds by placing words on a canvas randomly, with sizes proportional to their frequency in the text. We will now look at the code for displaying the word cloud:

```
>>> from wordcloud import WordCloud
>>> wcloud = WordCloud().generate_from_frequencies(frequency_dist)
>>> import matplotlib.pyplot as plt
>>> plt.imshow(wcloud, interpolation='bilinear')
>>> plt.axis("off")
(-0.5, 399.5, 199.5, -0.5)
>>> plt.show()
```

In the preceding code, we passed in the frequency distribution of words that we obtained earlier, with NLTK. The word cloud generated by the preceding code is shown in the following screenshot:

Based on our previous example, in the stop words section, we will look at how the distribution changes after we remove the stop words. After the removal of stop words, the word cloud looks more in line with the topic of the text:

In the preceding word cloud, common words such as when, with, from, and so on, have been removed. This can be directly verified in the dictionary of word frequency distribution, using the following code:

```
>>> words_in_webtext_without_sw = [word for word in webtext_words if word
not in sw_1]
>>> 'when' in words_in_webtext_without_sw
False
>>> 'from' in words_in_webtext_without_sw
False
```

Similarly, we can check for the presence of other words in the frequency distribution dictionary words_in_webtext_without_sw ,that appear in the word cloud before the removal of stop words.

POS tagging

We have analyzed some of the basic NLP preprocessing tasks, such as tokenization, stemming, and stop word removal. We have also explored how to determine and visualize word distribution in a text corpus. In this section, we will get deeper into NLTK by looking at POS tagging.

What is POS tagging?

POS refers to categorizing the words in a sentence into specific syntactic or grammatical functions. In English, the main parts of speech are **nouns, pronouns, adjectives, verbs, adverbs, prepositions, determiners**, and **conjunctions**. POS tagging is the task of attaching one of these categories to each of the words or tokens in a text. NLTK provides both a set of tagged text corpus and a set of POS trainers for creating custom taggers. The most common tagged datasets in NLTK are the **Penn Treebank** and **Brown Corpus**. The Penn Treebank consists of a parsed collection of texts from journal articles, telephone conversations, and so on. Similarly, the Brown Corpus consists of text from 15 different categories of articles (science, politics, religion, sports, and so on). This text data provides very fine granularity tagging, while many applications might need only the following universal tag set:

- VERB: Verbs (all tenses and modes)
- NOUN: Nouns (common and proper)
- PRON: Pronouns
- ADJ: Adjectives
- ADV: Adverbs
- ADP: Adpositions (prepositions and postpositions)
- CONJ: Conjunctions
- DET: Determiners
- NUM: Cardinal numbers
- PRT: Particles or other function words
- X-other: Foreign words, typos, abbreviations
- .: Punctuation

NLTK also provides mapping from a tagged corpus (such as the Brown Corpus) to the universal tags, as shown in the following code. The Brown Corpus has a finer granularity of POS tags than the universal tag set. For example, the tags VBD (for past tense verb) and VB (for base form verb) map to just VERB in the universal tag set:

```
>>> from nltk.corpus import brown
>>> brown.tagged_words()[30:40]
[('term-end', 'NN'), ('presentments', 'NNS'), ('that', 'CS'), ('the',
'AT'), ('City', 'NN-TL'), ('Executive', 'JJ-TL'), ('Committee', 'NN-TL'),
(',', ','), ('which', 'WDT'), ('had', 'HVD')]
>>> brown.tagged_words(tagset='universal')[30:40]
[('term-end', 'NOUN'), ('presentments', 'NOUN'), ('that', 'ADP'), ('the',
'DET'), ('City', 'NOUN'), ('Executive', 'ADJ'), ('Committee', 'NOUN'),
(',', '.'), ('which', 'DET'), ('had', 'VERB')]
```

Here, you can see that the word `City` is tagged as `NP-TL`, which is a proper noun (`NP`) appearing in the context of a title (`TL`) in the Brown Corpus. This is mapped to `NOUN` in the universal tag set. Some NLP tasks may need these fine-grained categories, instead of the general universal tags.

Applications of POS tagging

POS tagging finds applications in **Named Entity Recognition** (**NER**), sentiment analysis, question answering, and word sense disambiguation. We will look at an example of word sense disambiguation in the following code. In the sentences `I left the room` and `Left of the room`, the word `left` conveys different meanings. A POS tagger would help to differentiate between the two meanings of the word `left`. We will now look at how these two different usages of the same word are tagged:

```
>>> import nltk
>>> text1 = nltk.word_tokenize("I left the room")
>>> text2 = nltk.word_tokenize("Left of the room")
>>> nltk.pos_tag(text1,tagset='universal')
[('I', 'PRON'), ('left', 'VERB'), ('the', 'DET'), ('room', 'NOUN')]
>>> nltk.pos_tag(text2, tagset='universal')
[('Left', 'NOUN'), ('of', 'ADP'), ('the', 'DET'), ('room', 'NOUN')]
```

In the first example, the word `left` is a verb, whereas it is a noun in the second example. In NER, POS tagging helps in identifying a person, place, or location, based on the tags. NLTK provides a built-in trained classifier that can identify entities in the text, which works on top of the POS tagged sentences, as shown in the following code:

```
>>> import nltk
>>> example_sent = nltk.word_tokenize("The company is located in South
Africa")
>>> example_sent
['The', 'company', 'is', 'located', 'in', 'South', 'Africa']
>>> tagged_sent = nltk.pos_tag(example_sent)
>>> tagged_sent
[('The', 'DT'), ('company', 'NN'), ('is', 'VBZ'), ('located', 'VBN'),
('in', 'IN'), ('South', 'NNP'), ('Africa', 'NNP')]
>>> nltk.ne_chunk(tagged_sent)
Tree('S', [('The', 'DT'), ('company', 'NN'), ('is', 'VBZ'), ('located',
'VBN'), ('in', 'IN'), Tree('GPE', [('South', 'NNP'), ('Africa', 'NNP')])])
```

The ne_chunk() function uses the trained **named entity chunker** to identify South Africa as a **geopolitical entity** (GPE), in the example sentence. So far, we have seen examples using NLTK's built-in taggers. In the next section, we will look at how to develop our own POS tagger.

Training a POS tagger

We will now look at training our own POS tagger, using NLTK's tagged set corpora and the sklearn random forest **machine learning** (**ML**) model. The complete Jupyter Notebook for this section is available at Chapter02/02_example.ipynb, in the book's code repository. This will be a classification task, as we need to predict the POS tag for a given word in a sentence. We will utilize the NLTK treebank dataset, with POS tags, as the training or labeled data. We will extract the word prefixes and suffixes, and previous and neighboring words in the text, as features for the training. These features are good indicators for categorizing words to different parts of speech. The code that follows shows how we can extract these features:

```
def sentence_features(st, ix):
    d_ft = {}
    d_ft['word'] = st[ix]
    d_ft['dist_from_first'] = ix - 0
    d_ft['dist_from_last'] = len(st) - ix
    d_ft['capitalized'] = st[ix][0].upper() == st[ix][0]
    d_ft['prefix1'] = st[ix][0]
    d_ft['prefix2'] = st[ix][:2]
    d_ft['prefix3'] = st[ix][:3]
    d_ft['suffix1'] = st[ix][-1]
    d_ft['suffix2'] = st[ix][-2:]
    d_ft['suffix3'] = st[ix][-3:]
    d_ft['prev_word'] = '' if ix==0 else st[ix-1]
    d_ft['next_word'] = '' if ix==(len(st)-1) else st[ix+1]
    d_ft['numeric'] = st[ix].isdigit()
    return d_ft
```

The function sentence_features() converts the text input into a dictionary of features, d_ft. Each sentence, which is a Python list, is passed in along with the corresponding index of the current word, for which the feature is to be extracted. This index, ix, is used to obtain the neighboring word features, as well as the prefixes/suffixes. Later in the example, we will look at the importance of these features after training. We will now use the treebank tagged sentences, with the universal tags that we explained in the previous section, as the labeled or training data:

```
tagged_sentences = nltk.corpus.treebank.tagged_sents(tagset='universal')
```

We used the universal tags for simplicity, as specified in the `tagset` named argument passed to the `tagged_sents` function. Instead of the universal tags, we could also utilize the fine-grained treebank POS tags, which would result in a large number of labels. We will now extract the features for each tagged sentence in the corpus, along with the training labels. The features are stored in the X variable, and the POS tags, or labels, are stored in the y variable. We will use the following code to extract the features:

```
def ext_ft(tg_sent):
    sent, tag = [], []

    for tg in tg_sent:
        for index in range(len(tg)):
            sent.append(sentence_features(get_untagged_sentence(tg),
index))
            tag.append(tg[index][1])

    return sent, tag

X,y = ext_ft(tagged_sentences)
```

In `sklearn`, we utilize `DictVectorizer` to convert the feature-value dictionary to training vectors or instances. It should be noted that, for values that are strings, `DictVectorizer` transforms them to a one-hot encoded vector. For example, if the number of possible values for the `suffix3` feature is 50, then there will be 50 features in the output. We will use the following code to apply `DictVectorizer`:

```
n_sample = 50000
dict_vectorizer = DictVectorizer(sparse=False)
X_transformed = dict_vectorizer.fit_transform(X[0:n_sample])
y_sampled = y[0:n_sample]
```

A sample size of around 50,000 sentences was utilized, to speed up the training. The training instances are further split into 80% training and 20% test set (refer to the Notebook). An ensemble classifier, using `RandomForestClassifier` from sklearn, is utilized as the POS tagger model, as shown in the following code:

```
rf = RandomForestClassifier(n_jobs=4)
rf.fit(X_train,y_train)
```

After training, we can verify the POS tagger with an example sentence. Before passing it to the `predict()` function, we will extract the features by using the same function (`sentence_features()`) that we used for the NLTK labeled data, as shown in the following code:

```
def predict_pos_tags(sentence):
 tagged_sentence = []
 features = [sentence_features(sentence, index) for index in
range(len(sentence))]
 features = dict_vectorizer.transform(features)
 tags = rf.predict(features)
 return zip(sentence, tags)
```

We converted the `sentence` variable, which is a list of words into its corresponding features, using the `sentence_features()` function. The dictionary of features extracted from this function is vectorized using the previously trained `dict_vectorizer`:

```
test_sentence = "This is a simple POS tagger"
for tagged in predict_pos_tags(test_sentence.split()):
  print(tagged)
```

We pass the test sentence, as a list of words, to the `predict_pos_tags` function. This will output the tags for each of the words in the sentence. The output that follows shows the POS tags of the sample sentence:

```
('This', 'DET')
('is', 'VERB')
('a', 'DET')
('simple', 'ADJ')
('POS', 'NOUN')
('tagger', 'NOUN')
```

The output looks reasonable, as it can identify determiners, verbs, adjectives, and nouns in the sentence. To evaluate the accuracy, we can predict the POS tags for the test data, using the following code:

```
predictions = rf.predict(X_test)
accuracy_score(y_test,predictions)

Output
0.9452000000000004
```

The accuracy (of around 94%) looks reasonable. We will also look at the confusion matrix, to observe how well the tagger performs for each of the POS tags. We will utilize the `confusion_matrix` function from `sklearn`, as shown in the following code:

```
conf_matrix = confusion_matrix(y_test,predictions)
plt.figure(figsize=(10,10))
plt.xticks(np.arange(len(rf.classes_)),rf.classes_)
plt.yticks(np.arange(len(rf.classes_)),rf.classes_)
plt.imshow(conf_matrix,cmap=plt.cm.Blues)
plt.colorbar()
```

In the code for plotting the confusion matrix, we have used the classes from the random forest classifier as the x and y labels. These labels are the POS tags in the data that we utilized for training. The plot that follows shows the pictorial representation of the confusion matrix:

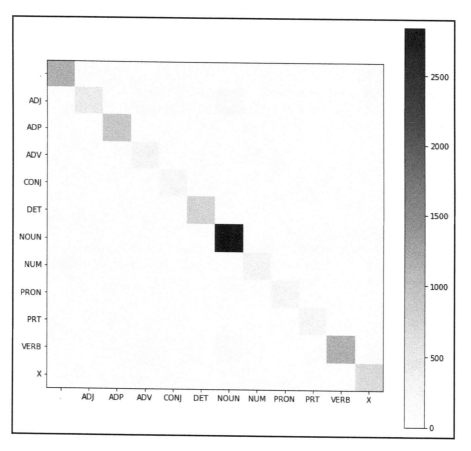

It looks like the tagger performs relatively well for nouns, verbs, and determiners in sentences, which can be seen in the dark regions in the plot. We will now look at the top features of the model, with the help of the following code:

```
feature_list =
zip(dict_vectorizer.get_feature_names(),rf.feature_importances_)
sorted_features = sorted(feature_list,key=lambda x: x[1], reverse=True)
print(sorted_features[0:20])
```

The random forest `feature importance` is stored in the Python `feature_importances` list. We will sort this list in descending order of feature importance, and will print the top 20 features, using the following code:

```
Output:

[('next_word=', 0.020920214730751722), ('capitalized',
0.01772036411509819), ('prefix1=,', 0.017100349286406635), ('suffix1=,',
0.013300188138108692), ('suffix2=ed', 0.012324641839199037), ('prefix1=*',
0.01184006667636649), ('suffix2=he', 0.010212280707210959), ('prefix2=th',
0.01012750927310713), ('suffix2=to', 0.010110760622078928), ('prefix3=the',
0.0094462675592230805), ('dist_from_first', 0.0093968467476374141),
('suffix1=f', 0.0092678798994399649), ('word=the', 0.0091584437614083847),
('dist_from_last', 0.0087969654754903419), ('prefix2=to',
0.0086095477647111125), ('suffix1=d', 0.0082316431932524976), ('word=a',
0.0077318882551946199), ('prefix2=an', 0.0074132280379715434),
('suffix1=s', 0.0067561700034315057), ('word=and', 0.0065749584774608179)]
```

You can see that some of the suffix features get higher importance scores. For example, words ending with `ed` are usually verbs in the past tense. We also find that some punctuation, such as commas, influence the tagging. Though POS tagging is also a type of text classification, we will look at the next most common NLP task, which is sentiment classification.

Training a sentiment classifier for movie reviews

We will now look at classifying sentiments in the movie reviews corpus in NLTK. The complete Jupyter Notebook for this example is available at `Chapter02/01_example.ipynb`, in the book's code repository.

First, we will load the movie reviews based on the sentiment categories, which are either positive or negative, using the following code:

```
cats = movie_reviews.categories()
reviews = []
for cat in cats:
    for fid in movie_reviews.fileids(cat):
        review = (list(movie_reviews.words(fid)),cat)
        reviews.append(review)
random.shuffle(reviews)
```

The `categories()` function returns either `pos` or `neg`, for positive and negative sentiments, respectively. There are 1,000 reviews in each of the positive and negative categories. We use the Python `random.shuffle()` function to convert the grouped positive and negative reviews into a random order. Next, we will select the top words in the reviews, and will use that as a base vocabulary for feature engineering or extraction, using the following code:

```
all_wd_in_reviews = nltk.FreqDist(wd.lower() for wd in
movie_reviews.words())
top_wd_in_reviews = [list(wds) for wds in
zip(*all_wd_in_reviews.most_common(2000))][0]
```

We have selected the top 2,000 words in the review to generate the features. We generate binary features from these words, based on their presence or absence in the review. Therefore, there will be `2000` features for each training set, with `1` at positions where the corresponding word is present in the review, and `0` otherwise:

```
def ext_ft(review,top_words):
    review_wds = set(review)
    ft = {}
    for wd in top_words:
        ft['word_present({})'.format(wd)] = (wd in review_wds)
    return ft
```

Each movie review is passed to the `ext_ft()` function, which returns the binary features in a dictionary. We will pass each review to the `ext_ft()` function, as shown in the following code:

```
featuresets = [(ext_ft(d,top_wd_in_reviews), c) for (d,c) in reviews]
train_set, test_set = featuresets[200:], featuresets[:200]
```

We have also split the labeled data into an 80% training and 20% test set. As an initial test, we will use the simple `Naive Bayes classifier` that comes with NLTK, as shown in the following code:

```
classifier = nltk.NaiveBayesClassifier.train(train_set)
print(nltk.classify.accuracy(classifier, test_set))
```

```
Output
0.805
```

Even with the simple Naive Bayes classifier, we can achieve about 80% accuracy for this dataset. We can also look at the most informative features that were learned by the classification model. Here, we will view the top 20 most important features, using the following code:

```
classifier.show_most_informative_features(10)
```

The `show_most_informative_features` function outputs the relevant features (with the number of top features as an argument), as shown in the following code:

```
Output:

Most Informative Features
word_present(seagal) = True        neg : pos  =    12.9 : 1.0
word_present(outstanding) = True   pos : neg  =    10.2 : 1.0
word_present(mulan) = True         pos : neg  =     7.0 : 1.0
word_present(wonderfully) = True   pos : neg  =     6.5 : 1.0
word_present(damon) = True         pos : neg  =     5.7 : 1.0
word_present(ridiculous) = True    neg : pos  =     5.6 : 1.0
word_present(awful) = True         neg : pos  =     5.6 : 1.0
word_present(lame) = True          neg : pos  =     5.5 : 1.0
word_present(era) = True           pos : neg  =     5.4 : 1.0
word_present(waste) = True         neg : pos  =     5.3 : 1.0
```

It looks like some of the words learned by the model, such as `waste`, `awful`, and `ridiculous`, convey negative connotations. Similarly, words such as `outstanding`, `wonderfully`, and `era` convey positive sentiments.

We will now evaluate with sklearn's random forest classifier model with the movie reviews data. But before that, we will vectorize the features using `DictVectorizer`, as we did in the previous section for training a POS tagger, as shown in the following code:

```
d_vect=None
def get_train_test(tr_set,te_set):
    global d_vect
    d_vect = DictVectorizer(sparse=False)
    X_tr, y_tr = zip(*tr_set)
    X_tr = d_vect.fit_transform(X_tr)
    X_te,y_te = zip(*te_set)
    X_te = d_vect.transform(X_te)
    return X_tr,X_te,y_tr,y_te
```

The `tr_set` and `te_set` are the training and test set instances that we obtained previously. The `get_train_test` function returns the vectorized features that can be passed to sklearn's random forest classifier, as shown in the following code:

```
X_train,X_test,y_train,y_test = get_train_test(train_set,test_set)
rf = RandomForestClassifier(n_estimators=100,n_jobs=4,random_state=10)
rf.fit(X_train,y_train)
```

Here, we used 100 estimators, or decision trees, for the classifiers. The `n_jobs` parameter is the number of parallel jobs, for faster training and prediction:

```
preds = rf.predict(X_test)
print(accuracy_score(y_test,preds))

Output
0.81
```

The accuracy (of around 81%) is a slight improvement from the Naive Bayes classifier. We will now remove all of the stop words in the reviews, and will again train the classifier to observe if there is any improvement in the model accuracy. We utilize the NLTK stop words corpora to remove the stop words. Just like earlier, we will select the top 2,000 words, as shown in the following code:

```
from nltk.corpus import stopwords
stopwords_list = stopwords.words('english')
all_words_in_reviews = nltk.FreqDist(word.lower() for word in
movie_reviews.words() if word not in stopwords_list)
top_words_in_reviews = [list(words) for words in
zip(*all_words_in_reviews.most_common(2000))][0]
```

`top_words_in_reviews` now excludes the stop words. Again, we will generate the features using this as our vocabulary and train a random forest classifier:

```
preds = rf.predict(X_test)
print(accuracy_score(y_test,preds))
0.76
```

The stop word removal for this dataset has not improved the model's accuracy, but has, in fact, reduced it. We can look at the most informative feature, as we did for the Naive Bayes classifier, by using the following code:

```
features_list =
zip(dict_vectorizer.get_feature_names(),rf.feature_importances_)
features_list = sorted(features_list, key=lambda x: x[1], reverse=True)
print(features_list[0:20])
```

Just like before, we have sorted the features based on their importance, learned by the random forest classifier. We will print the top 20 from the sorted Python list, `features_list`:

```
[('word_present(bad)', 0.012904816953952729), ('word_present(boring)',
0.006797056379259946), ('word_present(stupid)', 0.006742453545126172),
('word_present(awful)', 0.00605732124427093), ('word_present(worst)',
0.005618499631730539), ('word_present(waste)', 0.005091242651240423),
('word_present(supposed)', 0.005019844359438753),
('word_present(excellent)', 0.005002846831984908), ('word_present(mess)',
0.004735341799753426), ('word_present(wasted)', 0.004477280752464545),
('word_present(ridiculous)', 0.00435578373608493), ('word_present(lame)',
0.00404257877140679), ('word_present(also)', 0.003663095965733155),
('word_present(others)', 0.0035194019538410553), ('word_present(dull)',
0.003464806019875671), ('word_present(plot)', 0.0034406946286116035),
('word_present(nothing)', 0.0033285487918061265),
('word_present(performances)', 0.003286015291474251),
('word_present(outstanding)', 0.0032708132090801516),
('word_present(memorable)', 0.003265718932501386)]
```

Similar to the Naive Bayes classifier, we can find words that convey positive and negative sentiments. While binary features might be useful for rudimentary text classification tasks, they are not suitable for more complex text classification applications. We will look at better feature extraction techniques in the next section.

Training a bag-of-words classifier

In the previous section, we utilized simple binary features for the words in the reviews in order to learn positive and negative sentiments. A better approach would be to use latent features, such as the frequency of the words used in the text. Compared to a binary representation of the presence or absence of words, the count of the words may better capture the characteristics of the text or document. **Bag-of-words** is a vector representation of text. Each of the vector dimensions captures either the frequency, presence or absence, or weighted values of words in the text. A bag-of-words representation does not capture the order of the words.

The binary feature extraction that was discussed in the previous section is, therefore, a simple bag-of-words representation of text. We will now look at an example of classifying sentiments in tweets using better bag-of-words representations. The complete Jupyter Notebook for this example is available at `Chapter02/03_example.ipynb`, in the book's code repository. We will use the Twitter sample corpus provided in NLTK. The NLTK Twitter samples contain sentiment polarity, just like in the `movie_reviews` corpus:

```
pos_tweets = [(string, 1) for string in
twitter_samples.strings('positive_tweets.json')]
neg_tweets = [(string,0) for string in
twitter_samples.strings('negative_tweets.json')]
pos_tweets.extend(neg_tweets)
comb_tweets = pos_tweets
random.shuffle(comb_tweets)
tweets,labels = (zip(*comb_tweets))
```

Like before, we read the data from the JSON files and attach the sentiment labels. The JSON parsing and text extraction are done by NLTK, with the `strings` function. We attach the sentiment label, 1 ,to denote positive sentiment, and 0 to denote negative sentiment. We also shuffle the order of the positive and negative sentiments in the Python list of tweets and sentiment label tuples, using the following code:

```
count_vectorizer = CountVectorizer(ngram_range=
  (1,2),max_features=10000)
X = count_vectorizer.fit_transform(tweets)
```

We utilize the `CountVectorizer`, in sklearn, to generate the features. We limit the number of features to `10000`. We also use both unigram and bigram features. An *n*-gram denotes *n* number of contiguous word features sampled from the text. A unigram is the usual single word feature, and a bigram is two consecutive word sequences in the text. As bigrams are two consecutive words, they can capture short word sequences or phrases in the text. In this example, as `ngram_range` is (1, 2), `CountVectorizer` will extract both unigram and bigrams features from the tweets.

We will now train the model with the tweets, after splitting it into 80% training and 20% test sets, using the following code:

```
rf = RandomForestClassifier(n_estimators=100,n_jobs=4,random_state=10)
rf.fit(X_train,y_train)
X_train,X_test,y_train,y_test =
train_test_split(X,labels,test_size=0.2,random_state=10)
```

We will now evaluate the model with the test set to predict the sentiment labels, printing the accuracy score and confusion matrix:

```
preds = rf.predict(X_test)
print(accuracy_score(y_test,preds))
print(confusion_matrix(y_test,preds))

Output

0.758
[[796 173]
[311 720]]
```

The model provides an accuracy of around 75%. We will test the model with the `tfidf` vectorizer. `tfidf` is similar to the count based *n*-grams model, except that the counts are now weighted. It gives weights to the words, based on their appearances in all of the documents or text. This means that words more commonly used across the documents will get lower weights, compared to words appearing in specific documents:

```
from nltk.corpus import stopwords
tfidf = TfidfVectorizer(ngram_range=(1,2),max_features=10000)
X = tfidf.fit_transform(tweets)
```

Like before, we extract both unigram and bigram features from the text. We will evaluate this model based on the test data:

```
preds = rf.predict(X_test)
print(accuracy_score(y_test,preds))
print(confusion_matrix(y_test,preds))
```

Output

0.756

`TfidfVectorizer`, in this case, has not improved the model's accuracy. We will now remove the stop words from the tweets, using the NLTK stop words corpora:

```
from nltk.corpus import stopwords
tfidf = TfidfVectorizer(ngram_range=(1,2),max_features=10000,
stop_words=stopwords.words('english'))
X = tfidf.fit_transform(tweets)

preds = rf.predict(X_test)
print(accuracy_score(y_test,preds))
print(confusion_matrix(y_test,preds))
```

Output

0.736

An evaluation of the test data shows a reduction in the model's accuracy. Removing stop words may not always improve the accuracy, and accuracy also depends on the training data. It is possible that specific stop words occur across some common phrases that are good indicators of a tweet's sentiment.

Summary

In this chapter, we covered common NLP tasks, such as preprocessing and exploratory analysis of text using the NLTK library. The unstructured characteristics of real-world data need extensive preprocessing, such as tokenization, stemming, and stop word removal, to make it suitable for ML. As you saw in the examples, NLTK provides a very extensive API for carrying out these preprocessing steps. It provides built-in packages and modules, and supports flexibility to build custom modules, such as user-defined stemmers and tokenizers.

We also discussed using NLTK for POS tagging, which is another common NLP task, used for issues such as word sense disambiguation and answering questions. Applications such as sentiment classification are widely used for their research and business value. We covered some basic examples of text classification, in the context of sentiment analysis, for tweets and movie reviews, using the NLTK corpora and sklearn. While these can be used in simple NLP applications, more complex text classification, using deep learning, will be explained in subsequent chapters.

3
Deep Learning and TensorFlow

Applications that leverage **natural language processing** (**NLP**) have begun to achieve close to human-level accuracy in tasks such as language translation, text summarization, and text-to-speech, due to the adoption of deep learning models. This widespread adoption has been driven by two key developments in the area of deep learning. One of them is the rapid progress in discovering novel deep neural network architectures, realized by the availability of huge volumes of data. Such architectures can achieve superior performance compared to traditional approaches. The other development is the increasing availability of open source tools or libraries, such as TensorFlow, which make easy implementations of these modern architectures possible in practical or productive applications. The purpose of this chapter is to equip the reader with a necessary basic knowledge of deep learning and TensorFlow, so that later chapters can be approached with confidence.

The following topics will be covered in this chapter:

- Various concepts and terminologies in deep learning
- An overview of common deep learning architectures, such as CNNs and RNNs
- Installation, setup, and getting started with TensorFlow

Deep learning

Deep learning has grown in popularity in recent years, and has started a revolution in the adoption of **artificial intelligence** (**AI**). Though some of the techniques are not new, a growing volume of data and availability of cheap computing power has enabled deep learning's widespread adoption. In this chapter, you will learn the basic deep learning concepts and vocabulary that will be required in the rest of the book.

Deep learning is a technique that enables machines or computers to learn and make predictions from raw data, in contrast to the traditional method of hardcoded rules or algorithms. It is a branch of **machine learning** (**ML**) that is, in turn, a branch of AI. Deep learning techniques are loosely inspired by neuroscience.

Perceptron

To start, we will introduce the perceptron model. The perceptron is the simplest neural network model. It can learn a linear mapping based on the input and output when trained on a labeled training dataset. A linear mapping is the sum of a product of weights on a set of input variables, otherwise known as **features**. The final sum is passed through a step function to select one of the binary values in the case of a classification problem. The following diagram represents a perceptron:

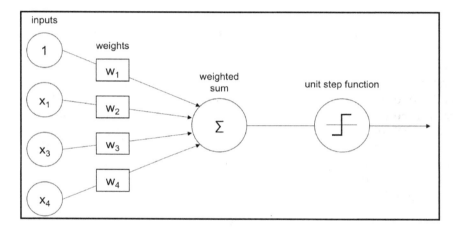

The weights are derived from the training data by a process called **learning**. The process of learning will be explained later in this chapter. The Perceptron uses the unit step function for the output prediction. The final activation output can be 0 or 1, corresponding to the binary class in the training data. While the unit step function is the simplest activation function, we will touch upon other types of activation functions that are widely used in modern deep learning architectures in the following section.

Activation functions

One of the important components in a neural network is the **activation function**. The activation function can transform the input of a neural network node into non-linear output. Such activation functions enable the neural network to learn arbitrary non-linear mappings or patterns from data. The activation can be thought of as an event of firing a node. As explained previously, in the case of a unit step function, the perceptron is either fired or not fired, corresponding to a value of 1 or 0, respectively. There are other kinds of activation functions, such as sigmoid, hyperbolic target, and **rectified linear unit (ReLU)**, which will be discussed next.

Sigmoid

A sigmoid can transform any input into a probability distribution. It basically squashes or maps any arbitrary range of values to a value between 0 and 1. Sigmoid functions are widely used in binary classification tasks with output that can be considered the probability of the class. The following diagram shows a graph of sigmoid activation:

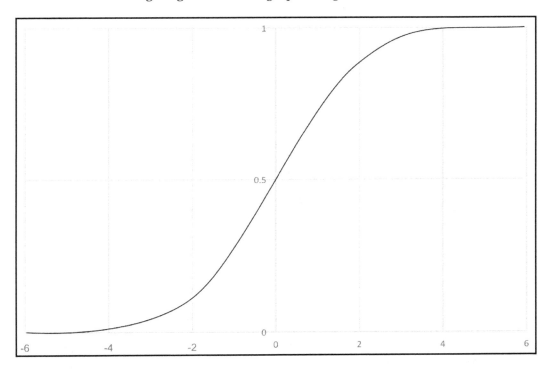

As the preceding diagram shows, the function resembles the unit function, but smoother. This smoothness ensures differentiation in the entire range of the function, which is necessary during the training of the network, as will be discussed in a later section.

Hyperbolic tangent

Hyperbolic tangent activation transforms the input into values ranging from -1 to 1. The following is a graph of a hyperbolic tangent function:

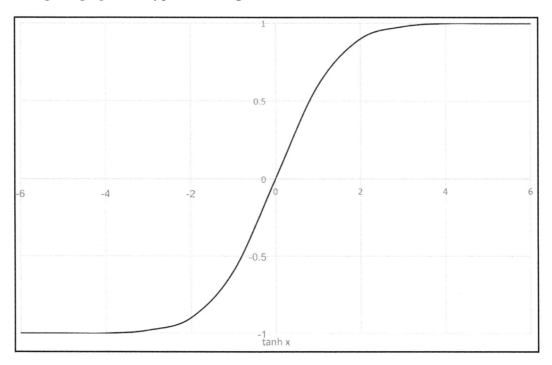

As shown in the preceding graph, this function is similar to a sigmoid function, but the y values vary from -1 to 1. The main advantage of the hyperbolic tangent function is that the values don't diminish for a negative x. The hyperbolic function also has a higher gradient over its range compared to a sigmoid function. This activation function is also referred to as a tanh function.

Rectified linear unit

ReLU caps the negative value to zero, but its output will be positive equal to the same values as the input. It has a constant gradient for positive values and a zero gradient for negative values. The following is a graph of ReLU:

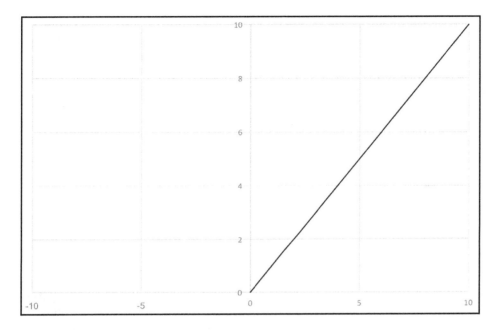

As shown, ReLU doesn't fire at all for negative values. The computational complexity of this activation function is lower than the functions described previously; hence, the prediction is faster. In the next section, you will see how to interconnect several perceptrons to form a deep neural network.

Neural network

A neural network is a network of interconnected perceptrons. An example of such a network is shown in the following diagram:

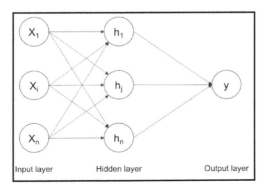

In the preceding diagram, the input layer is fed with input data, which are then passed to the hidden layer. Each unit, or node, in the hidden layer computes an activation based on the input, and then passes it to a final output node. The output node, in turn, computes the final output, based on all of the input from the hidden layer. Although the preceding diagram shows only one hidden layer, there can be multiple hidden layers for a given network. An activation function in the output can be used for categorical data with two classes. There are some additional techniques required to predict multi-label classes. We will learn about one-hot encoding, softmax, and cross-entropy in the following sections.

One-hot encoding

One-hot encoding is a vectorization technique for labeled data, especially categorical data. In the case of binary labels, target variables will be presented as [0, 1], [1, 0]. The same representation for three classes will appear as [0, 0, 1], [0, 1, 0], [1, 0, 0]. This type of representation can support any number of categories. The main advantage of one-hot encoding is that it treats all categorical data equally, in contrast to arbitrary categorical labels. For instance, categories to represent colors such as red, green, and blue, may use integers such as 0, 1, and 2. Although there is no intrinsic order for colors, some ML models may treat such input as if it has an order. This is avoided in one-hot encoding, as it does not assume any order in the categorical values since they are binary encoded.

Softmax

Softmax normalizes or squashes a vector of arbitrary values to a probability distribution between 0 and 1. The sum of the softmax output will be equal to 1. Therefore, it is commonly used in the last layer of a neural network to predict probabilities of the possible output classes. The following is the mathematical expression for the softmax function for a vector with j values:

$$Softmax(z_j) = \frac{\sum e^{z_j}}{\sum_{k=1}^{K} e^{z_k}}$$

Here z_j represents the *jth* vector value and K represents the number of classes. As we can see the exponential function smoothens the output value while the denominator normalizes the final value between 0 and 1.

Cross-entropy

Cross-entropy is the loss during training for classification tasks. A high-level description of cross-entropy is that it computes how much the softmax probabilities or the predictions differ from the true classes. The following is the expression for cross entropy for binary classification with output represented by probability $\hat{y}$ and the true values by y:

$$CrossEntropy = -y\log(\hat{y}) - (1-y)\log(1-\hat{y})$$

As we can see from the preceding expression, the cross-entropy will increase or penalize when the probability of prediction is close to 1 while the true output is 0 and vice versa. The same expression can be extended to K classes.

Training neural networks

Training deep neural networks is hard, as there are several **hyperparameters** to be optimized. The variables that define the structure of the network and how it is trained are called **hyperparameters**. The number of hidden layers and the activation function to be used are a couple of examples of architecture-defining hyperparameters. Similarly, the learning rate and batch size of the training data are examples of training-related hyperparameters. The other main parameters are the network weights and biases that have to be obtained by training the input data. The mechanism or method of obtaining these parameters of the network is called **training**.

Backpropagation

The goal of the training algorithm is to find the weights and biases of the network that minimize a certain loss function, which depends on the prediction output and the true labels or values. To accomplish this, the gradients of the loss function, with respect to the weights and biases, are computed at the output, and the errors are propagated backward, up to the input layer. These propagated errors are, in turn, used to compute the gradients of all of the intermediate layers, up to the input layer. This technique of computing gradients is called **backpropagation**. During each iteration of the process, the current error in the output prediction is propagated backward through the network, to compute gradients with respect to each layer's weights and biases.

This approach is depicted in the following diagram:

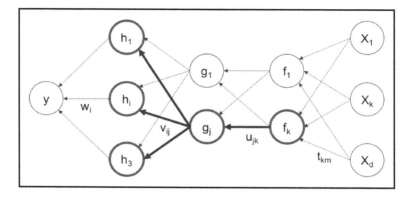

The training algorithm called **gradient descent**, utilizes backpropagation to update weights and biases. That algorithm will be explained next.

Gradient descent

Gradient descent is an optimization technique that utilizes the gradients computed from backpropagation to update the weights and biases, moving towards the goal of minimizing the loss. As shown in the following diagram, the cost (or loss) function is minimized by adjusting the weights, along the slope or gradient of the function:

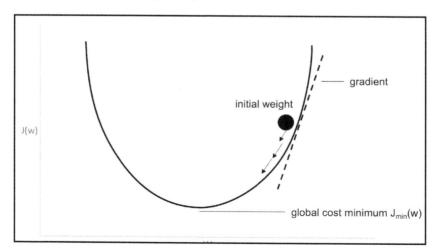

For a simple perceptron, this cost function is linear, with respect to the weights. But for deep neural networks, the cost function is most often high-dimensional and non-linear. As gradient descent has to traverse paths along all of the different dimensions, it may be difficult to arrive at the global minimum in an acceptable time. To avoid this problem and train faster, neural networks normally employ stochastic gradient descent, which is explained next.

Stochastic gradient descent

Stochastic gradient descent is a variation of the gradient descent algorithm to train deep learning models. The basic idea is that instead of training the whole set of the data, a subset is utilized. Theoretically, one sample is good enough for training the network. But in practice, a fixed number of the input data or a batch is usually used. This approach results in faster training, as compared to the vanilla gradient descent.

Regularization techniques

Overfitting is a problem in ML, where a model blindly learns all of the patterns in the data, including noise. A neural network can easily be overfitted during training, due to the availability of a large number of parameters. Theoretically, given any size of input data, a large enough **Artificial Neural Network** (**ANN**) can memorize all of the patterns in it, along with noise. Therefore, the weights of models have to be regularized to avoid overfitting the data.

We will look at three types of regularization:

- Dropout
- Batch normalization
- L1 and L2 normalization

Dropout

A dropout mechanism is a regularization technique where some neurons are left out during training; hence, the weights are regularized. The following diagram shows a neural network with dropout on the right-hand side, and a standard network on the left:

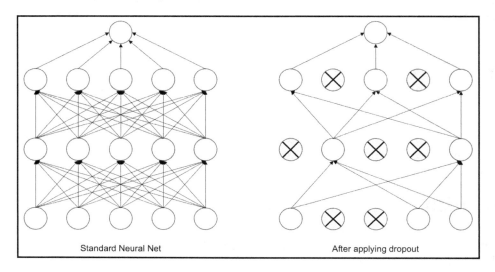

In effect, dropout prevents the network from giving too much importance to any single node or feature, which may result in overfitting. The weight values are therefore spread across different nodes, regularizing the output. Another regularization technique that works on the data itself is batch normalization, which will be explained next.

Batch normalization

Batch normalization rescales the input and all intermediate layer output of the network, making the training smoother and faster. The rescaling is done to achieve a 0 mean and a standard deviation of 1 for all of the input and output. This helps the neural network to train faster and leads to some regularization.

L1 and L2 normalization

L1 and L2 normalization are common regularization techniques that control how much the weights can grow or shrink in the network during training. It has the effect of not giving too much importance to a specific feature, similar to dropout. In L1 regularization, the loss function increases in direct proportion to the size of the weights, whereas in L2 normalization, it increases in proportion to the square of the weights.

Convolutional Neural Network

Convolutional Neural Networks (CNNs) learn the convolution kernel to transform the data. Convolution makes the transform invariant to translation. As layers progress, the depth of the features change, based on the number of filters assigned; the following diagram illustrates this:

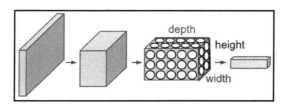

Kernel

The kernel is the small window used by a CNN to slide across the feature map. As shown in the following diagram, the kernel is used to go in a sliding window motion and produce output feature maps:

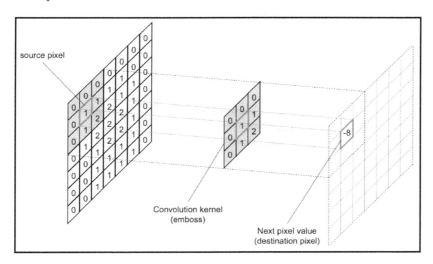

The kernel can come in various sizes of rectangles and can move in longer or shorter strides.

Max pooling

Max pooling picks the maximum value from a small window. This is a form of sub-sampling:

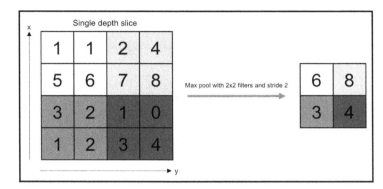

In the preceding diagram, the mechanism picks the maximum value from a window.

Recurrent neural network

A **recurrent neural network** (**RNN**) can be used to train a model with a temporal dependence, such as language. It can be used to train any kind of sequence data. The output of a neuron is fed back into itself in an RNN. An RNN, when unrolled, looks as follows:

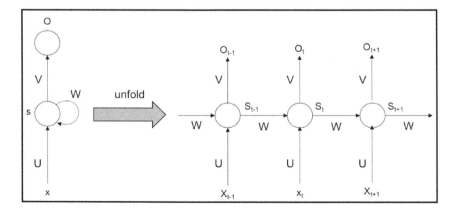

Due to its nature of taking input from previous time-steps, the data from a sequence that occurred long ago is lost.

Long-Short Term Memory

Long-Short Term Memory (**LSTM**) can remember things from a long time ago by using a **forget gate**. The advantage of LSTM (over RNN) is that it can remember over long periods of time. There are several gates in LSTM, such as the forget gate, the output gate, and the input gate. Each has its own function:

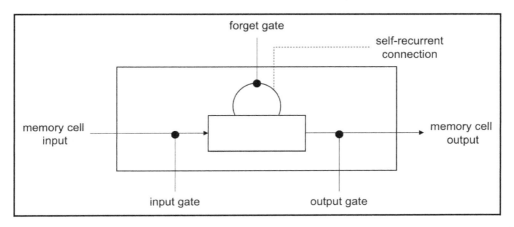

We have learned several techniques for deep learning in this section. Next, we will learn about TensorFlow.

TensorFlow

TensorFlow is a library provided by Google for ML. It is fast and scalable. TensorFlow has a wide variety of tools for visualization and deployment. It has gained popularity in the developer community and has been used in several organizations. In this section, you will see hardware requirements, installation, and a couple of simple examples.

General Purpose – Graphics Processing Unit

A **General Processing – Graphics Processing Unit** (**GPGPU**) can accelerate deep learning model training and inference to a great extent. Recent advances in deep learning have been possible because of big data and cheap computation. The company, Nvidia, provides GPUs and some libraries to accelerate deep learning. Having GPU hardware for training is useful, but not necessary.

CUDA

The **Compute Unified Device Architecture (CUDA)** library provided by Nvidia will install the required drivers for the GPU. Go to `https://developer.nvidia.com/cuda-downloads` and access the following screen:

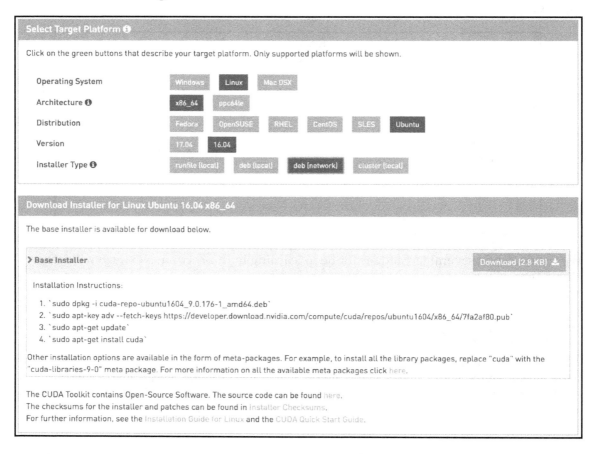

Based on the environment you are using, select a version, and install it with the provided instructions.

cuDNN

The **CUDA Deep Neural Network (cuDNN)** library is used to accelerate the training and inference of deep learning models when Nvidia hardware is used. The library can be downloaded from `https://developer.nvidia.com/cudnn`.

Installation

The installation of TensorFlow is straightforward in an environment where Python is installed. Depending on whether you have a GPU or not, you can use the following code:

```
sudo pip install tensorflow
```

You can also use the following:

```
sudo pip install tensorflow-gpu
```

Next, we will see a couple of examples.

Hello world!

Let's look at an example of `Hello, world!` using TensorFlow. We will go over this example directly in the Python shell:

1. Enter the Python shell.
2. Import TensorFlow with the following command:

   ```
   >>>import tensorflow as tf
   ```

3. TensorFlow can understand constants, variables, and operations, when defined with a `tf` base definition. Define a constant string as follows:

   ```
   >>>hello_world = tf.constant("Hello, world!")
   ```

4. Create a session:

   ```
   >>>sess = tf.Session()
   ```

5. Run the session:

   ```
   >>>print(sess.run(hello_world))
   ```

6. The output should be as follows:

```
Hello, world!
```

Congratulations! You have written your first program using TensorFlow. Next, we will introduce a few concepts for using TensorFlow.

Adding two numbers

We will look at an example of adding two numbers using TensorFlow. A placeholder is a node in a TensorFlow graph to which values can be passed during a session. A session is when the graph is initialized and ready to process the values:

1. We will define two placeholders to take two integer values:

```
a = tf.Placeholder(tf.int32)
b = tf.Placeholder(tf.int32)
```

2. Add these two variables and store them in a variable:

```
c = a + b
```

 Note that this operation is just defined and not yet executed.

3. A dictionary of values is created to load to the placeholders. The keys are variables with placeholders themselves, as shown here:

```
values = {a: 5, b: 3}
```

4. Create a session. Once a session is initialized, the graph is loaded into the memory and is ready for the consumption of values into placeholders, and to do the processing:

```
sess = tf.Session()
```

5. Run the session by passing values into the graph. The output from the c node is requested back, so use the following code:

```
print(sess.run([c], values))
```

The output should be [8.0]. This example illustrates how values can be fed into the graph and processed.

TensorBoard

Next, let's use TensorBoard to visualize the graph. Let's update the program of addition to include the instructions for TensorBoard. Any node can be assigned with a name, so that the node can be rendered with a corresponding name in TensorBoard:

1. In the following snippet, the names 'a', 'b', and 'c' are assigned to the placeholders:

```
a = tf.Placeholder(tf.int32, name='a')
b = tf.Placeholder(tf.int32, name='b')
c = tf.add(a, b, name='add')
values = {a: 5, b: 3}
sess = tf.Session()
```

2. The values are created and the session is started, as usual. Then, the summary writer is created, with a file path as an argument. The details needed for the summary will be stored in that file, and can be used to display TensorBoard:

```
summary_writer = tf.summary.FileWriter('/tmp/1', sess.graph)
```

3. Run the session, as described in the previous section:

```
sess.run([c], values)
```

4. Once the program has been run, you can go to the Command Prompt and type the following command, with the path of the summary file as an argument, as shown here:

```
tensorboard --logdir=/tmp/1
```

5. Go to the following link:

```
http://localhost:6006/
```

You will see the following view:

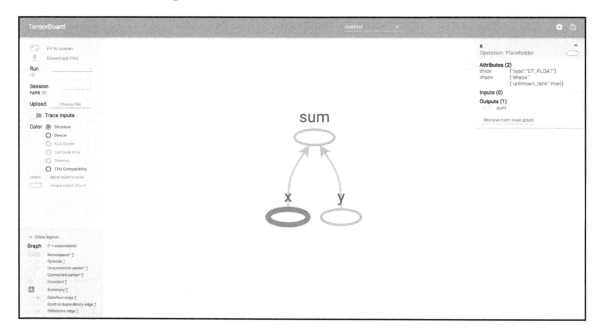

In subsequent chapters, you will learn about other uses of TensorBoard.

The Keras library

The Keras library is a simplified API to use multiple deep learning libraries at the backend. Keras is popular in the deep learning community, due to its simplicity. Keras can use TensorFlow or the Torch framework at its backend. In this book, TensorFlow and Keras are used as examples. TensorFlow also has a Keras version, under the `tf.keras` module.

Summary

In this chapter, you learned about the basics of deep learning and TensorFlow. The vocabulary that was covered in this chapter will be used throughout the book. Concepts such as CNN and LSTM are the fundamental building blocks for many of the applications.

In the next chapter, we will train a deep learning model to classify a text for various applications, using LSTM.

4
Semantic Embedding Using Shallow Models

In this chapter, we will discuss the motivation for understanding semantic relationships between words, and we will discuss approaches for identifying such relationships. In the process, we will obtain a vector representation for words, which will let us build vector representations at a document level.

We will cover the following topics in this chapter:

- Word embeddings, to represent words as vectors, trained by a simple shallow neural network
- **Continuous Bag of Words** (**CBOW**) embeddings, to predict a target from a source word, using a similar neural network
- Sentence embeddings, through averaging Word2vec
- Document embeddings, through averaging across the document

Word vectors

Word vectors are useful building blocks in many applications. They capture and encode the semantic relationships between words. As a consequence, they lead to the transformation of words into a sequence of numbers, forming a dense vector that is well-suited for training deep learning models. In this chapter, we will take a detailed look at the various approaches to building such semantically useful word embeddings.

The classical approach

Traditionally, the approach for building word representations used things such as the bag-of-words model. In this model, word representations considered individual words to be independent of one another. Hence, such representations often used a one-hot representation, which indicated the presence or absence of words in a sentence, to generate a vector representation in a sentence or document. However, such a representation is seldom useful in real-world applications, where word meanings change based on the words surrounding them. For example, let us consider the following sentences: *The cat sat on the broken wall*, and, *The dog jumped over the brick structure*. It is quite evident from these two sentences that although, they are discussing two separate events, the semantic meanings of the sentences are similar to one another. For instance, a *dog* is similar to a *cat*, as they share an entity called *animal*, while a *wall* could be viewed as similar to a *brick* structure. Hence, while the sentences discuss different events, they are semantically related to one another. In the classical approach for encoding words using the bag-of-words model (where words are encoded in their own dimensions), encoding such a semantic similarity is not possible.

Let us consider the following sentences:

- TensorFlow is an open source software library
- Python is an open source interpreted software programming language

If we consider the earlier two lines of text to be separate documents, we can construct two lists of words:

- [TensorFlow, is, an, open, source, software, library]
- [Python, is, an, open, source, interpreted, software, programming, language]

The vocabulary of the following documents can be written as: [TensorFlow, is, an, open, source, software, library, Python, interpreted, programming, language], which is 11 words long.

Hence, we can represent the first document as follows:

- [1, 1, 1, 1, 1, 1, 1, 0, 0, 0, 0]
- [0, 1, 1, 1, 1, 1, 0, 1, 1, 1, 1]

In the preceding representation, every number indicates the number of times the word in that position of the vocabulary repeats itself in the document. Hence, we can see that when the vocabulary increases, most of the words in the vocabulary will not be present in each document, making it a long, and mostly empty (zeros), vector representation. The size of the vector will be the size of the vocabulary, however large.

Another important aspect that is lost with classical methods is the order in which the words occur in the sentence. The traditional bag-of-words approach aggregates the vocabulary of the text present in the documents, in order to obtain a representation of the words that are present. However, this is a drawback where the context is lost; similar to the encoding discussed previously, it assumes that words in the document are independent of one another. Another pitfall of this approach is that such a representation leads to data sparsity, which would make it difficult to train statistical models. This forms the fundamental motivation for using vector representations for words, where the semantics of the words are encoded in the representation.

Word2vec

Vector representations of words allow for a continuous representation of semantically similar words, wherein words that are related to one another are mapped to points that are close to each other in a high dimensional space. Such an approach to word representations builds on the fact that words that share similar contexts also share semantic meanings. Word2vec is one such model, trying to directly predict a word by using its neighbors, learning small but dense vectors called **embeddings**. Word2vec is also a computationally efficient, unsupervised model that learns word embeddings from raw text. In order to learn these dense vectors, Word2vec is available in two flavors: the **CBOW** model and the **skip-gram** model (proposed by Mikolov et al.).

Word2vec is a shallow, three-layer neural network, where the first and last layers form the input and output; the intermediate layer builds latent representations, for the input words to be transformed into the output vector representation.

The Word2vec representation of words allows for exploring interesting mathematical relationships between word vectors, which is also an intuitive expression for words. For instance, we will be able to find out the value of this expression by using word representations:

king - man = queen - woman

Mathematically, what this expression evaluates is the equivalence of the latent space of the word vectors evaluated by the expressions. On the other hand, intuitively, we can understand that removing *man* from *king* and adding *woman* results in *queen*. Such a relationship can be built only when the contexts of the words are understood, which is possible when the positional relationships of the words are exploited. It is evident, from the semantics, that the word *king* occurs in a position along with *man*, in a manner similar to how the word *queen* and *woman* are present with one another:

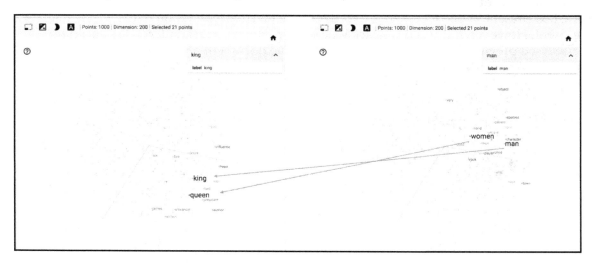

Transformation of word vectors

The preceding screenshot shows the transformation of the word vectors from *woman* to *queen*, and how this is analogous to the transformation of *man* to *king*. The process of understanding such a relationship is achieved using Word2vec, where a simple, three-layer neural network is used to predict surrounding words (given an input word), or to predict the word (given the surrounding words). Both of these approaches are variations of the Word2vec approach. The approach wherein the surrounding words are predicted using the input word is the skip-gram model, while the approach wherein the target word is predicted using the surrounding words is the CBOW model.

The CBOW model

The CBOW model of Word2vec predicts a target word from a set of source context words. What this means is that, in the sentence, *The cat sat on the dirty mat*, CBOW tries to predict the target word vector for *mat* by using the context words, *the, cat, sat, on,* and *dirty*. In order to achieve this, CBOW builds a tuple of context-target pairs of words. Hence, for the set of context words (the, cat, sat, on, dirty), we predict the word *mat*, which is represented as (the, mat), (cat, mat), (sat, mat), (on, mat), (dirty, mat).

The skip-gram model

On the other hand, the skip-gram model does the inverse of the CBOW task, predicting the context words by using the target words. Taking the example we discussed earlier, in the sentence, *The cat sat on the dirty mat*, skip-gram tries to predict the target word vectors for *the, cat, sat, on,* and *dirty*, using the context word vector for *mat*. Hence, for the context word *mat*, we predict the target words (the, cat, sat, on, dirty), which are represented as (mat, the), (mat, cat), (mat, sat), (mat, on), (mat, dirty).

A comparison of skip-gram and CBOW model architectures

The following diagram shows a comparison of the CBOW and skip-gram model architectures:

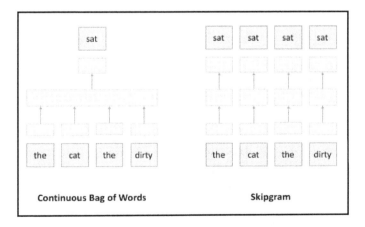

This diagram shows how skip-gram learns to predict the target word by using the words nearby. On the other hand, CBOW learns to predict the target word based on the words present in its context, which is represented as a bag-of-words, present in a fixed-size window that is around the target word.

In general, the skip-gram approach tends to produce better word representations when the datasets are larger. Hence, we will concentrate on building a skip-gram model for the rest of this chapter. We will also look at how to visualize the trained word embeddings by using TensorBoard. Such a visualization would allow us to get the intuitions behind word embeddings. The following section will walk through the code and analyze the results.

Building a skip-gram model

For our first step, we will import the Python modules necessary for our example:

```
from tensorflow.contrib.tensorboard.plugins import projector

import os
import numpy as np
import tensorflow as tf
```

The `projector` module from TensorFlow provides the necessary methods for us to add our word vectors for visualization on TensorBoard. Subsequently, we will create a dictionary with all of the model parameters that we will be using to train our Word2vec model:

```
# Parameters related to training the model

model_params = {
    "vocab_size": 50000,      # Maximum number of words
    "batch_size": 64,         # Batch size for every training step
    "embedding_size": 200,    # Dimensions of the word embedding vectors
    "num_negatives": 64,      # Number of negative words to be sampled
    "learning_rate": 1.0,     # Learning rate for the training
    "num_train_steps": 500000, # Number of steps to train the model
}
```

We will define a `Word2vecModel` class, which we will use for our model definition, training, and visualization routines. The class, with its __init__ method, looks as follows:

```
class Word2vecModel:
    """
    Initialize variables for Word2vec model
    """
```

```
    def __init__(self, data_set, vocab_size,
                     embed_size, batch_size, num_sampled, learning_rate):
        self.vocab_size = vocab_size
        self.embed_size = embed_size
        self.batch_size = batch_size
        self.num_sampled = num_sampled
        self.lr = learning_rate
        self.global_step = tf.get_variable('global_step',
                                              initializer=tf.constant(0),
                                              trainable=False)
        self.skip_step = model_params["skip_step"]
        self.data_set = data_set
```

We will use the __init__ method for initializing Word2vec model parameters. As shown previously, we will initialize the model's learning rate, batch size, vocabulary size, and embedding vector size, using the initialization method. We will then import the data using a generator, for which we use TensorFlow's Dataset API, as follows:

```
data_set = tf.data.Dataset.from_generator(generator,
                                           (tf.int32, tf.int32),
                         (tf.TensorShape([model_params["batch_size"]]),
                          tf.TensorShape([model_params["batch_size"],
1]))))
```

We use the Dataset API to produce samples from generator, and use the dataset's from_generator method to produce data whose elements are produced by generator. The generator argument should be a callable object that returns an object that supports the iter() protocol. This could be a generator function. The elements generated by generator must be compatible with the given output_types argument, and optionally, the output_shapes arguments. We can write a generator method as follows:

```
def generator():
    yield from batch_generator(model_params["vocab_size"],
                               model_params["batch_size"],
                               model_params["skip_window"],
                               file_params["visualization_folder"])
```

We will define a method to import the data for which we created generator. We will use TensorFlow's name_scope, to ensure that the graphs are well-defined for defining Python operations:

```
with tf.name_scope('nce_loss'):
    # construct variables for NCE loss
    nce_weight = tf.get_variable('nce_weight',
                            shape=[self.vocab_size, self.embed_size],
                            initializer=tf.truncated_normal_initializer(
```

```
                                    stddev=1.0 / (self.embed_size ** 0.5))))
        nce_bias = tf.get_variable('nce_bias',
                    initializer=tf.zeros([model_params["vocab_size"]])))

        # define loss function to be NCE loss function
        self.loss = tf.reduce_mean(tf.nn.nce_loss(weights=nce_weight,
                                biases=nce_bias,
                                labels=self.target_words,
                                inputs=self.embedding,
                                num_sampled=self.num_sampled,
                                num_classes=self.vocab_size),
                            name='loss')
```

We will then create another `name_scope`, to initialize an embedding matrix and an embedding lookup that can retrieve the embedding for any given word in the dataset. We will then create another `name_scope`, for defining the `loss` function. We will use **noise contrastive estimation** (**NCE**) loss, which converts a multinomial classification problem, such as the one encountered for predicting the next word, to a problem of binary logistic regression.

For each training sample in the dataset, the enhanced classifier is fed a true pair (one that appears in the center and another that appears in the context of the center word) and k number of randomly chosen negative pairs (consisting of the center word and a randomly chosen vocabulary word that does not occur in the context of the chosen word). By learning to distinguish the true pairs from the negative ones, the classifier learns the word vectors. In effect, this loss ensures that, instead of predicting the next word, the optimized classifier instead predicts whether a pair of words is good or bad. As the next step, we will define the optimizer that will be used for training:

```
        self.optimizer =
            tf.train.GradientDescentOptimizer(self.lr).minimize(self.loss,
                                        global_step=self.global_step)
```

`GradientDescentOptimizer` is an `optimizer` method that implements the gradient optimization algorithm, which allows for setting the learning rate parameter, as well as the step on which this optimization was performed.

Finally, we will create histogram and scalar summaries by using the loss values, so as to monitor the loss during training. We will merge all of the summaries, so that they can be displayed on TensorBoard:

```
        with tf.name_scope('summaries'):
            tf.summary.scalar('loss', self.loss)
```

```
tf.summary.histogram('histogram loss', self.loss)
self.summary_op = tf.summary.merge_all()
```

In these steps, we train the neural network for `train_steps` and monitor the loss. In general, the objective of the training is to reduce this loss value. However, if the training data is low, training for a longer period of time and using a higher dimensional word representation can often lead to overfitting. Hence, we need to ensure that the model does not overfit to the training data, while also ensuring that it generalizes well.

In the next section, we will visualize the embeddings by projecting them to a lower dimension, on TensorBoard.

Visualization of word embeddings

We will embed the trained word vectors into TensorBoard and visualize the learned vectors by projecting them down to two dimensions. For such a projection, we can use methods such as t-SNE or PCA, which are available in TensorBoard. The following screenshot shows how a projection using PCA appears on TensorBoard:

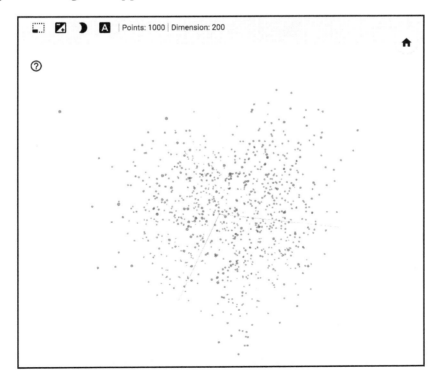

The preceding visualization illustrates how TensorBoard shows embeddings on its projector. However, this visualization does not look useful, and it makes no sense when it's viewed, as it uses PCA dimensionality reduction. Hence, we will switch the visualization mode to using t-SNE, which is another dimensionality reduction technique, well-suited for visualizing high dimensional data:

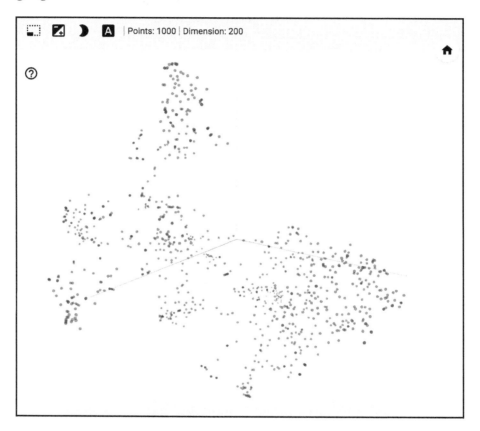

In the t-SNE projection, the word embeddings seem to have some patterns, apparent from the clusters appearing in different areas of the projection. In order to understand the topics that these clusters have discovered, TensorBoard allows for selectively zooming in on areas and viewing the underlying data in them. This operation can be viewed as follows:

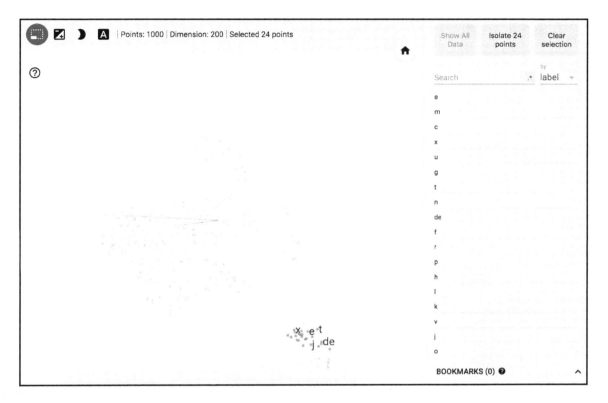

When we inspect an isolated cluster on TensorBoard, it becomes apparent that the vectors capture some general, semantic information about words and their relationships with one another. The words in the specific cluster that was selected have, interestingly, letters from the English alphabets of each just a single character long.

Next, we will search for a particular word and check its closest neighbors:

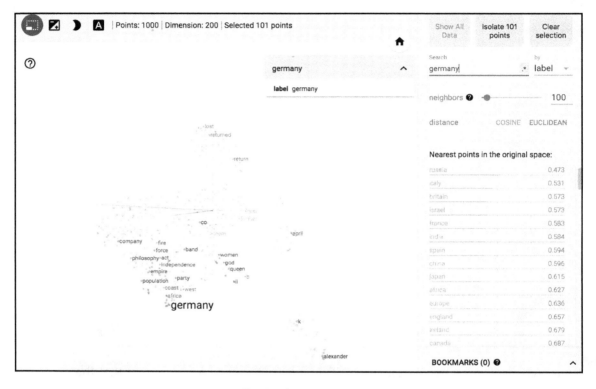

Clusterboard for the word Germany

In this case, we searched for the word `germany`, and found that the words closest to the given word are **russia**, **italy**, **britain**, and so on—all names of countries. It is very interesting to note that none of this information was provided to the model, in labels or any other form.

Another example of the model discovering semantic relationships between words is shown in the following screenshot:

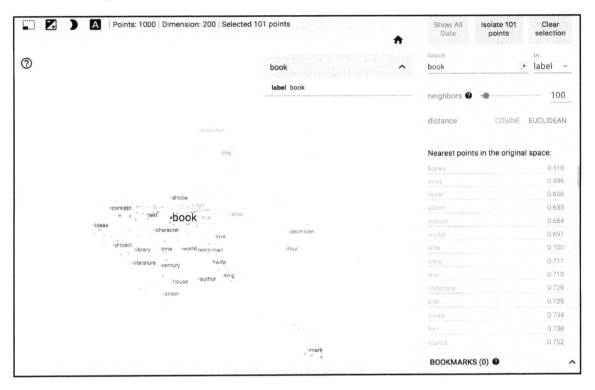

Clusterboard for the word book

This example shows how the closest words to the word `book` are found to be **story, novel**, and **album**. This semantic relationship was discovered by the model, an example of how Word2vec proves to be very useful, even with no prior information provided.

From word to document embeddings

Word2vec provided a very elegant method to produce good word vectors. However, sentence-or document-level vector representation is not inherently possible with word vectors, as the number of words in every document is variable. Hence, one of the simplest methods proposed in literature to extend word embeddings to a document is to average the individual word embeddings available in the document.

Therefore, document embedding can now be represented as follows:

$$Emb(d) = \sum_{i=1}^{m} w_i \times Emb(w_i)$$

In the preceding equation, since we are equally weighting all of the words in the sentence, $w_i = 1/m$. Hence, all of the weights are equally weighted to obtain the final document embedding. However, such an approach has the inherent assumption that all of the words in the document carry equal weightage in providing the meaning of the document.

Sentence2vec

One of the major drawbacks of the method that we discussed previously (for obtaining document-level vector representations) is that the words present in the document are given equal weight age. Such an approach suppresses the importance of certain words in the sentence, which actually add value to the meaning of the document. Let us discuss this point with a concrete example of how the method builds a document-level vector representation. Take a look at the sentence, *Jack and Jill went up the hill to fetch a pail of water*. In the sentence, the words that provide the most context about the action happening are *Jack, Jill, hill, fetch, pail*, and *water*. However, the preceding method builds the representation with equal weight given to every single word in the sentence.

An interesting approach that has been discussed is using the weighted average of word vectors, instead of equally weighting the words. One of the ways to calculate word weights is to use the tf-idf weights for every word, using tokens present in the document. The logic behind this approach is that frequently occurring words in a document do not convey much information. On the other hand, frequently occurring words across different documents convey more information about the importance of the word.

The tf-idf weighting can be explained using the following equation:

$$tf - idf_{t,d} = tf_{t,d} \times idf_t$$

In the preceding equation, *tf-idf*$_{t,d}$ issues a weight score, based on the term *t* and the document *d*, as follows:

- Highest if a term, *t*, is found across a few documents in the corpus
- Lower if the term occurs a fewer number of times in a document, or occurs in too many documents in the corpus (resulting in a lower relevance of the word)
- Lowest when the term, *t*, occurs in all of the documents and many times per document

Hence, the approach for getting a good document-level representation is to normalize the weights of individual words across a document, and to weight the words based on the normalized word weights. Such an approach is not only effective in document representations, but is also low in computational costs, as it ignores words with very low weights. Similar to the preceding method, we can represent the sentence2vec embedding as follows:

$$Emb(d) = \sum_{i-1}^{m} w_i \times Emb(w_i)$$

The major difference here is that the weights, w_i, are now different, and are calculated using the tf-idf. Hence, the final embedding is a weighted average of the word embedding vectors.

Alternative approaches to using raw weights include applying a threshold to the weights, to convert the weights into a binary format. Hence, the lower the threshold, the higher the number of words that will be used to produce the document representation, with more computing required. On the other hand, a high threshold for the weights would considerably reduce the number of words used in representing the document, lowering the computation cost, but this is at the risk of ignoring words that would be potentially useful for representing the document.

Doc2vec

A simple extension of the Word2vec model, applied to the document level, was proposed by Mikilov et al. In this method, in order to obtain document vectors, a unique document ID is appended to the document. It is trained with the words in the document to produce an average (or concatenated) of the word embeddings, in order to produce a document embedding. Hence, in the example that we discussed earlier, the doc2vec model data would look as follows:

- TensorFlow is an open source software library
- Python is an open source interpreted software programming language

Contrary to the earlier approach, the document lists now look as follows:

- [DOC_01, TensorFlow, is, an, open, source, software, library]
- [DOC_02, Python, is, an, open, source, interpreted, software, programming, language]

This doc2vec model looks very similar to the approach that we discussed with CBOW. Hence, the document vector, D, for every document, is trained simultaneously, when we train the word vectors, W. This results in training the word vectors as well as the document vectors, which are accessible to us when the training is complete. The reason that this method is similar to CBOW is that the model tries to predict the target word, given the context word. Hence, in the example, *DOC_01*, *TensorFlow*, *is*, and *an*, are used to predict *open*. This model is called the **Paragraph Vector Distributed Memory** (**PV-DM**). The idea behind a document vector is to represent the semantic context of the topic that is discussed in the document.

Similar to Word2vec, a variant of the PV-DM model is the **Paragraph Vector – Distributed Bag of Words** (**PV-DBOW**), which is similar to the skip-gram model of Word2vec. Hence, in this version, the model proposes the target word vectors, given a context word. For instance, *DOC_01* is used to predict the words, *TensorFlow*, *is*, *an*, and *open*. One potential advantage that doc2vec bears over Word2vec, is that the word vectors do not need to be stored.

Visualization of document embeddings

Similar to the earlier visualizations, let us look at how doc2vec trains documents, and how the final document embeddings can enable an understanding of the underlying topics of the documents:

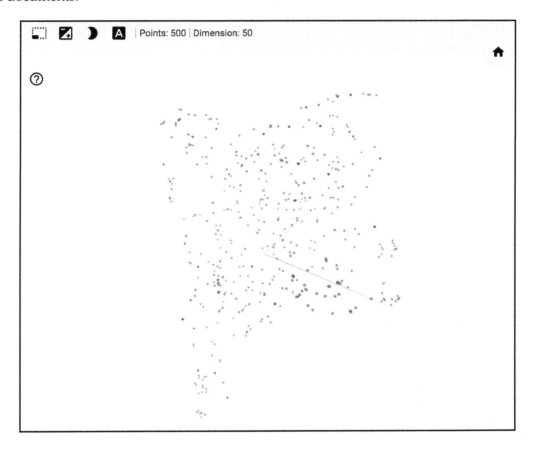

In the preceding visualization, you can see that there are some clusters visible in the upper-left corner and at the bottom of the screenshot. This visualization shows that we can figure out the topics of the documents without any explicit labeling of those topics. However, let us see what these clusters include:

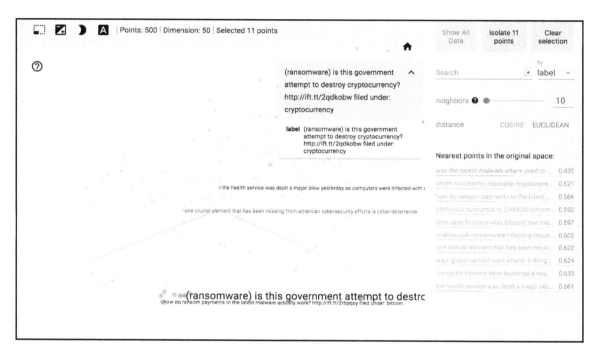

In the preceding cluster, we can see that the doc2vec model has discovered a cluster of documents that are discussing **malware attacks**. The visualization in the middle shows the cluster, while the list on the right shows the documents and their similarity scores, when compared to the document, **is this government attempt to destroy cryptocurrency**. It can be seen that, although this document does not have any words about malware or attack, doc2vec has discovered that the document is discussing malware attacks by using the contexts in which **ransomware** is present in other documents. Let us explore another cluster present in the embedding projector:

This cluster shows a set of documents that are completely separate from the other documents in the corpus. These documents discuss URLs from which they were archived and contain a URL along with the words archived from the document. The rest of the documents in this cluster are also URLs and text, similar to the other documents in the cluster:

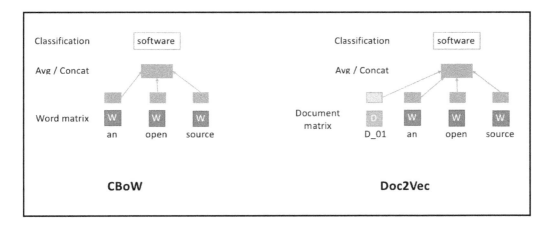

The preceding figure compares doc2vec with the CBOW model of Word2vec. This illustration shows the clear extension of Word2vec to the doc2vec model, an extension from learning word vectors to document vectors.

Summary

In this chapter, we discussed Word2vec and its variants, then walked through the code for developing a skip-gram model for understanding word relationships. We then used TensorBoard to visualize word embeddings, and looked at how its various projections can provide very useful visualizations. We then discussed a logical extension of Word2vec to produce a document representation, which we improved by leveraging the tf-idf weights. Finally, we discussed doc2vec and its variants for building document-level vector representations. We also looked at how document embeddings can discover the topics present in documents, using TensorBoard.

In the next chapter, we will look at using deep neural networks for text classification. We will look at the different neural networks that can be used to build a text classifier, and will discuss the pros and cons of each architecture.

Text Classification Using LSTM 5

Text classification is the task of tagging natural language texts or unstructured text to one of the categories from a predefined set. Identifying positive-negative sentiments in product reviews, categorizing news articles, and segmenting customers based on their conversations about products in social media are some of the applications of text classification. One real-world example is automatic spam detection using **machine learning (ML)** in Gmail. The main goal of this chapter is to make the reader understand and get familiar with hands-on deep learning approaches for text classification.

In the previous chapters (Chapter 2, *Text Classification and POS Tagging Using NLTK*), we briefly touched upon text classification using classic ML approaches using a bag-of-words models with NLTK and sklearn. In this chapter, we will dive deeper into classifying text using deep learning methods. The focus of this chapter will be mainly on using **recurrent neural networks (RNNs)**, such as **Long Short-Term Memory (LSTM)**, and **Gated Recurrent Units (GRUs)** for text classification. However, we will also cover **Convolutional Neural Networks (CNNs)** for completeness. To address the breadth of this topic, we will also touch upon a related unsupervised learning method called **topic modeling**. To summarize, the following will be the main topics covered in this chapter:

- Topic modeling
- Using CNNs to classify text
- RNNs for text classification
- Text classification with transfer learning
- A brief summary of state-of-the-art deep learning approaches to text classification

Data for text classification

Before diving into the **machine learning** (**ML**) problems in text classification, we will take a look at the different open datasets that are available on the internet. Many of the classification tasks may require large labeled text data. This data can be broadly grouped into those with binary classes, multi-classes, and multi-labels. The following are some of the popular datasets used for benchmarking in both research and some competitions, such as Kaggle:

	Dataset name	Class type	Source
1	IMDb movie Dataset	Binary classes	http://ai.stanford.edu/~amaas/data/sentiment/
2	Twitter Sentiment Analysis Dataset	Binary classes	http://thinknook.com/twitter-sentiment-analysis-training-corpus-dataset-2012-09-22/
3	YouTube Spam Collection Dataset	Binary classes	https://archive.ics.uci.edu/ml/datasets/YouTube+Spam+Collection
4	News Aggregator Dataset	Multiclass	https://archive.ics.uci.edu/ml/datasets/News+Aggregator
5	Yelp reviews	Multi-label	https://www.yelp.com/dataset
6	Amazon reviews dataset	Multiclass	http://jmcauley.ucsd.edu/data/amazon/
7	Reuters Corpora	Multi-label/Multiclass	http://trec.nist.gov/data/reuters/reuters.html

Some of the preceding datasets will also be used as examples for this chapter. While the preceding list is not exhaustive, these are provided for the reader so that they can start experimenting with text classification and topic categorization tasks.

 A comprehensive list of open datasets can also be found from the UCI repository at https://archive.ics.uci.edu/ml/datasets.html and from Kaggle at https://www.kaggle.com/datasets.

Topic modeling

When we have a collection of documents for which we do not clearly know the categories, topic models help us to roughly find the categorization. The model treats each document as a mixture of topics, probably with one dominating topic.

For example, let's suppose we have the following sentences:

- Eating fruits as snacks is a healthy habit
- Exercising regularly is an important part of a healthy lifestyle
- Grapefruit and oranges are citrus fruits

A topic model of these sentences may output the following:

- **Topic A**: 40% healthy, 20% fruits, 10% snacks
- **Topic B**: 20% Grapefruit, 20% oranges, 10% citrus
- **Sentence 1 and 2**: 80% Topic A, 20% Topic B
- **Sentence 3**: 100% Topic B

From the output of the model, we can guess that *Topic A* is about health and *Topic B* is about fruits. Though these topics are not known apriori, the model outputs corresponding probabilities for words associated with health, exercising, and fruits in the documents.

It is clear from these examples that topic modeling is an unsupervised learning method. It helps in discovering structures or patterns in documents when we have little or no labels for doing text classification. The most popular algorithm for topic modeling is **Latent Dirichlet Allocation (LDA)** for short. The original paper on LDA uses a variational Bayesian method for estimating the probabilities of words belonging to different topics. The details of the algorithm can be found in the paper *Latent Dirichlet Allocation* as this is out of the scope of this book (`https://dl.acm.org/citation.cfm?id=944937`). We will now look at an example of topic modeling using LDA. We will be using the `gensim` library for the LDA model to find topics in sample texts from the NLTK `webtext` corpus, which we introduced in `Chapter 2`, *Text Classification and POS Tagging Using NLTK*. The complete Jupyter Notebook for this example is available under the `Chapter05/01_example.ipynb` directory in this book's code repository. First, we will import the necessary Python modules for our example:

```
from nltk.corpus import webtext, stopwords
import gensim
import random
from pprint import pprint
import numpy as np
import logging
#logging.basicConfig(format='%(asctime)s : %(levelname)s : %(message)s',
level=logging.INFO)
```

Here, we import the `nltk`, `webtext`, and `stopwords` corpus. For using the `gensim` module, we have it using the `pip` installer:

```
pip install gensim
```

This will install `gensim` on the system. The code that follows reads the sentences from the corresponding text corpus:

```
firefox = webtext.sents('firefox.txt')
wine = webtext.sents('wine.txt')
pirates = webtext.sents('pirates.txt')
```

The `sents` function reads the sentence from the respective text corpus. The sentences from the Firefox discussion forum, the script of the movie *Pirates of the Caribbean*, and `wine` reviews are collected in a list, as shown in the following code:

```
all_docs = []
all_docs.extend(firefox)
all_docs.extend(pirates)
all_docs.extend(wine)
random.shuffle(all_docs)
```

This will collate all the text documents in a Python list, and we will shuffle the list to transform it into a random list collection of text. We will later verify if the topic model can distinguish between the three different topic categories we have chosen from the NLTK `webtext` corpus by using the following code:

```
docs = [[word for word in doc if word not in stopwords.words('english')]
for doc in all_docs]
docs = [doc for doc in docs if len(doc)&gt;1]
```

In the following code, we remove the stop words from the text using the NLTK `stopwords` corpus. We also discard all documents with length or number of words less than 1:

```
chunksize=len(docs)
dictionary = gensim.corpora.Dictionary(docs)
corpus = [dictionary.doc2bow(doc) for doc in docs]
model = gensim.models.LdaModel(corpus=corpus, id2word=dictionary,
num_topics=3,passes=20)
```

We use the gensim `dictionary` class to transform our text collection `docs` to a bag-of-words representation which is stored in the `corpus` variable. The dictionary transforms the documents into sparse bag-of-words vectors with corresponding IDs for each word or token. This is passed to the `LdaModel` along with the dictionary for the ID to word mapping training. We have also set the number of topics equal to 3, which is the same as the number of topics we obtained from the NLTK `webtext` corpus. Finally, the number of passes has been set to 20 for the model. The code that follows extracts the top topics from the corpus:

```
top_topics = model.top_topics(corpus)
print("Topic 1: ")
print(top_topics[0][0])
print("Topic 2: ")
print(top_topics[1][0])
print("Topic 3: ")
print(top_topics[2][0])
```

The following output shows the topics and the probability of words occurring in each topic:

```
Topic 1:
[(0.029538315, '.'), (0.025298702, '"'), (0.018974159, "'"), (0.017001661,
'-'), (0.0097839413, '('), (0.0089947991, 'page'), (0.0080595175, ')'),
(0.0076006982, 'window'), (0.0075753955, 'Firefox'), (0.0061700493,
'open'), (0.0058493023, 'menu'), (0.0057583884, 'bar'), (0.005752211, ':'),
(0.0057242708, 'tab'), (0.0054682544, 'new'), (0.0053855875, 'Firebird'),
(0.0052021407, 'work'), (0.0050605903, 'browser'), (0.00455163, '0'),
(0.0045419205, 'button')]

Topic 2:
[(0.10882618, '.'), (0.048713163, ','), (0.033278842, '-'), (0.019521466,
'I'), (0.018609792, '***'), (0.011298033, 'fruit'), (0.010273052, 'good'),
(0.0097078849, 'A'), (0.0089780623, 'wine'), (0.0089215562, '"'),
(0.0087491088, 'bit'), (0.0080983331, 'quite'), (0.0072782212, 'Top'),
(0.0061755609, '****'), (0.0060614017, '**'), (0.005842932, 'nose'),
(0.0057750815, 'touch'), (0.0049686432, 'Bare'), (0.0048470194, 'Very'),
(0.0047901836, 'palate')]

Topic 3:
[(0.051035155, ','), (0.043318823, ':'), (0.037644491, '.'), (0.029482145,
'['), (0.029230012, ']'), (0.023068342, '"'), (0.019555457, '!'),
(0.012494524, 'Jack'), (0.011483309, '?'), (0.010315109, '*'),
(0.008776715, 'JACK'), (0.008776715, 'SPARROW'), (0.0074223313, '-'),
(0.0061529884, 'WILL'), (0.0061529884, 'TURNER'), (0.0060977913, 'Will'),
(0.0055771996, 'I'), (0.0054870662, '...'), (0.0041205585, 'ELIZABETH'),
(0.0041205585, 'SWANN')]
```

We can see some patterns in the output of the model based on the word occurrences for each topic, though the output appears to include even punctuation characters. `Topic 1` appears to be about the `Firefox` discussion forum, `Topic 2` follows the theme of `wine` reviews, and `Topic 3` is from the *Pirates of the Caribbean* movie script.

Topic modeling versus text classification

Topic modeling, as we have seen in the previous example, is not mutually exclusive as it models documents as a mixture of topics. For example, a document can be categorized as 70% Topic A and 30% Topic B. Text classification, on the other hand, classifies documents exclusively belonging to a specific class. However, this requires labeled data that may not always be available. It is also possible to use the output of a topic model as a feature for text classification which might improve the classification's accuracy. Topic models can also be used to quickly create manual labeled data that can be subsequently used for training a text classifier. We have touched upon topic modeling and have seen how it differs from text classification or complements it. Let's now explore text classification using deep learning models.

Deep learning meta architecture for text classification

Deep learning text classification model architectures commonly consist of the following three components connected in sequence:

- Embedding layer
- Deep representation component
- Fully connected part

We will discuss each of them in the following topics.

Embedding layer

Given a sequence of word IDs as input, the embedding layer transforms these into an output list of dense word vectors. The word vectors capture the semantics of the words, as we have seen in `Chapter 3`, *Semantic Embedding using Shallow Models*. In the deep learning frameworks such as TensorFlow, this part is usually handled by an embedding lookup layer which stores a lookup table to map the words represented by numeric IDs to their dense vector representations.

Deep representation

Deep representation takes the sequence of embedding vectors as input and converts them to a compressed representation. The compressed representation effectively captures all the information in the sequence of words in the text. The deep representation part is usually an **RNN**, though a **CNN** can be utilized as well. For the RNN, the compressed representation of the text is the final hidden state of the network output after the last time step. In the CNN, this will be the output of the last layer, which would commonly be a max pooling layer. Both the RNN and CNN outputs, therefore, capture deep representations of the text inputs.

Fully connected part

The **fully connected part** takes the deep representation from either the RNN or CNN and transforms it into the final output classes or class scores. This component is comprised of fully connected layers along with batch normalization and optionally dropout layers for regularization.

We have now seen the general meta-architecture of a deep learning text classifier. In the following sections, we will dive into hands-on examples of text classifiers, incorporating this architecture as we go. Specifically, we will look at identifying spam in YouTube video reviews and classifying news articles.

Identifying spam in YouTube video comments using RNNs

As a first example, we will look into the problem of identifying spam in YouTube video comments. The complete Jupyter Notebook for this example is available under the `Chapter05/02_example.ipynb` directory in this book's code repository. The data contains the comments with binary labels specifying whether the comment is genuine or spam. The code that follows loads the comments in CSV format into a pandas DataFrame:

```
comments_df_list = []
comments_file = ['data/Youtube01-Psy.csv','data/Youtube02-
KatyPerry.csv','data/Youtube03-LMFAO.csv',
 'data/Youtube04-Eminem.csv','data/Youtube05-Shakira.csv']
for f in comments_file:
 df = pd.read_csv(f,header=0)
 comments_df_list.append(df)
comments_df = pd.concat(comments_df_list)
comments_df = comments_df.sample(frac=1.0)
print(comments_df.shape)
comments_df.head(5)
```

The following output shows a sample of the YouTube comments with the various fields:

	COMMENT_ID	AUTHOR	DATE	CONTENT	CLASS
102	z12dfr5irwr5chwm3232gvnq2laqcdezn04	Carlos Rueda	2015-05-22T15:04:20.310000	I am going to blow my mind	0
117	z133ibkihkmaj3bfq22rilaxmp2yt54nb	Debora Favacho (Debora Sparkle)	2015-05-21T14:08:41.338000	BEST SONG EVER X3333333333	0
331	_2viQ_Qnc68Qq98m0mmx4rlprYiD6aYgMb2x3bdupEM	Hidden Love	2013-08-01T09:19:56.654000	Hi. Check out and share our songs.	1
322	z13cedgolkfvw3xey22kcnzrfm3egjj0z	Rafael Diaz Jr	2015-01-25T20:57:46.039000	Check out this video on YouTube:	1
133	LneaDw26bFugQanw0UtVOqzEgWt6mBD0k6SsEV7u968	Jacob Johnson	NaN	You guys should check out this EXTRAORDINARY w...	1

Here, we load the `.csv` files from five popular YouTube videos and load them into a pandas DataFrame. We can see from the output that it shows both a valid comment and spam. The CONTENT column contains the comment text and the CLASS column is set to 1 for spam and 0 otherwise. We will use the average of all comments size as the maximum size of each comment by using the following code. Any comments with the number of words greater than this will be truncated to keep the training data of fixed length:

```
average_comments_size = int(sum([len(c) for c in
comments_df.CONTENT])/comments_df.shape[0])
print(average_comments_size)
```

We utilize the `vocabulary_processor` to preprocess all the comments and split the data into training and test, with an 80% to 20% ratio, as shown in the following code:

```
vocabulary_processor =
tf.contrib.learn.preprocessing.VocabularyProcessor(average_comments_size)
X_transform = vocabulary_processor.fit_transform(comments_df.CONTENT)
X_transform = np.array(list(X_transform))
y = comments_df.CLASS.values
X_train, X_test, y_train, y_test =
model_selection.train_test_split(X_transform,
 y, test_size=0.2, random_state=42)
n_words = len(vocabulary_processor.vocabulary_)
```

In this example and subsequent examples in this chapter, we will utilize the TensorFlow estimator API to create, train, and test the models. Estimators in TensorFlow provide an easy to use interface for building the graph, initializing variables, creating checkpoint files, and saving summaries for TensorBoard viewing. We will use the following code to create the `estimator`:

```
def get_estimator_spec(input_logits, out_lb, train_predict_m):
    preds_cls = tf.argmax(input_logits, 1)
    if train_predict_m == tf.estimator.ModeKeys.PREDICT:
        return tf.estimator.EstimatorSpec(
        mode=train_predict_m,
        predictions={
            'pred_class': preds_cls,
            'pred_prob': tf.nn.softmax(input_logits)
        })
    tr_l = tf.losses.sparse_softmax_cross_entropy(labels=out_lb,
logits=input_logits)
    if train_predict_m == tf.estimator.ModeKeys.TRAIN:
        adm_opt = tf.train.AdamOptimizer(learning_rate=0.01)
        tr_op = adm_opt.minimize(tr_l,
global_step=tf.train.get_global_step())
        return tf.estimator.EstimatorSpec(train_predict_m, loss=tr_l,
```

```
train_op=tr_op)
    eval_metric_ops = {'accuracy': tf.metrics.accuracy(labels=out_lb,
predictions=preds_cls)}
    return tf.estimator.EstimatorSpec(train_predict_m, loss=tr_l,
train_op=tr_op)
```

The `AdamOptimizer` is used for optimizing the `loss` function for which we use the `tf.losses.sparse_softmax_cross_entropy` function. This computes the cross-entropy given the logits with probability distribution across the two classes and the true labels:

```
def rnn_model_fn(features, labels, mode):
    comments_wd_vec = tf.contrib.layers.embed_sequence(
        features[COMMENTS_FT], vocab_size=n_words, embed_dim=EMBED_DIMENSION)
    comments_word_list = tf.unstack(comments_wd_vec, axis=1)
    rnn_cell = tf.nn.rnn_cell.GRUCell(average_comments_size)
    _, comments_encoding = tf.nn.static_rnn(rnn_cell, comments_word_list,
dtype=tf.float32)
    logits = tf.layers.dense(inputs=comments_encoding, units=2,
activation=None)
    return get_estimator_spec(input_logits=logits, out_lb=labels,
train_predict_m=mode)
```

As described in the previous section, on meta-architecture for text classification for the model, we utilize an embedding layer followed by a `GRUCell`. The output of the GRU is fed to a dense layer that computes the `logits`. The `logits` output is then passed to the `softmax` layer to compute the class predictions. The GRU cell used in this example is similar to the LSTM with the difference being it outputs the hidden state with no control gates. Therefore, the LSTM has one extra gate compared to the GRU. In addition to that, unlike LSTMs, GRUs may not be able to remember long-term word associations. However, for this specific task, the differences may not be significant. You can also experiment with replacing the GRU cell with an LSTM in the code, as shown here:

```
run_config = tf.contrib.learn.RunConfig()
run_config =
run_config.replace(model_dir='/tmp/models/',save_summary_steps=10,log_step_
count_steps=10)
classifier =
tf.estimator.Estimator(model_fn=rnn_model_fn,config=run_config)
```

We store the model checkpoint file under the `/tmp/models` directory using `RunConfig`. The logging and summary step frequency is also modified from its default value of 100 to 10 for better visualization in TensorBoard. You can also modify these values accordingly in the code. Finally, we train the model for 200 steps by using the following code:

```
train_input_fn = tf.estimator.inputs.numpy_input_fn(
        x={COMMENTS_FT: X_train},
        y=y_train,
        batch_size=128,
        num_epochs=None,
        shuffle=True)
classifier.train(input_fn=train_input_fn, steps=200)
Output
INFO:tensorflow:Saving checkpoints for 200 into /tmp/models/model.ckpt.
INFO:tensorflow:Loss for final step: 0.000836024.
```

The model is evaluated on the test data and we obtain an accuracy of 94%, as you can see from the following code:

```
test_input_fn = tf.estimator.inputs.numpy_input_fn(
        x={COMMENTS_FT: X_test},
        y=y_test,
        num_epochs=1,
        shuffle=False)
preds = classifier.predict(input_fn=test_input_fn)
y_predicted = np.array(list(p['pred_class'] for p in preds))
y_predicted = y_predicted.reshape(np.array(y_test).shape)

acc = metrics.accuracy_score(y_test, y_predicted)
print('Accuracy: {0:f}'.format(acc))
```

The following is the output of the preceding code:

```
INFO:tensorflow:Restoring parameters from /tmp/models/model.ckpt-200
Accuracy: 0.905612
```

To visualize the graph and training process, start TensorBoard with the `logdir` pointing to the same path we used in `RunConfig`. Point the browser to `localhose:6006` (default) to view the graphs and plots. We can see that the loss steadily decreases with the training step, as shown in the following screenshot:

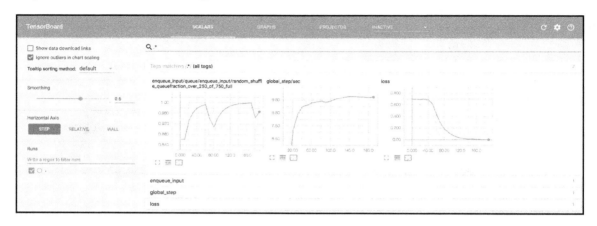

Training loss and steps/sec

Visualization of the model graph shows the input, embedding layer, RNN cell, the dense layer, and the softmax output:

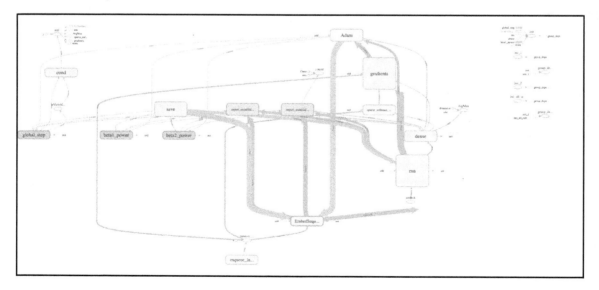

Text classification model

In the embedding projection, we can also see that there is a clear separation of the word embedding into the two clusters learned by the model. The following screenshot shows an example of the words associated with spam and those associated with a genuine comment. This shows how the model has pushed the word vectors associated with these two classes into separate clusters:

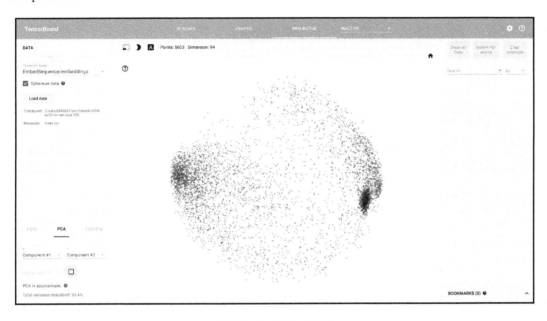

Word vector visualization with PCA

We have seen how an RNN-based deep learning model can be used for text classification. As explained previously, we can also use a CNN to do text classification, which we will explore next.

Classifying news articles by topic using a CNN

For this example, we will use the dataset of references to news web pages collected by a news aggregator. There are four categories in the dataset belonging to the news of science and technology, business, entertainment, and health. The complete Jupyter Notebook for this example can be found under the `Chapter05/03_example.ipynb` directory in this book's code repository.

We will first look at the sample of the data from this dataset:

```
news_df = pd.read_csv('data/newsCorpora.csv',delimiter='\t', header=None,
names=['ID','TITLE','URL','PUBLISHER','CATEGORY','STORY','HOSTNAME','TIMEST
AMP'])
news_df = news_df.sample(frac=1.0)
news_df.head(5)
```

The dataset is represented in the table format as follows:

ID	TITLE	CATEGORY
225897	Fed's Dudley sees *relatively slow* rate hike...	b
26839	L'Wren Scott's death officially ruled as suicide	e
32332	Idina Menzel Says She *Benefited* From John Tr...	e
188058	Weak earnings and the dark cloud of Ukraine co...	b
22176	Android Wear- Google's latest PLAY	t

Here, we are only interested in the TITLE and CATEGORY columns. The CATEGORY column will be set to one of the four categories to which the news belongs to. This is represented by characters t, b, e, and m for science and technology, business, entertainment, and health, respectively. As in the previous example, we take the average size of the TITLE as the maximum document size to fix the length of the training instances.

The TensorFlow vocabulary_processor is used for preprocessing each TITLE text to a list of words with the length of the list fixed to the average title size. If the number of words is greater than the average title size, the text is truncated. If it is less than the average title size, it is padded with zeros. This is achieved with the following code:

```
lencoder = LabelEncoder()
voc_processor =
tf.contrib.learn.preprocessing.VocabularyProcessor(average_title_size)
X_transform = voc_processor.fit_transform(news_df.TITLE)
X_transform = np.array(list(X_transform))
y = lencoder.fit_transform(news_df.CATEGORY.values)
X_train, X_test, y_train, y_test =
model_selection.train_test_split(X_transform,
                                  y, test_size=0.2, random_state=42)
n_words = len(voc_processor.vocabulary_)
n_classes = len(lencoder.classes_)
```

The `AdamOptimizer` with sparse softmax cross-entropy is used for training the model, like before. For the model, we replace the `GRUCell` in the previous example with a convolutional layer followed by max pooling. The number of filters is set to 5 while the filter height is set to 3, with the width equal to the embedding size. Therefore, the filter convolution is performed three words at a time with a single stride, as specified in the stride parameters. The number of convolutional layers is set to one for a simple architecture and faster training. You can experiment with increasing both the number of filters as well as the convolutional layers. Note that we have also reshaped the input embeddings to four-dimensional tensors with the last channel dimension being 1. The following code shows how the CNN model is constructed:

```
filter_size=3
num_filters=5
def cnn_model_fn(features,labels,mode):
    news_word_vectors = tf.contrib.layers.embed_sequence(features[NEWS_FT],
vocab_size=n_words,
embed_dim=WORD_EMBEDDING_SIZE)
    news_word_vectors = tf.expand_dims(news_word_vectors, -1)
    filter_shape = [filter_size, WORD_EMBEDDING_SIZE, 1, num_filters]
    W = tf.Variable(tf.truncated_normal(filter_shape, stddev=0.1),
name="W")
    b = tf.Variable(tf.constant(0.1, shape=[num_filters]), name="b")
    conv1 = tf.nn.conv2d(news_word_vectors,
            W,
            strides=[1, 1, 1, 1],
            padding="VALID",
            name="conv1")
    relu1 = tf.nn.relu(tf.nn.bias_add(conv1, b), name="relu")
    pool1 = tf.nn.max_pool(
            relu1,
            ksize=[1, average_title_size - 3 + 1, 1, 1],
            strides=[1, 1, 1, 1],
            padding='VALID',
            name="pool1")
    activations1 = tf.contrib.layers.flatten(pool1)
    logits =
tf.contrib.layers.fully_connected(activations1,n_classes,activation_fn=None
)
    return get_estimator_spec(input_logits=logits, out_lb=labels,
train_predict_m=mode)
```

As before, we train the model for 200 training steps and evaluate it on the test data by using the following code:

```
run_config = tf.contrib.learn.RunConfig()
run_config =
run_config.replace(model_dir='/tmp/models/',save_summary_steps=10,log_step_
count_steps=10)
classifier =
tf.estimator.Estimator(model_fn=cnn_model_fn,config=run_config)
train_input_fn = tf.estimator.inputs.numpy_input_fn(
        x={NEWS_FT: X_train},
        y=y_train,
        batch_size=len(X_train),
        num_epochs=None,
        shuffle=True)
classifier.train(input_fn=train_input_fn, steps=100)
```

The following is the output result for the test data:

```
INFO:tensorflow:Restoring parameters from /tmp/models/model.ckpt-27
Accuracy: 0.903094
[[20990    534    108   1559]
 [  410  29606    142    331]
 [  493   1432   5741   1381]
 [ 1266    369    162  19960]]
```

We can see both the accuracy and the confusion matrix. The accuracy is around 93% and the diagonal column of the confusion matrix shows the correct predictions for the document type. We can visualize the model graph and learning metrics plots in TensorBoard:

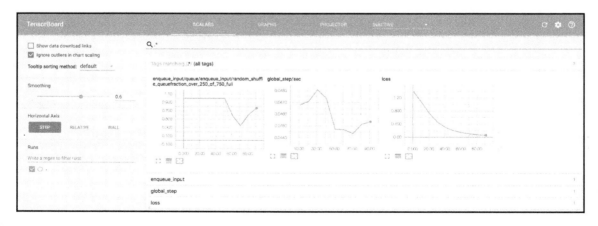

Training loss and steps/sec

We can see the training loss decreasing with the number of training steps. The accuracy can be improved by adding more convolutional layers and increasing the number of filters, as shown in the following screenshot:

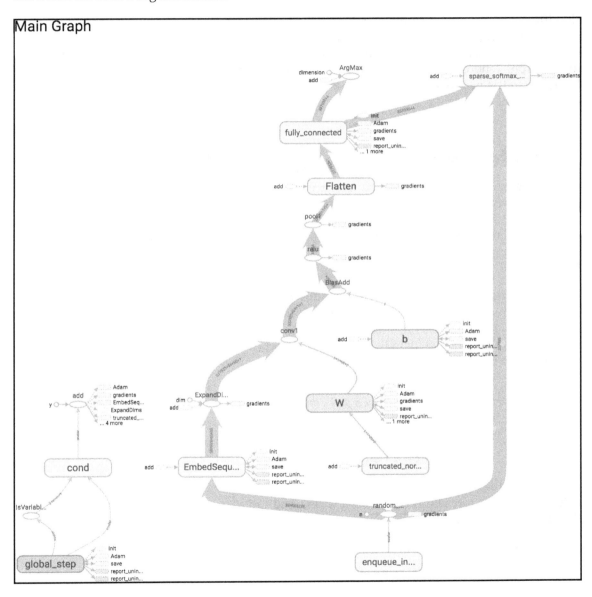

CNN model for text classification

The graph shows the input, embedding layer, convolutional layer, max pooling, dense layer, and the softmax output.

We have seen how the same neural network meta-architecture can be utilized for text classification. The only difference between the two examples was that the first used an RNN as the deep representation whereas the latter example used a CNN. But in both examples, the input word embedding's were learned from scratch using the training data. In situations where we have less training data, we can turn to other approaches like transfer learning. In the next example, we will use pre-learned word embedding for text classification.

Transfer learning using GloVe embeddings

Global Vectors (**GloVe**) uses global word-word co-occurrences statistics in a large text corpus to arrive at dense vector representations of words. It is an unsupervised learning method with the objective of making the dot product of the learned vectors equal to the logarithm of the probability of co-occurrences. This translates to differences in vectors in the embedding space as the ratio of logarithms of ratio equals to the difference in logarithms.

For this example, we will use the GloVe embedding, which is pre-trained on Twitter data. This data consists of around 2 billion tweets with a vocabulary size of 1.2 million. For the classification task, we use the customer reviews or ratings of Amazon instant videos. First, we must load the reviews data in JSON format and convert it to a pandas DataFrame, as shown in the following code:

```
json_data = []
with gzip.open('data/reviews_Amazon_Instant_Video_5.json.gz', 'rb') as
json_file:
for json_str in json_file:
  json_data.append(json.loads(json_str))
  reviews_df = pd.DataFrame.from_records(json_data)
```

For our classification task, we are only interested in the `reviewText` fields and `overall` columns which represent the user review text and rating, respectively. We print the sample data to see the ratings and review text, as shown in the following code:

```
reviews_df[['overall','reviewText']].head(5)
```

The following is the output of the preceding code:

	overall	reviewText
9102	4.0	I enjoy this show because it shows old stuff t...
22551	5.0	I really enjoy these programs. I am a pretty g...
33811	3.0	Decent cast, but it seems a little formulaic...
8127	5.0	My kids love this show. It's one of my 3 year...
17544	5.0	How they keep coming up with the shenanigans t...

The word vectors are then loaded from the GloVe embeddings text file using the following code:

```
def build_word_vector_matrix(vector_file):
    np_arrays = []
    labels_array = []
    with codecs.open(vector_file, 'r', 'utf-8') as f:
        for i, line in enumerate(f):
            sr = line.split()
            if(len(sr)&lt;26):
                continue
            labels_array.append(sr[0])
            np_arrays.append(np.array([float(j) for j in sr[1:]]))
    return np.array(np_arrays), labels_array
```

Each line in the file consists of the word followed by its corresponding vector representation. This is read into the numpy array np_arrays and the corresponding word is read into the labels_array. The build_word_vector_matrix, when called, returns the word token and the word vector arrays. Like before, we transform the reviews data to fixed length sentences of maximum length equal to the average size of all reviews with TensorFlow's vocabulary_processor. We pass the review DataFrame to the vocabulary_processor to achieve this, as shown in the following code:

```
lencoder = LabelEncoder()
voc_processor =
tf.contrib.learn.preprocessing.VocabularyProcessor(average_review_size)
voc_processor.fit(vocabulary)
X_transform = voc_processor.transform(reviews_df.reviewText)
X_transform = np.array(list(X_transform))
y = lencoder.fit_transform(reviews_df.overall.values)
X_train, X_test, y_train, y_test =
model_selection.train_test_split(X_transform,
                                 y, test_size=0.2, random_state=42)
n_words = len(voc_processor.vocabulary_)
n_classes = len(lencoder.classes_)
```

The model function for the estimator uses an RNN, as in our previous example, except that we set the `Trainable=False` for the input embedding variable `word_embeddings`. This ensures that during the model's training, the embeddings are not learned again. Note that the `word_embeddings` variable contains the lookup table for the GloVe embeddings. The code that follows shows the function utilized for creating the RNN model:

```
def rnn_model_fn(features,labels,mode):
    em_plholder = tf.placeholder(tf.float32, [voc_size, WD_EMB_SIZE])
    Wt = tf.Variable(em_plholder,trainable=False, name='Wt')
    comments_word_vec = tf.nn.embedding_lookup(Wt, features[REVIEW_FT])
    comments_wd_l = tf.unstack(comments_word_vec, axis=1)
    rnn_cell = tf.nn.rnn_cell.GRUCell(WD_EMB_SIZE)
    _, comments_encoding = tf.nn.static_rnn(rnn_cell, comments_wd_l,
dtype=tf.float32)
    dense = tf.layers.dense(comments_encoding, units=512,
activation=tf.nn.relu)
    dropout = tf.layers.dropout(inputs=dense,
rate=0.4,training=(mode==tf.estimator.ModeKeys.TRAIN))
    logits = tf.layers.dense(inputs=dropout, units=n_classes)
    return get_estimator_spec(input_logits=logits, out_lb=labels,
train_predict_m=mode,
embedding_placeholder=em_plholder)
```

Like we did previously, we can view the model graph and training in TensorBoard. We can see the steady decrease in the learning rate with the step count:

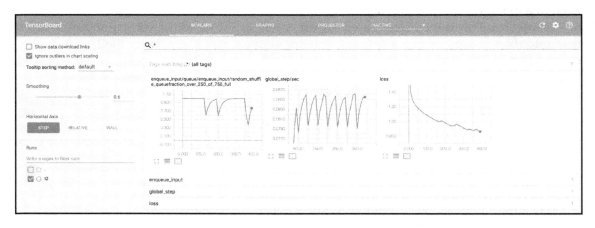

Training loss and steps/sec

The following graph shows the network with `word_embedding` input, RNN layer, FC layer, and finally the softmax output:

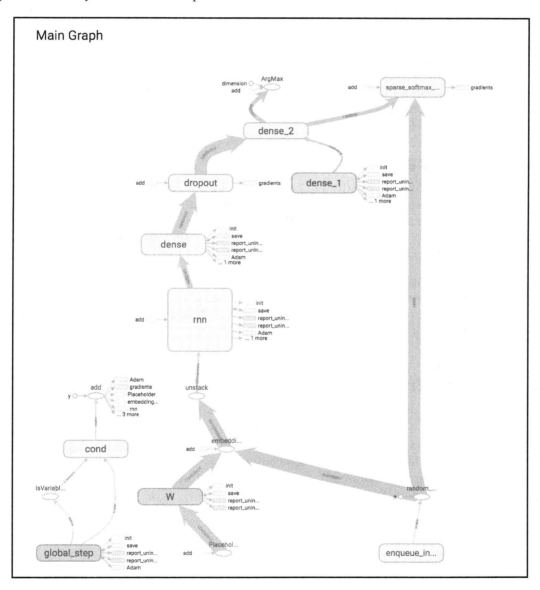

Model with GloVe embeddings

Multi-label classification

So far, we have seen problems in which we need to classify text into one of the classes or labels. There are text classification problems in which we might need to attach multiple categories to the same document. For example, in the `Yelp reviews` dataset, the reviewer might be talking about different aspects of a restaurant such as the food, ambiance, quality of service, and so on. In this case, we need to identify what categories the review belongs to so that we can understand the overall review. We will now look at some of the existing approaches to this problem.

Binary relevance

Multi-label classification for identifying L labels of a document can be transformed to an L binary classification problem. In this approach, we pass a document into the L binary classifiers, where each are trained for identifying one of the L classes. The output of the L classifiers is merged to produce a vector of class labels to which the document belongs. Even for simple models such as decision trees, SVMs can be used for the binary classifiers.

Though this is the simplest approach, the disadvantage is that it assumes the categories are independent of each other, which may not always be the case. For example, in our Yelp review example, the ambiance and service categories may be correlated. We will now look at other approaches for handling this.

Deep learning for multi-label classification

In the paper on *Large-scale Multi-label Text Classification – Revisiting Neural Networks* (https://arxiv.org/abs/1312.5419), Nam et al. approaches this problem by using a deep **multi-layer perceptron** (**MLP**) with a hidden layer and output units producing scores for the labels. They use a label predictor which converts the label scores from the deep network to binary classes using thresholding based on a rank loss function. The details of this approach can be found in the aforementioned paper.

The following diagram illustrates this approach:

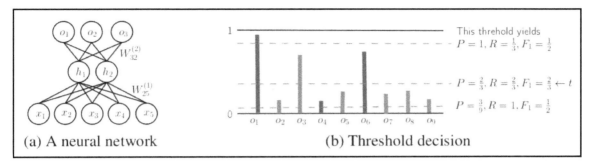

(a) A neural network   (b) Threshold decision

Approach for multi-label classification

In the preceding diagram, the output consists of nine possible labels on which thresholding is applied. The threshold which yields the highest **F1** score, which is the middle one is picked. The blue bars are the relevant labels for a training example.

While there are many state-of-the-art deep learning text classification approaches for multi-class problems, they can also output top-k class predictions (or we can apply thresholding) for multi-labels. We will look at some of these multi-class models that can be used for multi-label classification. One recent popular deep learning method is fastText, as explored in the paper *Bag of Tricks for Efficient Text Classification* (https://arxiv.org/abs/1607.01759) by A Joulin et al. In fastText, a document is represented by averaging the word embedding vectors of the words appearing in the document. This averaged document vector is then passed to a softmax layer that outputs the class probabilities. This approach, therefore, does not take into consideration the word order. In the paper *Convolutional Neural Networks for Sentence Classification* (http://www.aclweb.org/anthology/D14-1181) by Kim et al., a CNN is used on the concatenation of word embeddings of a document. Several filters are used on the document whose output is fed to a max overtime pooling layer. This is followed by a fully connected layer with softmax outputs corresponding to *L* labels. This was the approach we used in one of our examples for text classification using a CNN. In the paper *Deep Learning for Extreme Multi-label Text Classification* (https://dl.acm.org/citation.cfm?id=3080834), Liu et al. utilizes the XML-CNN architecture for multi-label classification. In particular, the previous approaches may not work well with a large number of labels and/or a skewed distribution of labels. The XML-CNN architecture tries to address this problem.

The following diagram illustrates this architecture:

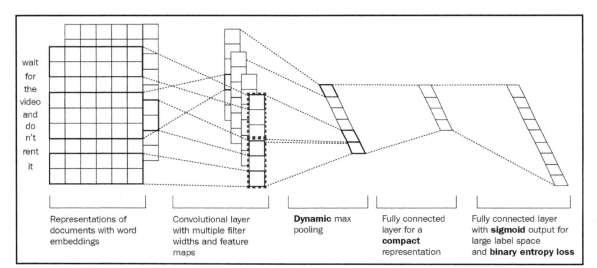

In the preceding diagram, the model uses a CNN with dynamic max pooling and a fully connected sigmoid output for the large label space. Another recent state-of-the-art method in text classification is attention-based networks, which have shown promising improvements compared to all the methods we have described so far. We will look at one of the recent papers on this in the following topic.

Attention networks for document classification

In the paper *Hierarchical Attention Networks for Document Classification* (http://www.cs.cmu. edu/~./hovy/papers/16HLT-hierarchical-attention-networks.pdf), Yang et al. have used a hierarchical deep learning architecture for classifying documents. The main intuition of their idea is that documents have inherent hierarchical structures such as words form sentences and sentences form documents. Moreover, not all parts of a document are equally important in capturing the semantics and meaning required for answering a specific query. They utilize two types of attention, one at the word level and another at the sentence level. In addition to that, the text representation is also split into a sentence level and document level. The following diagram shows the different components of the network that are capturing the word level and sentence level deep representations and the corresponding attention mechanisms:

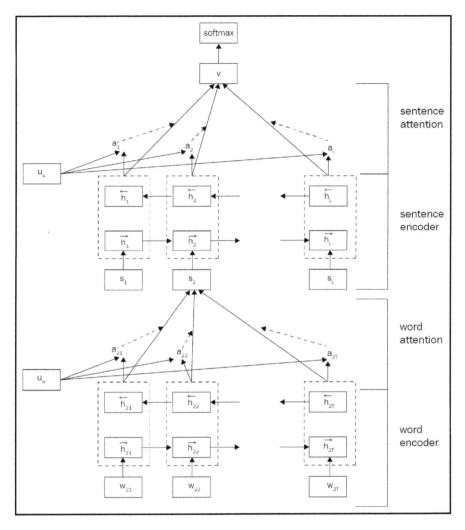

Components of the attention network

A Keras implementation of the model presented in the paper is available in GitHub `https://github.com/richliao/textClassifier` and the TensorFlow implementation can be found under `https://github.com/ematvey/hierarchical-attention-networks`.

Summary

In this chapter, we have explored different techniques for text classification using LSTM, GRU, and CNN-based networks. We also touched upon topic modeling, which is a related problem in text classification. A simple example using `gensim` for topic modeling was introduced. We saw some solutions to sentiment classification, review rating prediction, and spam detection using real-world datasets. This gave us an overview of how to approach text classification problems with deep learning techniques using recurrent neural networks and convolutional networks. An example using transfer learning using pre-trained word embeddings was also covered. Finally, we discussed the state-of-art techniques such as extreme multi-label classification and attention networks that can be applied in complex text classification scenarios.

In the next chapter, we will look at deep learning approaches regarding search and de-duplication for identifying similar documents.

6
Searching and DeDuplicating Using CNNs

Deep neural networks have been proven to work extremely well when provided with a large number of data points. However, a dearth of data for building large search engines has been a primary issue for most engines. Traditional approaches to searching in text data involved domain understanding and keyword mapping. These provided search engines with a knowledge graph that included sufficient information about the topics, so that the engine would be able to find answers. The search engine would then also be able to expand to new topics, by obtaining the relationships between topics.

In this chapter, we will explore how to build a search engine using **machine learning** (**ML**), and we will use it for tasks such as matching and deduplication. In order to understand how deep learning can improve our searches, we will build baseline methods, using traditional methods such as TF-IDF and latent semantic indexing. Subsequently, we will develop a **Convolutional Neural Network** (**CNN**) that learns to identify duplicate texts. We will compare traditional approaches to CNNs, in order to understand the pros and cons of each approach.

We will approach the task of searching as the ability to understand the semantics of sentences. Searching for text in a large corpus of data requires the ability to get an appropriate representation of the text. We will tackle the task of deduplication as an extension of the classifier.

Data

In order to build our search and retrieval system, we will use the same data for training and testing. We will use the **Quora** duplicate questions data for building our approach to searching and retrieving. The task of the Quora duplicate question pair is to determine whether two pairs of questions have the same meaning. The data contains a pair of questions and a ground truth label, marked by a human expert, mentioning whether the pairs of questions are duplicates. The ground truth data provided also mentions that these labels are subjective, meaning that not all human experts might agree on whether the pair of questions is similar. Hence, the data should be taken as *informed*, and not 100% accurate, due to the inherent subjectivity in the text data.

Data description

The data provided is in the form of id, qid1, qid2, question1, question2, and is_duplicate, where the id field provides the ID for the training pair, qid and qid2 provide the ID for each question, and question1 and question2 are the full text for each question used for training, and is_duplicate is a Boolean or target value, set to 1 if the pair of texts are duplicates (semantically meaning the same) and 0 if they are not duplicates. The data that we will be using to train contains approximately 404,000 question pairs, along with their labels.

Training the model

We will train a model for matching these question pairs. Let's start by importing the relevant libraries, as follows:

```
import sys
import os
import pandas as pd
import numpy as np
import string
import tensorflow as tf
```

Following is a function that takes a pandas series of text as input. Then, the series is converted to a list. Each item in the list is converted into a string, made lower case, and stripped of surrounding empty spaces. The entire list is converted into a NumPy array, to be passed back:

```
def read_x(x):
    x = np.array([list(str(line).lower().strip()) for line in x.tolist()])
    return x
```

Next up is a function that takes a pandas series as input, converts it to a list, and returns it as a NumPy array:

```
def read_y(y):
    return np.asarray(y.tolist())
```

The next function splits the data for training and validation. Validation data is helpful to see how well the model trained on the training data generalizes with unseen data. The data for validation is randomly picked by shuffling the indices of the data. The function takes question pairs and their corresponding labels as input, along with the ratio of the split:

```
def split_train_val(x1, x2, y, ratio=0.1):
    indicies = np.arange(x1.shape[0])
    np.random.shuffle(indicies)
    num_train = int(x1.shape[0]*(1-ratio))
    train_indicies = indicies[:num_train]
    val_indicies = indicies[num_train:]
```

The ratios of training and validation are set to 10%, and accordingly, the shuffled indices are separated for training and validation by slicing the array. Since the indices are already shuffled, they can be used for splitting the training data. The input data has two question pairs, x1 and x2, with a y label indicating whether the pair is a duplicate:

```
    train_x1 = x1[train_indicies, :]
    train_x2 = x2[train_indicies, :]
    train_y = y[train_indicies]
```

Similar to the training question pairs and labels, the validation data is sliced, based on a 10% ratio split of the indices:

```
    val_x1 = x1[val_indicies, :]
    val_x2 = x2[val_indicies, :]
    val_y = y[val_indicies]

    return train_x1, train_x2, train_y, val_x1, val_x2, val_y
```

The training and validation data are picked from the shuffled indices, and the data is split based on the indices.

> Note that the question pairs have to be picked from the indices, for both training and testing.

Encoding the text

Next, a function is created to convert the list of strings into vectors. The character set is made first by concatenating the English characters, and the dictionary is created with those characters as keys, while the integers are the values:

```
def get_encoded_x(train_x1, train_x2, test_x1, test_x2):
    chars = string.ascii_lowercase + '? ()=+-_~"`<>,./\|[]{}!@#$%^&*:;' +
"'"
```

The preceding example is just a set of characters from the English language. Other language characters can also be included, to make the approach generic for different languages.

> Note that this character set can be inferred from the dataset, to include non-English characters.

Next, a character map is formed between the set of characters and integers. The character map is formed as a dictionary, as shown in the following code snippet:

```
char_map = dict(zip(list(chars), range(len(chars))))
```

Next, a maximum sentence length is obtained from the dataset by going through every question. First, a list of the length of every individual line is formed, and the maximum value is taken from that:

```
max_sent_len = max([len(line) for line in np.concatenate((train_x1,
    train_x2, test_x1, test_x2))])
print('max sentence length: {}'.format(max_sent_len))
```

We need to preset the maximum length of all of the questions, to quantize the vector to that size. Whenever a question is smaller in length (when compared to the maximum length), spaces are simply appended to the text:

```
def quantize(line):
        line_padding = line + [' '] * (max_sent_len - len(line))
        encode = [char_map[char] if char in char_map.keys() else char_map['
'] for char in line_padding]
        return encode
```

The train and test question pairs are encoded by calling the preceding `quantize` function and converting them to a NumPy array. Every question is iteratively quantized, as shown here:

```
train_x1_encoded = np.array([quantize(line) for line in train_x1])
train_x2_encoded = np.array([quantize(line) for line in train_x2])
test_x1_encoded = np.array([quantize(line) for line in test_x1])
test_x2_encoded = np.array([quantize(line) for line in test_x2])
return train_x1_encoded, train_x2_encoded, test_x1_encoded,
   test_x2_encoded, max_sent_len, char_map
```

Next, there is quantization where every character is split and encoded using the character map after padded with spaces. Then, the array of integers is converted to a NumPy array. The next function combines the preceding functions to preprocess the data. The data, present in the form of `.csv`, is read for both training and testing. Question 1 and question 2 are from different columns of the data frame, and are split accordingly. The data is a binary, whether the question is duplicate or not.

First, load the `.csv` file of the train and test dataset using the pandas framework:

```
def pre_process():
    train_data = pd.read_csv('train.csv')
    test_data = pd.read_csv('test.csv')
```

Then, pass the pandas DataFrames to the functions defined at the beginning, to covert the raw text to a NumPy array, shown as follows. The question pandas series are subset before passing them to the functions:

```
train_x1 = read_x(train_data['question1'])
train_x2 = read_x(train_data['question2'])
train_y = read_y(train_data['is_duplicate'])
```

Convert the test question pairs to NumPy arrays by using the same functions shown here:

```
test_x1 = read_x(test_data['question1'])
test_x2 = read_x(test_data['question2'])
```

Next, pass the NumPy arrays of the train and test data for encoding, and get back the encoded question pairs, the maximum sentence length, and the character map:

```
    train_x1, train_x2, test_x1, test_x2, max_sent_len, char_map =
get_encoded_x(train_x1, train_x2, test_x1, test_x2)
    train_x1, train_x2, train_y, val_x1, val_x2, val_y =
split_train_val(train_x1, train_x2, train_y)

    return train_x1, train_x2, train_y, val_x1, val_x2, val_y, test_x1,
test_x2, max_sent_len, char_map
```

The encoding can be called during the training process.

Modeling with CNN

Next, we will build a character based CNN model. We will start by creating embedding lookup with dimensions a number of characters and 50. First, the character set length is obtained from the character map:

```
def character_CNN(tf_char_map, char_map, char_embed_dim=50):
    char_set_len = len(char_map.keys())
```

Each convolution layer is initiated with a random variable for weights and biases. The convolution layer function will be called when the model is constructed:

```
def conv2d(x, W, b, strides=1):
        x = tf.nn.conv2d(x, W, strides=[1, strides, strides, 1],
            padding="SAME")
        x = tf.nn.bias_add(x, b)
        return tf.nn.relu(x)
```

Each layer is also followed by a max pooling layer, defined as follows:

```
def maxpool2d(x, k=2):
        return tf.nn.max_pool(x, ksize=[1, k, k, 1], strides=[1, k, k,
            1], padding="SAME")
```

Next, an embedding for the input is created and initialized with random values:

```
with tf.name_scope('embedding'):
        embdded_chars =
tf.nn.embedding_lookup(params=tf.Variable(tf.random_normal([char_set_len,
char_embed_dim])), ids=tf_char_map, name='embedding')
        embedded_chars_expanded = tf.expand_dims(embdded_chars, -1)
```

At the end, the layer is flattened. Then, four layers of convolution are created, with increasing filters and stride lengths. The bigger stride looks at a long temporal dimension of the text:

```
prev_layer = embedded_chars_expanded
with tf.name_scope('Character_CNN'):
    for idx, layer in enumerate([[3, 3, 1, 16], [3, 3, 16, 32], [3, 3, 32, 64], [3, 3, 64, 128]]):
        with tf.name_scope('Conv{}'.format(idx)):
            w = tf.Variable(tf.truncated_normal(layer, stddev=1e-1), name='weights')
            b = tf.Variable(tf.truncated_normal([layer[-1]], stddev=1e-1), name='bias')
            conv = conv2d(prev_layer, w, b)
            pool = maxpool2d(conv, k=2)
            prev_layer = pool

    prev_layer = tf.reshape(prev_layer, [-1, prev_layer.shape[1]._value * prev_layer.shape[2].value * prev_layer.shape[3]._value])

    return prev_layer
```

Next, a function is created and two of the previous described CNN are created and concatenated for each question pair. Then, three fully connected layers are created by reducing the dimensions to form the final activation:

```
def model(x1_pls, x2_pls, char_map, keep_prob):
    out_layer1 = character_CNN(x1_pls, char_map)
    out_layer2 = character_CNN(x2_pls, char_map)
    prev = tf.concat([out_layer1, out_layer2], 1)
```

The model is a similar to a siamese network, where two encoders are trained at the same time:

```
with tf.name_scope('fc'):
    output_units = [1024, 512, 128, 2]
    for idx, unit in enumerate(output_units):
        if idx != 3:
            prev = tf.layers.dense(prev, units=unit, activation=tf.nn.relu)
            prev = tf.nn.dropout(prev, keep_prob)
        else:
            prev = tf.layers.dense(prev, units=unit, activation=None)
            prev = tf.nn.dropout(prev, keep_prob)
    return prev
```

This completes the model construction, with a few convolution layers followed by max pooling layers.

Training

Next, a function is created to train the data. The placeholders are created for the question pairs and their labels. The output of the model created in the preceding function is taken through cross-entropy softmax as the loss function. Using the Adam optimizer, the model weights are optimized, as follows:

```
def train(train_x1, train_x2, train_y, val_x1, val_x2, val_y, max_sent_len,
char_map, epochs=2, batch_size=1024, num_classes=2):
    with tf.name_scope('Placeholders'):
        x1_pls = tf.placeholder(tf.int32, shape=[None, max_sent_len])
        x2_pls = tf.placeholder(tf.int32, shape=[None, max_sent_len])
        y_pls = tf.placeholder(tf.int64, [None])
        keep_prob = tf.placeholder(tf.float32)   # Dropout
```

Next, the model is created and followed by logit computation. The loss is computed between the logits and the one-hot encoding of the labels. The loss is optimized using the Adam optimizer, with a learning rate of 0.001. The correct prediction and accuracy is calculated, as follows:

```
    predict = model(x1_pls, x2_pls, char_map, keep_prob)
    with tf.name_scope('loss'):
        mean_loss = tf.losses.softmax_cross_entropy(logits=predict,
onehot_labels=tf.one_hot(y_pls, num_classes))
    with tf.name_scope('optimizer'):
        optimizer = tf.train.AdamOptimizer(learning_rate=0.001)
        train_step = optimizer.minimize(mean_loss)
    with tf.name_scope('accuracy'):
        correct_prediction = tf.equal(tf.argmax(predict, 1), y_pls)
        accuracy = tf.reduce_mean(tf.cast(correct_prediction, tf.float32))
    saver = tf.train.Saver()
```

The session is initialized for all of the weights. For every epoch, the encoded data is shuffled and fed through the model. The same procedure is also followed by the validation data:

```
    with tf.Session() as sess:
        sess.run(tf.global_variables_initializer())
        train_indicies = np.arange(train_x1.shape[0])
        variables = [mean_loss, correct_prediction, train_step]
```

Next, the epochs are iterated, and for each epoch, the training data is shuffled, to provide robust training:

```
iter_cnt = 0
for e in range(epochs):
    np.random.shuffle(train_indicies)
        losses = []
        correct = 0
```

Next, the batches of data are iterated and sliced, shown as follows. The data is then used for training and validating the model:

```
for i in range(int(math.ceil(train_x1.shape[0] / batch_size))):
        start_idx = (i * batch_size) % train_x1.shape[0]
        idx = train_indicies[start_idx:start_idx + batch_size]
```

Next, the `feed` dictionary is assembled and passed through the session, as shown here:

```
feed_dict = {x1_pls: train_x1[idx, :],
             x2_pls: train_x2[idx, :],
             y_pls: train_y[idx],
             keep_prob: 0.95}
 actual_batch_size = train_y[idx].shape[0]

 loss, corr, _ = sess.run(variables, feed_dict=feed_dict)
```

Next, using the computed loss and the correct duplicates, the accuracy is calculated:

```
        corr = np.array(corr).astype(np.float32)
        losses.append(loss * actual_batch_size)
        correct += np.sum(corr)
        if iter_cnt % 10 == 0:
            print("Minibatch {0}: with training loss = {1:.3g} and
accuracy of {2:.2g}" \
                .format(iter_cnt, loss, np.sum(corr) /
actual_batch_size))
            iter_cnt += 1
        total_correct = correct / train_x1.shape[0]
        total_loss = np.sum(losses) / train_x1.shape[0]
        print("Epoch {2}, Overall loss = {0:.5g} and accuracy of
{1:.3g}" \
            .format(total_loss, total_correct, e + 1))
```

For every five iterations, the validation data is prepared and validation accuracy is calculated, as shown here:

```
            if (e + 1) % 5 == 0:
                val_losses = []
                val_correct = 0
                for i in range(int(math.ceil(val_x1.shape[0] /
batch_size))):
                    start_idx = (i * batch_size) % val_x1.shape[0]

                    feed_dict = {x1_pls: val_x1[start_idx:start_idx +
batch_size, :],
                                 x2_pls: val_x2[start_idx:start_idx +
batch_size, :],
                                 y_pls: val_y[start_idx:start_idx +
batch_size],
                                 keep_prob: 1}
                    print(y_pls)
                    actual_batch_size = val_y[start_idx:start_idx +
batch_size].shape[0]
                    loss, corr, _ = sess.run(variables,
feed_dict=feed_dict)
                    corr = np.array(corr).astype(np.float32)
                    val_losses.append(loss * actual_batch_size)
                    val_correct += np.sum(corr)
```

Next, the accuracy of the matches is calculated:

```
                total_correct = val_correct / val_x1.shape[0]
                total_loss = np.sum(val_losses) / val_x1.shape[0]
                print("Validation Epoch {2}, Overall loss = {0:.5g} and
accuracy of {1:.3g}" \
                    .format(total_loss, total_correct, e + 1))
            if (e+1) % 10 == 0:
                save_path = saver.save(sess, './model_{}.ckpt'.format(e))
                print("Model saved in path:{}".format(save_path))
```

The model is saved, and it can be restored for inference, as shown in the next section.

Inference

Next, a function is created to perform the inference for the test data. The model was stored as a checkpoint in the preceding step, and it is used here for inference. The placeholders for the input data are defined, and a saver object is also defined, as follows:

```
def inference(test_x1, max_sent_len, batch_size=1024):
    with tf.name_scope('Placeholders'):
        x_pls1 = tf.placeholder(tf.int32, shape=[None, max_sent_len])
        keep_prob = tf.placeholder(tf.float32)   # Dropout

    predict = model(x_pls1, keep_prob)
    saver = tf.train.Saver()
    ckpt_path = tf.train.latest_checkpoint('.')
```

Next, a session is created and the model is restored:

```
with tf.Session() as sess:
        sess.run(tf.global_variables_initializer())
        saver.restore(sess, ckpt_path)
        print("Model restored.")
```

With the model loaded into the session, the data is passed in batches, and the predictions are stored:

```
        prediction = []
        for i in range(int(math.ceil(test_x1.shape[0] / batch_size))):
            start_idx = (i * batch_size) % test_x1.shape[0]
            prediction += sess.run([tf.argmax(predict, 1)],
                                 feed_dict={x_pls1:
test_x[start_idx:start_idx + batch_size, :], keep_prob:1})[0].tolist()
        print(prediction)
```

Next, all of the functions are called, in order to preprocess the data, train the model, and perform inference on the test data:

```
train_x1, train_x2, train_y, val_x1, val_x2, val_y, test_x1, test_x2,
max_sent_len, char_map = pre_process()
train(train_x1, train_x2, train_y, val_x1, val_x1, val_y, max_sent_len,
char_map, 100, 1024)
inference(test_x1, test_x2, max_sent_len)
```

Once the training starts, you can see the training and the results, as follows:

```
Validation Epoch 25, Overall loss = 0.51399 and accuracy of 1
Epoch 26, Overall loss = 0.19037 and accuracy of 0.889
Epoch 27, Overall loss = 0.15886 and accuracy of 1
Epoch 28, Overall loss = 0.15363 and accuracy of 1
Epoch 29, Overall loss = 0.098042 and accuracy of 1
Epoch 30, Overall loss = 0.10002 and accuracy of 1
Tensor("Placeholders/Placeholder_2:0", shape=(?,), dtype=int64)
```

After 30 epochs, the model is able to provide 100% accuracy on the validation data. We have to see how to train a model to detect duplicates, using the Quora question pair as an example.

Summary

In this chapter, we saw how to use character-based CNN, by training a model to search for duplicate pairs. Character CNN gives us the flexibility to train models with unknown characters, and it is more generic than word-level embedding. Similar kinds of networks can be used for searching, matching, and deduplication.

In the next chapter, we will learn how to train a model for **Named Entity Recognition** (**NER**) using LSTM.

7
Named Entity Recognition Using Character LSTM

Human beings, when provided with repetitive tasks, are prone to committing errors, owing to muscle memory and loss of concentration. Loss of concentration is often known as **brain fatigue**, wherein the brain tends to operate in an autopilot state, without the need to think about actions and reactions. Hence, there is a pressing need to improve conventional user interfaces, changing the way that we fundamentally interact with machines, to cater to answer questions without any loss of information or errors. Such user interfaces are also a very important area of research, owing to their impact on a multitude of applications, in customer service, search interfaces, and human-computer interactions.

In order to develop such interfaces, one of the fundamental tasks is to understand and interpret a sentence provided as input by a user. Such an interface should be able to recognize words in a sentence, along with what they convey to the user reading the sentence. Such a process is called **Named Entity Recognition** (**NER**), wherein the objective is to find (and classify) named entities in a text. NER falls under the broader area of information retrieval, and it is commonly known by names such as **entity identification**, **entity chunking**, and **entity extraction**.

In NER, entities are predefined categories, such as peoples' names, organization names, location names, times, and so on. NER allows a computer program to interpret the sentence, *I will meet you at Burj Khalifa for a cup of coffee at 7:30 PM tomorrow*, as, *I will meet you at (Burj Khalifa)$_{Location}$ for a cup of (coffee)$_{Food}$ at (7:30 PM)$_{Time}$ (tomorrow)$_{Date}$*. In this example, the algorithm detects and classifies a two-token location, a single-token food item with, and a temporal expression, and a date.

NER is often considered a sequence labeling problem, using approaches such as the **Hidden Markov Model (HMM)**, **decision trees**, **maximum entropy (ME)** models, **Support Vector Machines (SVMs)**, and **Conditional Random Fields (CRFs)**. However, in recent literature, deep learning has been extensively leveraged for recognizing named entities. With large amounts of data available for applications to build its algorithms, deep learning has shown that it can outperform conventional methods, while also being robust in generalizing its learning capabilities.

It has to be noted that state-of-the-art NER systems for the English language produce near-human performance. For example, the best system scored an F-measure of 93.39%, while human annotators scored approximately 97%.

NER with deep learning

Deep learning provides a good opportunity to leverage large amounts of data, to extract the best possible features for NER. In general, the deep learning approaches of NER use the **recurrent neural network (RNN)**, as the problem is posed as a sequence labeling task. RNNs do not only have the capability to process variable length inputs; variants of such neural networks, called **Long Short-Term Memory (LSTM)**, possess long-term memory, which is useful for understanding non-trivial dependencies in the words of a given sentence. Variations of LSTM, called **bidirectional LSTM**, have the ability to understand not only long-term dependencies, but also the relationships of words in a sentence, from both sides of a sentence.

In this chapter, we will build an NER system using deep learning with LSTM. However, before we try to understand how to build such a system, we will look at the data (and the format in which we will be processing the data) that will be used in our deep learning model.

Data

The data that is most commonly used to test and benchmark NER is the `CoNLL2003` dataset, which is a shared task for language-independent NER. The dataset contains a training, development, and test file, along with a large file of unannotated data. The development file is used for tuning the parameters of the learning method, while the training data is used for training the model, using the tuned parameters, and testing on the test dataset.

The CoNLL data, split between the development and the test, is provided to avoid tuning systems on the test data. The data for the English language is taken from news stories between August 1996 and August 1997, from the Reuters Corpus. A sample sentence from the CoNLL dataset, with its accompanying entity annotations, is shown as follows:

```
Only RB B-NP O
France NNP I-NP B-LOC
and CC I-NP O
Britain NNP I-NP B-LOC
backed VBD B-VP O
Fischler NNP B-NP B-PER
' s POS B-NP O
proposal NN I-NP O
. . O O
```

Each line of the CoNLL data contains four fields: the word, the **part of speech (POS)** tag of the word, the chunk tag of the word, and its named entity tag. The tag, O , is given to words outside of the named entities.

In order to handle entities where there are two tokens (for example, New York) a **tagging scheme** is used to distinguish different entity cases. When two entities of an <entity> type are next to one another, the first word of the second entity is tagged as B-<entity>, to show that it starts another entity. The entities provided by the CoNLL2003 task are LOC, PER, ORG, and MISC, which are locations, persons, organizations, and miscellaneous, respectively.

Another dataset that is commonly used for building NER systems is the **Groningen Meaning Bank (GMB)**, which has many more annotations that are useful for the task of building an NER system. In this chapter, however, we will be using the CoNLL2003 data for our experiments and evaluation.

A couple of widely used open source frameworks? for off-the-shelf NER systems are Stanford's NLTK and Explosion AI's spaCy. While both of these frameworks provide excellent off-the-shelf performance for various tasks, we are interested in developing a flexible, state-of-the-art deep learning model for an NER system.

Model

As discussed earlier, we can consider the problem of named entity recognition a sequence problem. A common deep learning approach, followed by most NLP systems, is to use RNNs. However, before we decide on the architecture for our RNN model, we need to think about how we will be providing our input and processing the output from our model.

As our input data is in the form of words, we need a dense vector representation for each word, $w \in \mathbb{R}^n$. Such a representation is also known as a **word embedding**; commonly available, pretrained word embeddings include Word2vec, GloVe, and fastText. Such pretrained word vectors provide very good semantic representations for each word, without the need to train them for every task. As there are quite a few entities that do not have pretrained word vectors, we can extract character-level vector representations, to take occurrences like hyphenated words or words that begin with a capital letter into consideration. This provides the model with valuable information about the entity discussed in the current context.

As we have decided to use a variant of RNNs, such as LSTM, to obtain a semantic representation of our input that is present in its context, we will obtain a vector representation for each word, in order to make a prediction about the entity.

Word embeddings

As discussed in the chapter on word embeddings, we would like to build a dense vector that is capable of capturing the semantic meaning of the context in which the word is being used. In this task, however, we will build our word embeddings as a concatenation of pretrained embeddings extracted at the word level and trained embeddings from the character level. Hence, the word embedding, $w \in \mathbb{R}^d$, is composed of a pretrained word-level vector, $w_{pretrain} \in \mathbb{R}^{d_1}$, and a trained character-level vector, $w_{char} \in \mathbb{R}^{d_2}$.

Although it is possible to encode the character-level vector as a one-hot encoding or use any other hand-crafted feature, such a feature might not be easily scalable to other datasets and languages. A robust method for encoding the character-level embedding is to learn it directly from the data. In this chapter, we will utilize a bidirectional LSTM to learn such an embedding:

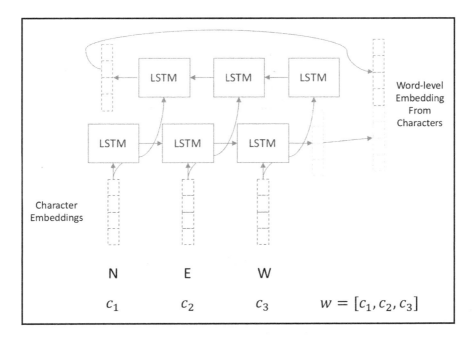

Hence, every character, c_i, in a word, $w = [c_1, c_2,..., c_k]$, has an associated vector, $c_i \in \mathbb{R}^{d_2}$. It has to be noted that we do not perform any preprocessing on the data to remove punctuation or change the words to lowercase, as such characters have an impact on the meaning conveyed by a word in a given position. For instance, the word *Apple* in the sentence, *They had to get an Apple product to complete their tech eco-system*, refers to the organization (ORG), while the word *apple* in the sentence, *They had to get an apple a day to keep the doctor away*, refers to the fruit. The distinction in the words can be easily identified when the uppercase usage of the word is considered. The character-level embedding vector tries to learn the structures, words, to arrive at the final forms in which they are being used. In other words, a character-level vector learns the morphology of the word that it represents.

Finally, we will concatenate the character embedding, $w_{char} \in \mathbb{R}^{d_2}$, with the word embedding, $w_{pretrain} \in \mathbb{R}^{d_1}$, to obtain the word representation, $w = [w_{pretrain}, w_{char}] \in \mathbb{R}^d$, with $d = d1 + d2$. Now that we have prepared our input, we will proceed to walk through the code to build our input and the model.

Walking through the code

In this section, we will be walking through the TensorFlow code for building the input. The following sections discuss the different parts of the code that we will be walking through.

Input

As we are looking at providing input dynamically, we will use TensorFlow's **placeholder** for our input. As we have a definite shape for the data, in terms of batch size and the number of words we can process per batch, we need to first pad the sentences in our dataset, to make them of the same length. Hence, we will define two placeholders, as follows:

```
# Define input placeholder for the word indices of shape = (batch size,
length of padded sentence)
word_indices = tf.placeholder(tf.int32, shape=[None, None])

# Placeholder for the sequence lengths of shape = (batch size)
sequence_lengths = tf.placeholder(tf.int32, shape=[None])
```

The sequence length placeholder allows the computation graph to utilize the actual length of the input data, as we padded the initial input to make it all of the same max_length.

Word embedding

Now that we have defined our input placeholders, we will define a TensorFlow Variable to hold our pretrained embeddings for the vocabularies in the data. The approach that we will follow, in this case, is an indexed array, which can fetch the embedding corresponding to a word index at i as pre_trained_embedding[i]. Since we would like to look up from an embedding matrix, we will load the pretrained embedding array into the TensorFlow variable. The TensorFlow code is defined as follows:

```
# Define a lookup table using the pre-trained embedding matrix
lookup_word_mat = tf.Variable(embedding_matrix, dtype=tf.float,
trainable=False)

# Define an embedding lookup using TensorFlow's in-built function
pre_trained_embedding = tf.nn.embedding_lookup(lookup_word_mat,
word_indices)
```

In the preceding code block, we defined the TensorFlow variable with trainable = False, as we do not want the algorithm to train our embeddings any further. This block defines the vector representation at the word level.

We will build the character-level vector representation in a similar method, using two placeholders, as follows:

```
# Define input placeholder for character indices of shape = (batch size,
maximum length of sentence, maximum length of a word)
char_indices = tf.placeholder(tf.int32, shape=[None, None, None])

# Placeholder for the word lengths of shape = (batch size, maximum length
of a sentence)
word_lengths = tf.placeholder(tf.int32, shape=[None, None])
```

As you can see, we chose to dynamically set the sentence and word lengths, based on the data available in the batch that is being processed during every iteration. Having defined how we will be building our word embeddings using characters, we will now look at how to train the embeddings.

Unlike in the earlier case, we do not have any pretrained embeddings at the character-level to look up in an embedding matrix. Hence, we will initialize the character embeddings by using random vectors, as follows:

```
# Define a variable lookup with default initialiser
lookup_char_mat = tf.get_variable(name="character_embeddings",
dtype=tf.float32, shape=[num_characters, dim_character])

# Define a character embedding lookup using TensorFlow's in-built function
character_embedding = tf.nn.embedding_lookup(lookup_char_mat, char_indices)
```

As shown in the previous figure, we will define a bidirectional LSTM that takes the characters from the data available in each batch as input:

```
# Define the LSTM to accept characters for forward RNN
bi_dir_cell_fw = tf.contrib.rnn.LSTMCell(char_hidden_dim,
state_is_tuple=True)

# Define the LSTM to accept characters for backward RNN
bi_dir_cell_bw = tf.contrib.rnn.LSTMCell(char_hidden_dim,
state_is_tuple=True)

# Define the bidirectional LSTM which takes both the forward and backward
RNNs, the inputs and the sequence lengths
_, ((_, out_fw), (_, out_bw)) =
tf.nn.bidirectional_dynamic_rnn(bi_dir_cell_fw, bi_dir_cell_bw,
character_embedding, sequence_length=word_lengths, dtype=tf.float32)
```

As we only need the output vectors, we will not store the rest of the return statements provided by the `bidirectional_dynamic_rnn` function. To derive the output, we will concatenate the forward and backward output produced, resulting in an output dimension twice the size of the original character's hidden dimension size. Consequently, we will obtain the representations for the characters as well as the words, by reshaping the output of the concatenation:

```
# Concatenate the two output vectors of the forward and backward RNNs
resulting in a vector of shape = (batch size x sentence, 2 x
char_hidden_dim)
output_fw_bw = tf.concat([out_fw, out_bw], axis = -1)

# Obtain character embedding by reshaping the output vector in the previous
step resulting in a vector of shape = (batch size, sentence length, 2 x
char_hidden_dim)
char_vector = tf.reshape(output_fw_bw, shape=[-1,
tf.shape(character_embedding)[1], 2*char_hidden_dim])

# Final word embedding is obtained by concatenating the pre-trained word
embedding and the character embedding obtained from the bidirectional LSTM
word_embedding = tf.concat([pre_trained_embedding, char_vector], axis = -1)
```

The effects of different pretrained word embeddings

There are a number of pretrained word embeddings available for us to leverage. In effect, these are words and their corresponding *n*-dimensional word vectors, made by different research teams. Notable pretrained word vectors are GloVe, Word2vec, and fastText. In our work, we use the pretrained Word2vec word vectors, although any of the preceding word embeddings should be useful in building the NER system that we have discussed in this chapter. The reading and processing of these pretrained word embedding models will be different:

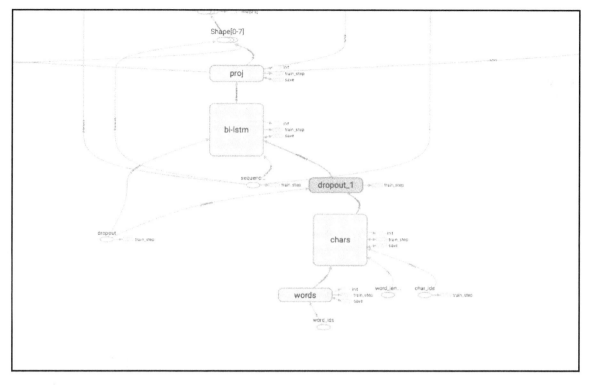

TensorBoard graph

The graph in the preceding diagram, from TensorBoard, shows how the words and character embeddings are used as input for the bidirectional LSTM.

Neural network architecture

As we have now built the word vectors from the character-word embedding concatenation, we will run a bidirectional LSTM over the sequence of word embeddings, to get a semantic representation of the embeddings, using the concatenated hidden states (forward and backward) of the bidirectional LSTM. This is shown in the following figure:

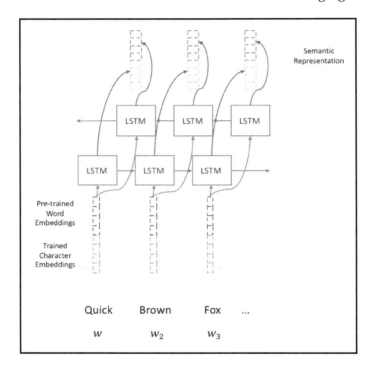

Using TensorFlow to implement this is straightforward, and is quite similar to how we implemented the earlier character-level embedding learning LSTM. However, unlike in the earlier case, we are interested in the hidden states of each time step:

```
bi_dir_cell_fw = tf.contrib.rnn.LSTMCell(hidden_state_size)

bi_dir_cell_cell_bw = tf.contrib.rnn.LSTMCell(hidden_state_size)

(out_fw, out_bw), _ = tf.nn.bidirectional_dynamic_rnn(bi_dir_cell_fw,
bi_dir_cell_bw, word_embedding, sequence_length=sequence_lengths,
dtype=tf.float32)

semantic_representation = tf.concat([out_fw, out_bw], axis=-1)
```

Hence, a semantic representation, h, captures the meaning of each available word, w, using the pretrained word vectors, the characters, and the context in which these words are available to the model. With such a vector made available, we can use a dense neural network to get a vector, where each element in the vector corresponds to a tag that we would like to predict as an entity:

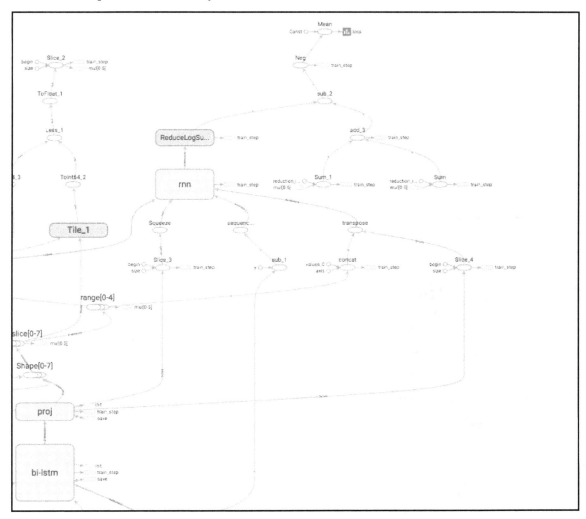

Semantic graph representation

The preceding figure shows how the bidirectional LSTM output is fed into:

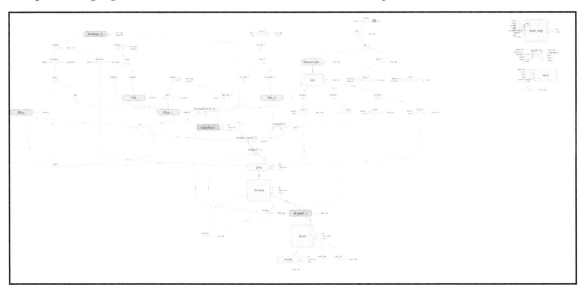

Bidirectional LSTM

Decoding predictions

Suppose that we would like to classify into five classes; we would compute a five-dimensional vector, $s \in \mathbb{R}^5 = \mathbb{W}.h + b$. This five-dimensional vector could be interpreted as the probability of representing each class. What this means is that the i-th component of s provides the probability, or the score, for the i class, given the word, w.

This dense vector can be computed in TensorFlow as follows:

```
# Weights matrix initialised with the default initialiser
W = tf.get_variable("W", shape=[2 * hidden_state_size, ntags],
dtype=tf.float32)

# Bias vector initialised using a zero initialiser
b = tf.get_variable("b", shape=[ntags], dtype=tf.float32,
initializer=tf.zeros_initializer())
```

```
# Getting number of time steps
num_time_steps = tf.shape(semantic_representation)[1]

# Using flattened (using reshape) vector to calculate prediction scores
prediction = tf.matmul(semantic_representatio_flatten, W) + b
```

Given that we can compute a dense vector that provides the score that a given word belongs to an *i* class, there are two methods that we can use to make our prediction.

The first method is the obvious approach of using softmax activation to normalize the scores into a vector, $p \in \mathbb{R}^5$. This method uses a non-linear activation, where the elements of the vector are calculated as follows:

$$p[i] = \frac{e^{s[i]}}{\sum_{j=1}^{5} e^{s[j]}}$$

The second method is a smarter way of labeling words, by using neighboring tags that are made available through an approach likely similar to the first step. For example, if we consider the words *New Delhi*, the NER system could potentially classify *New* as the beginning of a location, based on the fact that it classified the word nearby, *Delhi*, as a location. This method, also known as a linear-chain **conditional random field** (**CRF**), defines a global score that takes into consideration the cost of beginning or ending with a given tag.

The training step

In previous sections, we discussed the input, the network architecture, and how we plan to decode the hidden states to predict the output vectors. Now, we will define the object function that we will be using to train our developed model.

In our case, cross-entropy loss works well as a loss for the case that we are dealing with. We will be using the second method to decode the output states, using a CRF. However, we will rely on TensorFlow to provide an easy-to-use function to implement such a complex concept, as follows:

```
# Define the labels as a placeholder with shape = (batch size, sentences)
labels = tf.placeholder(tf.int32, shape=[None, None], name="labels")

log_likelihood, transition_params = tf.contrib.crf.crf_log_likelihood(
scores, labels, sequence_lengths)
```

The implementation of CRF is made quite simple, with TensorFlow coming to the rescue. We can finally calculate the loss by using the log likelihood value that we just calculated, as follows:

```
# Negate log-likelihood value to obtain a distance measure
loss = tf.reduce_mean(-log_likelihood)
```

Implementing the `softmax` method to compute the loss value is the classic method for obtaining the scores. However, we need to pay attention to the padding:

```
loss_values =
 tf.nn.sparse_softmax_cross_entropy_with_logits(logits=scores,
 labels=labels)

loss = tf.reduce_mean(loss_values)
```

The training is finally done, using either of the loss functions that we just defined. In our case, we are choosing to use `AdamOptimizer` (although other optimizers can also be used) to minimize our loss value:

```
opt = tf.train.AdamOptimizer(learning_rate)

training_op = opt.minimize(loss)
```

With the CRF method, an F1 score of around 88 can be obtained, with an accuracy of about 92%. One of the dependencies of this current approach is the pretrained word embedding. Hence, we will train another network, where all of the word embeddings are trained from scratch. The training losses for both of these methods are shown in the following screenshot:

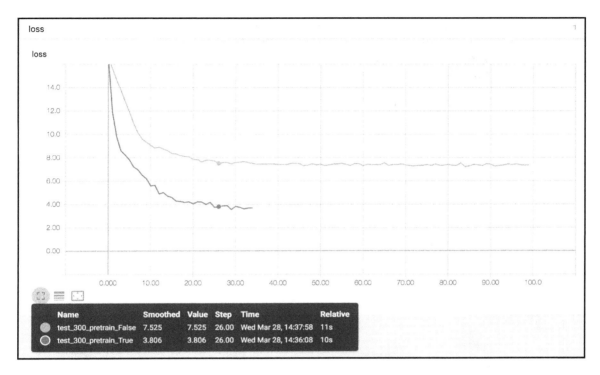

Training loss graph

In this training, we ran the model for 100 epochs and monitored the training loss. We will monitor the validation and quit the training if the validation accuracy does not improve for a fixed number of epochs. When we use the pretrained word embeddings, the loss is considerably lower, and the training stops at 35 epochs, since the performance did not improve. Training without using pretrained word embeddings results in a final accuracy of about 69%.

The training steps shown previously use a word embedding size of 300 dimensions. However, larger word embeddings require larger storage requirements, and, in turn, larger loading times, when we would like to perform inference. Hence, we will repeat the preceding experiments with word embeddings of 100 dimensions:

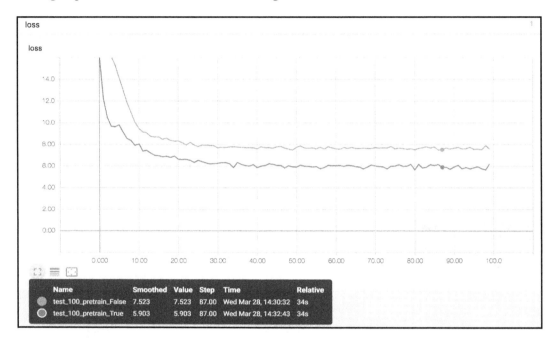

Training loss graph

With a reduced word embedding dimension, representation of the words becomes challenging, resulting in a loss of data, although it reduces the model (as well as the initial pretrained word embedding file) required for us to train the model.

Training with pretrained word embedding vectors results in considerably lower training loss, and a final test accuracy of about 74% and a reduction of 14%, when compared to the pretrained word embedding of 300 dimensions. Similarly, training without pretrained word embedding vectors results in a lower accuracy of about 64% and a 5% reduction, when compared to training with a word vector dimension of 300:

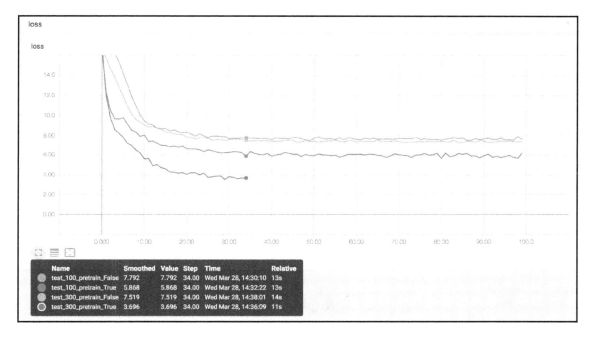

Training loss graph

When we compare the performance of the training with 300 dimensions and the training with 100 dimensions, we get a better picture of the impact of model performance in both approaches. With a word embedding size of 300, it is evident that the model is able to extract much more information than with the word embedding size of 100 dimensions. It is also evident that using pretrained word embedding provides a considerable reduction in training time and results in far better model performance:

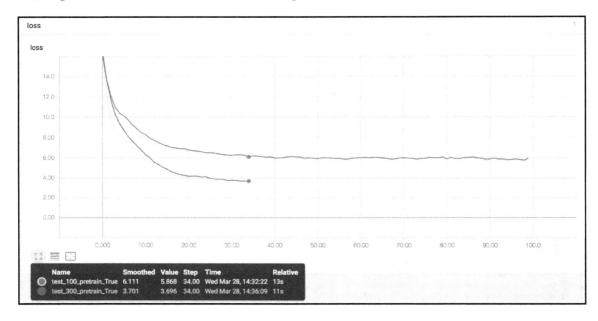

Training loss graph

When we compare the performances of the best performing models across the different dimensions, it is evident that the model trained with a word embedding size of 300 performs considerably better. At epoch 34, the model trained with 300 dimensions not only has a lower loss value, but it also trains much more quickly, as shown in the preceding figure illustrating the training log.

Another evaluation that we can perform uses classic softmax activation, instead of using CRF, for the final scoring. To make an objective evaluation of the advantage of using CRF, we will use a pretrained model with 300 dimensions, the best performing model from the earlier run:

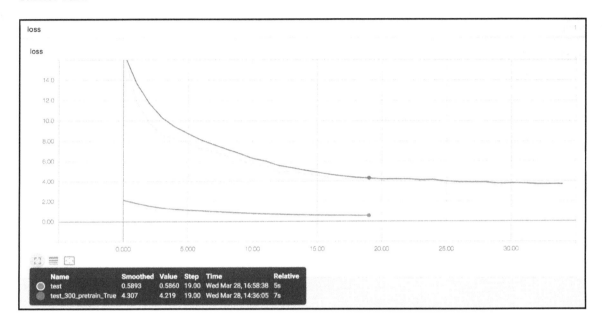

Training loss graph

The preceding figure shows a training comparison of both methods. The softmax-based method achieves about 74% accuracy and trains for just 20 epochs. However, the softmax based method is not as powerful as the CRF-based model, in terms of its performance, as shown by the accuracy scores that we obtain after training completes. The lower loss value reflected in the chart is due to a difference in loss metrics when using CRF and softmax.

Scope for improvement

While the framework discussed in this chapter worked very well for the data that we have in hand, this might not be case when the dataset is small, or if the data is imbalanced.

Summary

In this chapter, we implemented a character-level, LSTM-based neural network for developing an algorithm to detect named entities. We showed that complex methods can be implemented easily by using TensorFlow, and we looked at methods to improve the performance of our model.

In the next chapter, we will discuss how to develop a deep neural network for text generation.

8
Text Generation and Summarization Using GRUs

In this chapter, we will describe methods for generating and summarizing text using deep learning techniques. Text generation is the process of automatically generating text, based on context and scope, by using an input source text. Some applications involving text generation include automatic weather report generation, medical report generation, and translating a given representation of input text into multiple languages. Text summarization is a related technique, in which a summary is generated from a source text. Some example tasks include generating news, product reviews, and business report summaries.

In this chapter, the main focus will be on providing the reader with approaches to text generation and summarization using **recurrent neural networks** (**RNNs**). The following topics will be covered in this chapter:

- Generating text using RNNs
- Summarizing text using RNNs
- A summary of state-of-the-art approaches to text generation and summarization

Generating text using RNNs

We used **Long Short-Term Memory** (**LSTMs**) and **Gated Recurrent Units** (**GRUs**) in previous chapters for text classification. In addition to being used for predictive tasks, RNNs can be used to create generative models, as well. RNNs can learn long-term dependencies from an input text, and can therefore generate completely new sequences. This generative model can be either character or word-based. In the next section, we will look at a simple word-based text generation model.

Generating Linux kernel code with a GRU

We will now look at a simple, fun example, to generate Linux kernel code using an RNN. The complete Jupyter Notebook for this example is available in the book's code repository, under `Chapter08`. For the training data, we will first extract the kernel code from the Linux source. You can download the latest (or an earlier) version of the Linux kernel from the kernel archives at `https://www.kernel.org/`.

We will extract the `tar` file and use only the core kernel under the kernel/directory in the source. Execute the following from the root directory of the `kernel` tree to extract code from all of the `*.c` files:

```
cd kernel
find . -name "*.c" -exec cat &gt;&gt; /tmp/kernel.txt {} \;
```

This will concatenate all of the `*.c` files from the core `kernel` directory, and will write it to the `kernel.txt` file, under `/tmp`. You can use any directory, other than the `/tmp` directory. First, we will prepare the training data from the raw kernel code file:

```
with codecs.open('/tmp/kernel.txt', 'r', encoding='utf-8', errors='ignore')
as kernel_file:
    raw_text = kernel_file.read()
kernel_words = re.split('(\-\&gt;)|([\-
\&gt;+\=\&lt;\/\&\|\(\))\:\*])',raw_text)
kernel_words = [w for w in kernel_words if w is not None]
kernel_words = kernel_words[0:300000]
kernel_words = set(kernel_words)
kword_to_int = dict((word, i) for i, word in enumerate(kernel_words))
int_to_kword = dict((i, word) for i, word in enumerate(kernel_words))
vocab_size = len(kword_to_int)
kword_to_int['&lt;UNK&gt;'] = vocab_size
int_to_kword[vocab_size] = '&lt;UNK&gt;'
vocab_size += 1
X_train = [kword_to_int[word] for word in kernel_words]
y_train = X_train[1:]
y_train.append(kword_to_int['&lt;UNK&gt;'])
X_train = np.asarray(X_train)
y_train = np.asarray(y_train)
X_train = np.expand_dims(X_train,axis=1)
y_train = np.expand_dims(y_train,axis=1)
print(X_train.shape, y_train.shape)
```

In the code, the regular expression, `re.split(' (\-\&gt;) | ([\-`
`\&gt;+\=\&lt;\/\&\|\(\)\:\*])'`, `raw_text`), splits sentences that include some of
the C language operators, such as pointers, arithmetic, and logical operators. While this is
not necessary when a character-level text generator is used, we do use it here, since we are
generating text at the word level. We will also create a dictionary, mapping words to
integer IDs (and vice versa), in the `kword_to_int` and `int_to_kword` variables,
respectively. The `numpy` variables, `X_train` and `y_train` , hold the training data and
labels, respectively. In `X_train`, we have a list of word IDs taken from `kword_to_int`,
while `y_train` contains the next word, corresponding to each word in `X_train`. These
`numpy` arrays are reshaped into a single dimension vector of word IDs using
the `numpy.expand_dims` function.

As in the previous chapters, we will use the TensorFlow estimator API for our model
training and validation:

1. We will look at the code for the `model` function:

```
def rnn_model_fn(features, labels, mode):
    embedding = tf.Variable(tf.truncated_normal([v_size,
EMBED_DIMENSION],
stddev=1.0/np.sqrt(EMBED_DIMENSION)),
                            name="word_embeddings")
    word_emb = tf.nn.embedding_lookup(embedding, features['word'])
    rnn_cell = tf.nn.rnn_cell.GRUCell(HIDDEN_SIZE)
    outputs, _ = tf.nn.dynamic_rnn(rnn_cell, word_emb,
dtype=tf.float32)
    outputs = tf.reshape(outputs, [-1, HIDDEN_SIZE])
    flayer_op = tf.layers.dense(outputs, v_size, name="linear")
    return estimator_spec_for_generation(flayer_op, labels, mode)
```

We use a simple network, with an input embedding layer followed by a `GRUCell`
and a dense layer.

Note that `EMBED_DIMENSION` and `HIDDEN_SIZE` are defined as `50` and
`256`, respectively. You can try them with different values to experiment
with the generated output.

2. The output of the dense layer is then fed to the optimizer that is defined in the
estimator specification function, which we will explore next:

```
def estimator_spec_for_generation(flayer_op, lbls, md):
    preds_cls = tf.argmax(flayer_op, 1)
    if md == tf.estimator.ModeKeys.PREDICT:
```

```
        prev_op = tf.reshape(flayer_op, [-1, 1, v_size])[:, -1, :]
        preds_op = tf.nn.softmax(prev_op)
        return tf.estimator.EstimatorSpec(
        mode=md,
        predictions={
            'preds_probs': preds_op
        })
    trng_loss = tf.losses.sparse_softmax_cross_entropy(labels=lbls,
logits=flayer_op)
    if md == tf.estimator.ModeKeys.TRAIN:
        optimizer = tf.train.AdamOptimizer(learning_rate=0.01)
        trng_op = optimizer.minimize(trng_loss,
global_step=tf.train.get_global_step())
        return tf.estimator.EstimatorSpec(md, loss=trng_loss,
train_op=trng_op)
    ev_met_ops = {'accy': tf.metrics.accuracy(labels=lbls,
predictions=preds_cls)}
    return tf.estimator.EstimatorSpec(md, loss=trng_loss,
train_op=trng_op)
```

During the training, we use `AdamOptimizer` to minimize the
`sparse_softmax_cross_entropy` loss, with the labels specifying the next
words in the sequence. During prediction time, we take the `softmax` output as
the probability of the next word. This softmax output represents the probability
distribution of the next word in the list of all of the words in the vocabulary of the
length, `v_size`.

3. We will create the `estimator` for training, and we will set up the training
   configuration:

```
run_config = tf.contrib.learn.RunConfig()
run_config = run_config.replace(model_dir='/tmp/models/',
            save_summary_steps=10,log_step_count_steps=10)
generator =
  tf.estimator.Estimator(model_fn=rnn_model_fn,config=run_config)
```

We configured logging the step summary so it step counts every 10 training
steps. We then created `estimator` with the `model` function and the
configuration.

4. We will now train the model:

```
train_input_fn = tf.estimator.inputs.numpy_input_fn(
    x={'word': X_train},
    y=y_train,
    batch_size=1024,
```

```
        num_epochs=None,
        shuffle=True)
generator.train(input_fn=train_input_fn, steps=300)
```

5. We create a training input function, `train_input_fn`, with the input training data, `X_train` and `y_train`. We set the batch size to `1024` and train the model with a step count of `300`. When it has executed, we will implement the following loss in the output:

```
INFO:tensorflow:global_step/sec: 0.598131
INFO:tensorflow:Saving checkpoints for 300 into
/tmp/models/model.ckpt.
INFO:tensorflow:Loss for final step: 0.0061470587.
```

6. Finally, we will use the trained model to generate the text, one word at a time. For this, we will use `generator` to predict the next word, given an initial word. The predicted word will then be used as the next input for predicting the subsequent word, and so on. We will concatenate all of these predicted words as the final generated text:

```
maxlen = 40
next_x = X_train[0:60]
text = "".join([int_to_kword[word] for word in next_x.flatten()])
for i in range(maxlen):
    test_input_fn = tf.estimator.inputs.numpy_input_fn(
        x={'word': next_x},
        num_epochs=1,
        shuffle=False)
    predictions = generator.predict(input_fn=test_input_fn)
    predictions = list(predictions)
    word = int_to_kword[np.argmax(predictions[-1]['preds_probs'])]
    text = text + word
    next_x = np.concatenate((next_x, [[kword_to_int[word]]]))
    next_x = next_x[1:]
```

We should pick a random sequence of words as the initial text. Here, we picked the first `60` words. You can select any other consecutive list of words from the original kernel code. We store that in the `next_x` variable, to keep track of the next word in the sequence. The `int_to_kword` dictionary, which was created during data preparation, is used to transform the predicted IDs into words that are appended to the `text` output variable. Note that we loop for `maxlen` number of iterations, which is set as `40` in the code. This can be increased or decreased, to experiment with increasing or decreasing the number of words in the generated text.

We can now look at the final output that is generated:

```
static int blk_trace_remove_queue Initialize POSIX timer handling for a
thread group.
  PAGE_SHIFT;
    if !rb_threads[cpu]s, const struct pci_dev ;
  check_mm the filter_hash does not exist or is empty,

    return NULL;

  memsetkexec_image;
struct kimage ;
}

power_attr_rostruct hist_field module_add_modinfo_attrs Fake ip  data;
  struct page
{
  return arg ? GFP_ATOMIC  PM_SUSPEND_ON
    goto fail_free_buffers;

  ret  sec;
  }

static struct ftrace_ops trace_ops __initdata  into them directly.
    !is_sampling_eventholders_dir, mod MIN_NICE can be offsets in the trace
data.
  to the buffer after this will fail and return NULL.
  ring_buffer_record_enable_cpu  {
    area[pos] ;

#ifdef CONFIG_SUSPEND
  if  hist_field_u16;
    break;
  case 1 representing a file path of format and ;

#endif ;
    goto out;
  }

  ftrace_graph_return  Pipe buffer operations for a buffer.  val;
  arch_spin_unlock If we fail, we do not register this tracer.
  return ret;
}
```

While the preceding output closely resembles kernel code, it does not make much sense.
Note that the output might differ on each run, and it might also be different in the
Notebook found in the book's code repository.

It does appear that the model has learned some of the classic Linux kernel idioms, such as the usage of `goto` in the code. It might be possible to generate more realistic kernel code with a character-level model, using deeper networks, bidirectional LSTMs, and so on. The reader can experiment with such approaches to get better results.

We will now look at the loss functions and the model graph in TensorBoard. We will look at the model graph first:

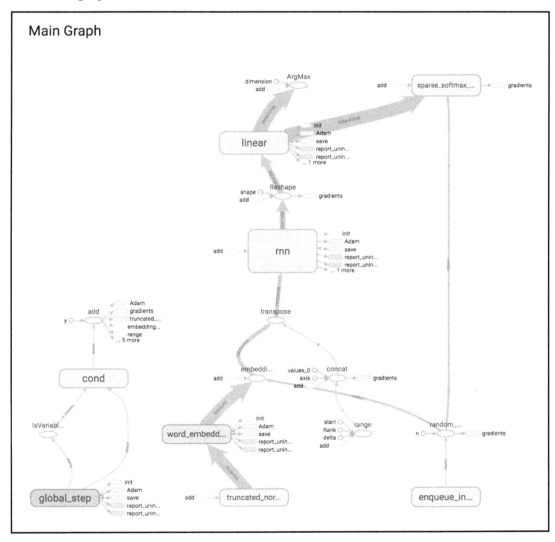

loss functions and the model graph in TensorBoard

The graph shows the input of the word embeddings, followed by the RNN cell and the dense layer. The sparse softmax layer gives the final output probabilities of the words in the input vocabulary. `AdamOptimizer` is used for minimizing the loss function, which takes the gradients as input. We will now look at how the `loss` function varies in the training steps:

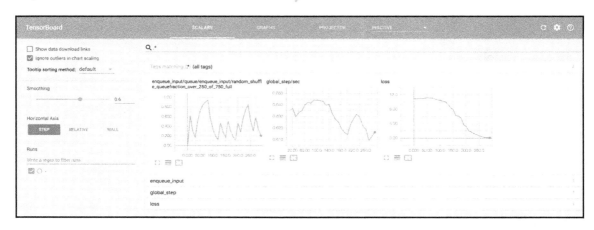

Varying loss function in the training

As you can see, the loss starts at around `11` and falls close to `0.1`.

Although this example is not practically useful by itself, the goal was to show the reader that such generative models can be used to learn the underlying structure and essence of the input text. Creating such sequence models, therefore, can help us to understand the structure of the text for a given domain. The domain that we used in the example was operating system code. The reader can explore further, with other texts and deeper models.

Text summarization

Text summarization is the process of transforming an input document into a short summary, to help us understand the main content of the document in a short amount of time. Fundamentally, there are two types of summarization. One of them is extractive summarization and the other is abstractive summarization. We will briefly look at descriptions of these types of summaries.

Extractive summarization

In this type of summarization, the important phrases or keywords in a document are extracted and concatenated to get a short summary.

The main advantage is that it is simple and robust, since the extracted text is taken directly from the document. The disadvantage of this method is that we may not be able to obtain new paraphrasing, which produces clarity in the summary. In the next section, we will briefly look at extractive summarization using gensim.

Summarization using gensim

Gensim has a summarizer that is based on an improved version of the **TextRank** algorithm by Rada Mihalcea et al. This is a graph-based algorithm that uses keywords in the document as vertices. The weight of the edges between the keywords is determined based on their co-occurrences in the text. An algorithm, similar to **PageRank**, is used to determine the importance of the keywords. Finally, a summary is extracted by ranking important sentences containing highly ranked keywords. It is clear, from this description, that TextRank is one example of an extractive summarizer. We will look at a simple example, using the gensim summarizer. As test data, we will use the nltk product review corpus:

```
from nltk.corpus import product_reviews_1
from gensim.summarization import summarizer
```

We have also imported the gensim summarizer. We will use it to generate the product review summary:

```
product_review_raw =
product_reviews_1.raw('Apex_AD2600_Progressive_scan_DVD player.txt')
product_summary = summarizer.summarize(product_review_raw,word_count=100)
print("Raw Text Length: ", len(product_review_raw.split()))
print("Summary Length: ", len(product_summary.split()))
print("Summary: ", product_summary)
```

We have chosen one of the products (DVD player) in the nltk corpus. We will limit the summary to 100 words, as passed in the word_count parameter of the summarize function. We will print the original text and the summary text word lengths to see the difference between the two :

```
Raw Text Length: 13014
Summary Length: 88
Summary: player[+2]##i bought this apex 2600 dvd player for myself at
christmas because it got good reviews as a good value for the money on a
```

```
variety of different sites . remote[-2]##we 've purchased 3 universal
remotes so far-all claiming to work " apex " dvd players and none worked .
##after having bought and been disappointed in another brand of dvd player
, i purchased the apex ad2600 from amazon and first of all i should say it
was delivered much more quickly than i had expected .
```

The output shows the summary text as having around 88 words, compared to 13014 words in the original product review. We can also look at the keywords that are extracted by the summarizer:

```
from gensim.summarization import keywords
keywords(product_review_raw).split("\n")[0:20]
```

The `keywords` module will extract the main keywords in the document. We will print the top 20 keywords in the review text:

```
['players',
 'dvd player',
 'dvds',
 'play',
 'playing',
 'plays',
 'apex',
 'picture',
 'pictures',
 'pictured',
 'remotes',
 'work',
 'works',
 'working',
 'worked',
 'customer',
 'customers',
 'disks types played',
 'problems',
 'problem']
```

The output also shows that some of the keywords are different tenses of the same word.

Next, we will look at an abstractive summarizer, using deep learning.

Abstractive summarization

This type of summarization can produce output summaries containing words or phrases that are not in the original text but preserving the original intent of the input document. This can result in novel phrases and thereby natural summaries. We will first look at an overview of abstractive text summarization using deep learning approaches. In text summarization, as the input and output, are both sequences of text, the deep learning model commonly used in practice is the sequence-to-sequence model. We will briefly describe this approach to text summarization next.

Encoder-decoder architecture

As the name encoder-decoder suggests, this architecture consists of an encoder and a decoder component. This is illustrated in the following diagram. The function of the **encoder** is to take an input text sequence and convert it into a dense vector representation, also known as a **thought vector** or **context vector**. The thought vector, in essence, is an internal representation that captures the context and meaning of the whole input text. The **decoder** takes the dense vector representation of the original, complete text and generates the output summary, one word at a time:

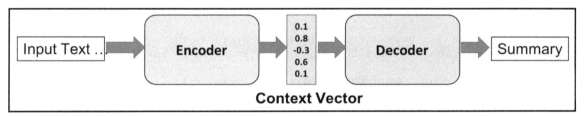

Encoder

The most common type of encoder uses bidirectional RNNs, with either LSTM or GRU units. In such cases, the input to the encoder is a distributed representation of words or word embeddings.

Decoder

The decoder is another bidirectional LSTM or GRU network. It takes the vector representation of the input text emitted by the encoder and the previously generated summary word and generates the next summary word.

News summarization using GRU

In this example, we will look into summarizing news articles using LSTMs. The data for this example was taken from CNN. The complete Python Notebook for this example can be found at `Chapter08/02_example.ipynb`, in the book's code repository. In addition to the basic architecture described previously, we will use an additional attention layer. It has been determined from text summarization research work that a model with an attention mechanism can perform better than a model without one.

Data preparation

First, we will load the original news file and the summaries into a pandas `DataFrame`:

```
titledata=[]
artdata=[]
with gzip.open('data/news.txt.gz') as artfile:
    for li in artfile:
        artdata.append(li)
with gzip.open('data/summary.txt.gz') as titlefile:
    for li in titlefile:
        titledata.append(li)
news = pd.DataFrame({'Text':artdata,'Summary':titledata})
news = news.sample(frac=0.1)
news['Text_len'] = news.Text.apply(lambda x: len(x.split()))
news['Summary_len'] = news.Summary.apply(lambda x: len(x.split()))
```

We will take a look at some sample news `Text` and `Summary`:

```
print(news['Text'].head(2).values)
print(news['Summary'].head(2).values)
```

```
Output:
[b'chinese president hu jintao said here monday that china will work with
romania to promote bilateral trade and economic cooperation .\n'  b'federal
reserve policymakers opened a two-day meeting here tuesday to debate us
monetary moves , a fed source reported .\n']

[b'chinese president meets romanian pm\n'  b'federal reserve policymakers
open two-day meeting\n']
```

For the word embeddings, we will utilize the `glove.6B` vector corpus. We will load this into an embeddings matrix:

```
def build_word_vector_matrix(vector_file):
    embedding_index = {}
```

```
    with codecs.open(vector_file, 'r', 'utf-8') as f:
        for i, line in enumerate(f):
        sr = line.split()
        if(len(sr)&lt;26):
            continue
        word = sr[0]
        embedding = np.asarray(sr[1:], dtype='float32')
        embedding_index[word] = embedding
        return embedding_index

embeddings_index =
    build_word_vector_matrix('/Users/i346047/prs/temp/glove.6B.50d.txt')
```

embeddings_index contains the word to the corresponding word vector mappings. Next, we will create a mapping from words to integer indexes (and vice versa), for all of the words in both the news text and summary:

```
word2int = {}
count_threshold = 20
value = 0
for word, count in word_counts_dict.items():
    if count &gt;= count_threshold or word in embeddings_index:
        word2int[word] = value
        value += 1


special_codes = [TOKEN_UNK,TOKEN_PAD,TOKEN_EOS,TOKEN_GO]

for code in special_codes:
    word2int[code] = len(word2int)

int2word = {}
for word, value in word2int.items():
    int2word[value] = word
```

Note that we also include special codes for words that are not present in the vocabulary (UNK), padding tokens (PAD), an end of a sentence (EOS), and starting tokens (GO). These are defined by the corresponding constants in the code. The padding token will be used to pad sentences to fixed lengths, in both the news text and summary. The start and end of sentence tokens are prefixed and appended, respectively, to the input news text, during training and inference. Next, we will convert the news text and summaries to integer IDs:

```
def convert_sentence_to_ids(text, eos=False):
    wordints = []
    word_count = 0
    for sentence in text:
        sentence2ints = []
```

```
        for word in sentence.split():
            word_count += 1
            if word in word2int:
                sentence2ints.append(word2int[word])
            else:
                sentence2ints.append(word2int[TOKEN_UNK])
        if eos:
            sentence2ints.append(word2int[TOKEN_EOS])
        wordints.append(sentence2ints)
    return wordints, word_count
```

Note that for words not in the vocabulary, we have assigned the UNK token ID. Likewise, we will end sentences with the EOS token. Next, we will drop all input texts and summaries not within a specified minimum and maximum sentence length. We will also remove the sentences with a number of unknown words greater than the limit:

```
news_summaries_filtered = []
news_texts_filtered = []
max_text_length = int(news.Text_len.mean() + news.Text_len.std())
max_summary_length = int(int(news.Summary_len.mean() +
news.Summary_len.std()))
min_length = 4
unknown_token_text_limit = 10
unknown_token_summary_limit = 4
for count,text in enumerate(id_texts):
    unknown_token_text = unknown_tokens(id_texts[count])
    unknown_token_summary = unknown_tokens(id_summaries[count])
    text_len = len(id_texts[count])
    summary_len = len(id_summaries[count])
    if((unknown_token_text&gt;unknown_token_text_limit) or
(unknown_token_summary&gt;unknown_token_summary_limit)):
        continue
    if(text_len&lt;min_length or summary_len&lt;min_length or
text_len&gt;max_text_length or      summary_len&gt;max_summary_length):
        continue
    news_summaries_filtered.append(id_summaries[count])
    news_texts_filtered.append(id_texts[count])
```

We have used the minimum and maximum lengths within one standard deviation of the average length for the input text and summaries. The reader can try this with different limits and a different number of unknowns by changing the variables, `max_summary_length`, `max_text_length`, `unknown_token_text_limit`, `unknown_token_summary_limit`, **and** and `min_length`.

Now, we will look at model creation.

Encoder network

For the encoder component, we utilize a bidirectional RNN with GRU cells. In place of the GRU cell, we could also use an LSTM. The reader may experiment with an LSTM to look at the differences in the model's performance:

```
def get_cell(csize,dprob):
    rnc = GRUCell(csize)
    rnc = DropoutWrapper(rnc, input_keep_prob = dprob)
    return rnc

def encoding_layer(csize, len_s, nl, rinp, dprob):
    for l in range(nl):
        with tf.variable_scope('encoding_l_{}'.format(l)):
            rnn_frnt = get_cell(csize,dprob)
            rnn_bkwd = get_cell(csize,dprob)
            eop, est = tf.nn.bidirectional_dynamic_rnn(rnn_frnt, rnn_bkwd,
                                                                rinp,
                                                                len_s,
dtype=tf.float32)
    eop = tf.concat(eop,2)
    return eop, est
```

Note that we have concatenated the encoder's output, as this is bidirectional.

Decoder network

Like the encoder, for the decoder network, we will utilize an RNN with GRU cells. We will also have `nlyrs` number of GRU layers, created with `dropout`, using the `tf.contrib.rnn.DropoutWrapper` wrapper class. We will utilize the `BahdanauAttention` mechanism to incorporate attention on the output of the encoder:

```
def decoding_layer(dec_emb_op, embs, enc_op, enc_st, v_size, txt_len,
                    summ_len,mx_summ_len, rnsize, word2int, dprob,
batch_size, nlyrs):
    for l in range(nlyrs):
        with tf.variable_scope('dec_rnn_layer_{}'.format(l)):
            gru = tf.contrib.rnn.GRUCell(rnn_len)
            cell_dec = tf.contrib.rnn.DropoutWrapper(gru,input_keep_prob =
dprob)
    out_l = Dense(v_size, kernel_initializer =
tf.truncated_normal_initializer(mean = 0.0, stddev=0.1))
```

```
attention = BahdanauAttention(rnsize, enc_op,txt_len,
                                        normalize=False,
                                        name='BahdanauAttention')
cell_dec = AttentionWrapper(cell_dec,attention,rnn_len)
attn_zstate = cell_dec.zero_state(batch_size , tf.float32 )
attn_zstate = attn_zstate.clone(cell_state = enc_st[0])
with tf.variable_scope("decoding_layer"):
    tr_dec_op = trng_dec_layer(dec_emb_op,
                                    summ_len,
                                    cell_dec,
                                    attn_zstate,
                                    out_l,
                                    v_size,
                                    mx_summ_len)
with tf.variable_scope("decoding_layer", reuse=True):
    inf_dec_op = infr_dec_layer(embs,
                                    word2int[TOKEN_GO],
                                    word2int[TOKEN_EOS],
                                    cell_dec,
                                    attn_zstate,
                                    out_l,
                                    mx_summ_len,
                                    batch_size)

    return tr_dec_op, inf_dec_op
```

For the attention and sequence to sequence generation, we will use classes from the `seq2seq` library in TensorFlow. Now, we can look at how decoding is performed during training:

```
def trng_dec_layer(dec_emb_inp, summ_len, cell_dec, st_init, lyr_op,
                        v_size, max_summ_len):
    helper = TrainingHelper(inputs=dec_emb_inp, sequence_length=summ_len,
time_major=False)
    dec = BasicDecoder(cell_dec,helper,st_init,lyr_op)
    logits, _, _ =
dynamic_decode(dec,output_time_major=False,impute_finished=True,
                            maximum_iterations=max_summ_len)
    return logits
```

We use the `tf.contrib.seq2seq.TrainingHelper` class to feed the ground truth summaries to the decoder input for the training. The attention state is also passed as input to the decoder, through the `initial_state` tensor. Finally, the `tf.contrib.seq2seq.dynamic_decode` function performs the decoding on this input.

Sequence to sequence

Next, we will look at the sequence to sequence high-level function that wraps all of this together. This takes the word embeddings of the input text sentence, creates the encoding/decoding layer, and produces the `logits` as output. The op_tr and op_inf objects represent the predictions during training and inference, respectively:

```
def seq2seq_model(data_inp, data_summ_tgt, dprob, len_txt, len_summ,
max_len_summ,
                  v_size, rnsize, nlyrs, word2int, batch_size):
    inp_emb = word_emb_matrix
    word_embs = tf.Variable(inp_emb, name="word_embs")
    inp_enc_emb = tf.nn.embedding_lookup(word_embs, data_inp)
    op_enc, st_enc = encoding_layer(rnsize, len_txt, nlyrs, inp_enc_emb,
dprob)
    inp_dec = process_encoding_input(data_summ_tgt, word2int, batch_size)
    inp_dec_emb = tf.nn.embedding_lookup(inp_emb, inp_dec)
    op_tr, op_inf = decoding_layer(inp_dec_emb,
                                                   inp_emb,
                                                   op_enc,
                                                   st_enc,
                                                   v_size,
                                                   len_txt,
                                                   len_summ,
                                                   max_len_summ,
                                                   rnsize,
                                                   word2int,
                                                   dprob,
                                                   batch_size,
                                                   nlyrs)

    return op_tr, op_inf
```

The output training logits, `op_tr`, is used (along with the ground truth summary) to compute the cost during training.

We will now look at building the graph.

Building the graph

The graph is built using the high-level `seq2seq_model` function. Let's look at the code for building the graph and optimizer:

```
train_graph = tf.Graph()
with train_graph.as_default():
    data_inp, tgts, lrt, dprobs, len_summ, max_len_summ, len_txt =
```

```
model_inputs()

    tr_op, inf_op = seq2seq_model(tf.reverse(data_inp, [-1]),
                                                tgts,
                                                dprobs,
                                                len_txt,
                                                len_summ,
                                                max_len_summ,
                                                len(word2int)+1,
                                                rnn_len,
                                                n_layers,
                                                word2int,
                                                batch_size)
        tr_op = tf.identity(tr_op.rnn_output, 'tr_op')
        inf_op = tf.identity(inf_op.sample_id, name='predictions')
        seq_masks = tf.sequence_mask(len_summ, max_len_summ, dtype=tf.float32,
name='masks')

    with tf.name_scope("optimizer"):
        tr_cost = sequence_loss(tr_op,tgts,seq_masks)
        optzr = tf.train.AdamOptimizer(lrt)
        grds = optzr.compute_gradients(tr_cost)
        capped_grds = [(tf.clip_by_value(grd, -5., 5.), var) for grd, var
in grds
                        if grd is not None]
        train_op = optzr.apply_gradients(capped_grds)
    tf.summary.scalar("cost", tr_cost)
print("Graph created.")
```

We utilized `AdamOptimizer` to minimize the cost, computed with the training logits and the target summary words. Note that because we are using RNNs, we cap the gradients, to avoid the problem of exploding gradients.

Training

For the training, we will use a slice of the input data, which can be increased to improve the model's performance:

```
min_learning_rate = 0.0006
display_step = 20
early_stop_cnt = 0
early_stop_cnt_max = 3
per_epoch = 3


update_loss = 0
```

```
batch_loss = 0
summary_update_loss = []

news_summaries_train = news_summaries_filtered[0:3000]
news_texts_train = news_texts_filtered[0:3000]
update_check = (len(news_texts_train)//batch_size//per_epoch)-1
checkpoint = logs_path + 'best_so_far_model.ckpt'
with tf.Session(graph=train_graph) as sess:
    tf_summary_writer = tf.summary.FileWriter(logs_path, graph=train_graph)
    merged_summary_op = tf.summary.merge_all()
    sess.run(tf.global_variables_initializer())
    for epoch_i in range(1, epochs+1):
        update_loss = 0
        batch_loss = 0
        for batch_i, (summaries_batch, texts_batch, summaries_len,
texts_len) in enumerate(
                get_batches(news_summaries_train, news_texts_train,
batch_size)):
            before = time.time()
            _,loss,summary = sess.run(
                [train_op, tr_cost,merged_summary_op],
                {data_inp: texts_batch,
                 tgts: summaries_batch,
                 lrt: lr,
                 len_summ: summaries_len,
                 len_txt: texts_len,
                 dprobs: dr_prob})
```

The batch data for training is obtained from the get_batches function, which formats the input text and summaries with the padding start and end tokens. You can change the parameters, such as the learning rate, layers, and dropout probabilities, to experiment with the model's performance. The epochs can also be increased, to improve the accuracy of the model. The model is also saved whenever there is an improvement in the batch loss.

We can now look at the final output of the training:

```
No Improvement.
** Epoch  20/20 Batch    20/1048 - Batch Loss:   1.454, seconds: 16.15
Average loss: 1.383
Saving model
** Epoch  20/20 Batch    40/1048 - Batch Loss:   1.362, seconds: 17.11
Average loss: 1.353
```

We can see that the loss decreased to around 1.353, from an initial value of 9.254. Note that this may vary for each run.

Inference

We will now load the saved model file and test it with sample data from the input text that was not seen by the model. We will load the `logits` tensor from the model, and use that to infer the summary text prediction output on unseen or test data:

```
INFO:tensorflow:Restoring parameters from
/tmp/models/best_so_far_model.ckpt

Text
Word Ids:    [33, 687, 145, 2047, 33, 5800, 1133, 2016, 19, 526, 6626, 3,
6842, 526, 1716, 5573, 11024, 128, 526, 3591, 1607, 1272, 3024, 19, 81,
8167, 19, 774, 526, 594, 1716, 65, 10590, 11026]

Input Words: a taiwan official gave a cautious welcome tuesday to the idea
of having the olympic torch through the island if beijing were to be chosen
to host the #### olympic games .

Summary
Word Ids:          [687, 605, 19, 81, 39, 740]
Response Words: taiwan launches to be &lt;unk&gt; wins
Ground Truth:     cautiously welcomes idea of allowing passage of
                  olympic torch
```

We will also run the inference on the training data. While the predictions or summary of the unseen input text is far from the ground truth, the predictions for the training data are quite close as the following output shows.

```
INFO:tensorflow:Restoring parameters from
/tmp/models/best_so_far_model.ckpt

Text
Word Ids:    [10651, 1190, 910, 2324, 457, 178, 1203, 3909, 126, 7746, 909,
910, 29, 33, 4642, 745, 10903, 581, 13, 33, 911, 2796, 19, 2156, 115, 526,
11024, 1871, 10589, 5672, 702, 10590, 11026]

Input Words: japanese share prices closed #.## percent higher thursday as
easing oil prices and a weaker yen buoyed confidence in a market continuing
to recover from the shock , dealers said .

Summary
Word Ids:          [548, 492, 493, 457, 178, 457]
Response Words: tokyo shares close #.## percent #.##
Ground Truth:     tokyo stocks close up #.## percent
```

It should be noted that the poor performance of the model with the test data can be attributed to the small dataset that we utilized for the training (with a training size of 3,000 samples). The reader can use the same model to train on a larger dataset, probably on a GPU, to get better results.

TensorBoard visualization

We will now take a brief look at the graphs and the loss function, with TensorBoard. First, we will look at the graph output from TensorBoard:

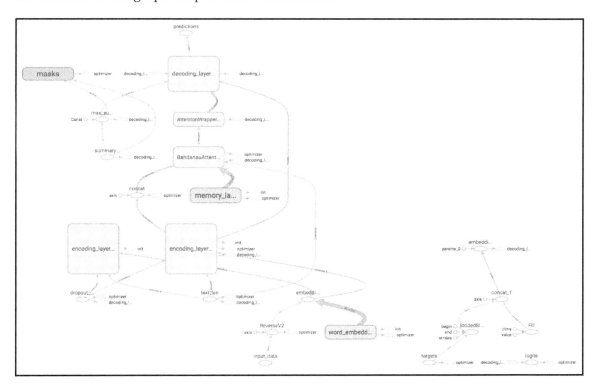

Graph output on TensorBoard

We can clearly see that the encoding layer and decoding layer form the main components of the model, with the Bahdanau attention mechanism as another input in the decoding layer. The input embeddings are first fed into the encoding layer, whose output is fed to the attention mechanism, as well as the decoding layer. Finally, the decoding layer provides the predictions as output. The optimizer takes in the decoding layer output, the attention mechanism output, and the targets, to optimize on the cost function:

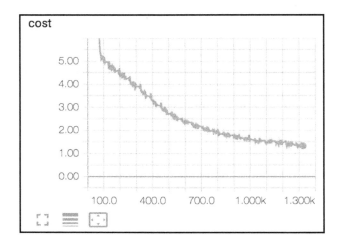

We also find that the cost steadily decreases with the number of training steps. In the next section, we will look at some recent papers that describe enhancements to the encoder-decoder model, with attention described here.

State-of-the-art abstractive text summarization

In this section, we will look at two recent papers that describe enhancements to the model used in our news text summarization example from the previous section.

In the first paper, *Abstractive Text Summarization Using Sequence-To-Sequence RNNs and Beyond* (https://arxiv.org/abs/1602.06023), from IBM, Ramesh Nallapati, et al., applied the model for neural machine translation to text summarization and achieved better performance, as compared to state-of-the-art systems. This model uses a bidirectional GRU-RNN as an encoder, and a unidirectional GRU-RNN as a decoder. Note that this is the same model architecture that we used in our news summarization example.

The following are the main additional enhancements that they proposed:

- In addition to word embeddings, they enhanced the input features to include POS tags, named entity tags, and the TF-IDF statistics of the words. This helps to identify the key concepts and entities in the document, improving the summarization text.
- These additional features are concatenated with the existing word vectors and fed into the encoder.

The following diagram illustrates the use of the additional features - word embeddings (**W**), parts of speech (**POS**), named entity tags (**NER**), and term frequency, inverse-document frequency (**TF-IDF**):

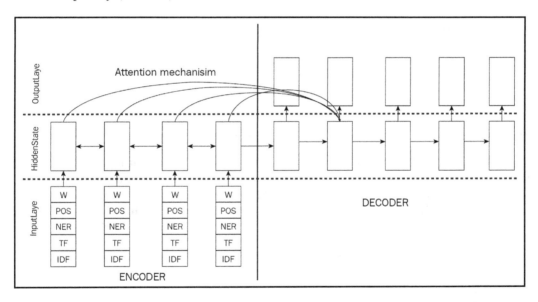

In order to handle unseen or **out-of-vocabulary** (**OOV**) words in the test data, they used a generator-pointer network that copied words from the source document position when activated. The news summarization example that we described earlier simply ignores OOV words and replaces them with UNK tokens, which may not generate coherent summaries.

The architecture, including the pointer-generator network, is illustrated in the following figure:

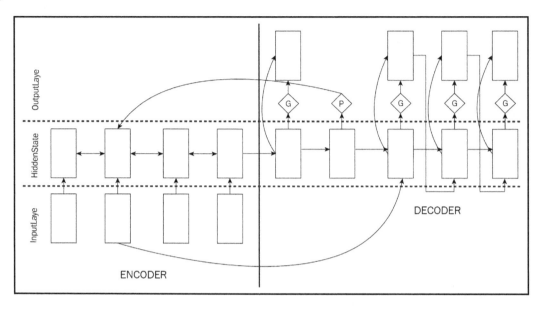

For source datasets with long document sizes and many sentences, it is also necessary to identify key sentences that should be used for the summary. For this, they used a hierarchical network, with two bidirectional RNNs, on the encoding side. One was used at the word level and the other at the sentence level. More details on this paper can be found at https://arxiv.org/abs/1602.06023.

In their paper, *Get to the Point: Summarization with Pointer-Generator Networks,* from Google, Abigail See et al. used a pointer-generator network, similar to the approach taken by Ramesh Nallapati et al. But, in addition to handling only OOV words, they also considered the copy distribution and vocabulary distribution. The copy distribution considers the repetitive use of a specific word in the source document, in addition to its attention. This raises the probability of the word being chosen in the summary. The following figure shows how vocabulary distribution and attention distribution are combined to generate the final summary. The detailed paper can be found at https://arxiv.org/abs/1704.04368:

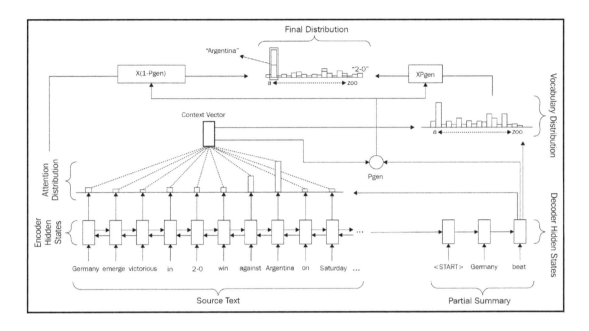

Summary

In this chapter, we focused on text generation and text summarization. Using GRU and RNN, we illustrated an example text generation model that can generate Linux kernel code. Such models, when applied to different domains or source input texts, can help us to understand the underlying structure and context. Next, we described the different types of text summarization. We explained a simple extractive summarization approach, using `gensim` to generate product review summaries. While extractive summarization reproduces words from the source text, abstractive summarization can generate novel and intuitive summaries.

To cover abstractive summarization, we introduced an encoder-decoder model, using GRU and RNN to summarize news text. We used CNN news text as input data to produce short summaries of the news. Finally, we looked at some state of the art approaches to improve upon our base encoder-decoder model (with attention). You can build on the base model that we developed, in order to incorporate these enhancements. One simple enhancement would be to add additional features, such as POS, NER, and TF-IDF, to the word embedding of the input text. In the next Chapter, we will look at another interesting topic of question-answering and chatbots. We will be developing a question answering model and build a chatbot using generative RNN model.

9
Question-Answering and Chatbots Using Memory Networks

Natural language understanding (NLU) tasks can be thought of as an umbrella term encompassing research areas that involve reasoning over text in both syntactic and semantic ways, such as text summarization, machine translation, and conversation modelling (that is, chatbots).

An interesting line of **natural language processing (NLP)** research deals with decomposing all NLU tasks into a simple **Question-Answer (QA)** framework, where the model must reason over an input text (for example, a Wikipedia article on dogs), to answer questions such as, *What is the most common breed of dogs? What is the summary of the article? What is the translation into French?*.

In this chapter, we will understand the QA task and introduce a class of deep learning models known as **memory networks** to build QA systems. We shall then learn about the various components of an end-to-end trained chatbot model and extend memory networks to build conversational chatbots.

The Question-Answering task

On the surface, the Question-Answering task seems straightforward—given a question and (optionally) some related facts, the model must produce an answer.

Traditional approaches to QA include rule-based models or information retrieval methods based on word overlap or tf-idf scores. However, training a model to understand the input as well as the facts in terms of both syntax and semantics can be challenging due to the inherent complications of natural language. Deep neural networks can learn to model these complexities without handcrafting or feature engineering, and have emerged as the state-of-the-art networks for these tasks.

Question-Answering datasets

Question-Answering datasets can have differences based on the form in which a response or answer is required. We will briefly summarize a few popular academic datasets for QA along with their key characteristics:

Dataset name	Description	Category	URL
bAbI text understanding tasks	This suite of 20 synthetically generated tasks was aimed to test some fundamental skills that models for NLU should possess. Each task trains a model to answer a question on the state of its environment based on a paragraph where various actions are taken in the environment.	Answer selection	https://research.fb.com/downloads/babi/
SQuAD: Stanford Question Answering Dataset	SQuAD contains questions associated with Wikipedia articles, and requires the model to select an answer span in the article itself as an answer to the question. It is the most popular QA dataset today.	Answer spanning	https://stanford-qa.com/
VQA: Visual Question Answering Dataset	In VQA, the input to be reasoned over is an image instead of text. The model must learn to reason over pixels to select answers to textual questions about the image.	Answer selection	http://www.visualqa.org/
AI2 Reasoning Challenge	The ARC dataset contains science multiple choice questions to select answers from. It was specially designed to expose the shortcomings of recent neural network models that claim to do language understanding for easy datasets such as SQuAD and bAbI!	Multiple choice	http://data.allenai.org/arc/

Memory networks for Question-Answering

Memory networks are a general class of neural network models for NLU tasks introduced by Weston et al. in 2014 in the context of end-to-end trained QA systems. Given a question and some supporting facts or relevant information, the task is to generate or select an appropriate answer. The model stores these facts in a persistent memory and is trained to perform reasoning based on them to produce an appropriate response.

 The first paper on this topic was titled *Memory Networks* by Jason Weston, Sumit Chopra, and Antoine Bordes, and can be found at http://arxiv.org/abs/1410.3916.

As QA tasks come in many varieties, memory networks offer a flexible and modular framework where facts stored in memories could range from text to images, and answers can be generated or retrieved from a set of candidates.

Memory network pipeline overview

A generic memory network's architecture can be decomposed into four parts: a **Question Module**, an **Input Module**, a **Memory Module**, and an **Output Module**. As is common practice in neural networks, information passes from one module to the other through dense vectors/embeddings, making the parameters of the model end-to-end trainable using gradient descent:

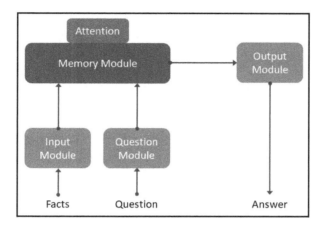

The working of this model is as follows:

- The **Input Module** receives multiple facts and encodes each of them in vectors.
- The **Question Module**, similar to the **Input Module**, is responsible for encoding the question in a vector.
- The **Memory Module** receives the encoded facts (from the **Input Module**) and the encoded question (from the **Question Module**), and performs a soft attention mechanism on the facts to figure out their relevance to the question. The result of the attention is a context vector for the given question, encoding the question, as well as all the contextual information required to answer it.
- The **Output Module** receives the context vector and is responsible for producing an answer in the desired format. This could mean the selection of an appropriate response from a candidate set, the prediction of answer spans, or the generation of a token-by-token response.

Writing a memory network in TensorFlow

In the following sections, we will look under the hood of a simple memory network architecture described by Sukhbaatar et al. in 2015 for building a retrieval-based QA system. We will provide code snippets to build a generic memory network class, explaining the working and details of the model along the way

 Details about the model can be found in the paper *End-to-End Memory Networks* by Sainbayar Sukhbaatar, Arthur Szlam, Jason Weston, and Rob Fergus at `http://arxiv.org/abs/1503.08895`.

Class constructor

We will define the constructor for initializing the memory network's `initializer` object, `optimizer` object, mini-batch size, and so on. We will also write high-level TensorFlow operations for the loss, prediction, and training. All of them hinge on the `_inference` method, which we will implement in the following sections:

```
class MemoryNetwork(object):
    def __init__(self, sentence_size, vocab_size, candidates_size,
                 candidates_vec, embedding_size, hops,
                 initializer=tf.random_normal_initializer(stddev=0.1),
                 optimizer=tf.train.AdamOptimizer(learning_rate=0.01),
                 session=tf.Session()):
        self._hops = hops
        self._candidates_vec = candidates_vec
        # Define placeholders for inputs to the model
        self._facts = tf.placeholder(
            tf.int32, [None, None, sentence_size], name="facts")
        self._questions = tf.placeholder(
            tf.int32, [None, sentence_size], name="questions")
        self._answers = tf.placeholder(
            tf.int32, [None], name="answers")

        # Define trainable variables used for inference
        with tf.variable_scope("MemoryNetwork"):
            # Word embedding lookup matrix for input facts and
              questions
            self.word_emb_matrix = tf.Variable(initializer(
                [vocab_size, embedding_size]), name="A")
            # Matrix used for linear transformations during inference
            self.transformation_matrix = tf.Variable(initializer(
                [embedding_size, embedding_size]), name="H")
```

```
# Word embedding lookup matrix for output responses
self.output_word_emb_matrix = tf.Variable(initializer(
    [vocab_size, embedding_size]), name="W")

# Compute cross entropy error on inference predictions
logits = self._inference(self._facts, self._questions)
cross_entropy = tf.nn.sparse_softmax_cross_entropy_with_logits(
    logits=logits, labels=self._answers, name="cross_entropy")
cross_entropy_sum = tf.reduce_sum(
    cross_entropy, name="cross_entropy_sum")

# Define loss operation
self.loss_op = cross_entropy_sum

# Define gradient pipeline
grads_and_vars = optimizer.compute_gradients(self.loss_op)
# Define training operation
self.train_op = optimizer.apply_gradients(
    grads_and_vars, name="train_op")

# Define prediction operation
self.predict_op = tf.argmax(logits, 1, name="predict_op")

# Load session and initialize all variables
self._session = session
self._session.run(tf.initialize_all_variables())
```

Input module

The input module does a word embedding lookup for all the words in each input fact, and then builds a single embedding for each fact by summing across the temporal direction, that is, summing the word embeddings for each word in a fact:

```
def _input_module(self, facts):
    with tf.variable_scope("InputModule"):
        facts_emb = tf.nn.embedding_lookup(self.word_emb_matrix,
                                           facts)
        return tf.reduce_sum(facts_emb, 2)
```

Question module

The question module does the same embedding lookup and temporal summation as the input module. The embedding matrix, and hence the word vocabulary, is shared between the two modules:

```
def _question_module(self, questions):
    with tf.variable_scope("QuestionModule"):
        questions_emb = tf.nn.embedding_lookup(
            self.word_emb_matrix, questions)
        return tf.reduce_sum(questions_emb, 1)
```

Since we are building the most conceptually simple memory network possible, we do not make use of more sophisticated sentence representation models, such as **recurrent neural networks** (**RNNs**) or **Convolutional Neural Networks** (**CNNs**). The modular nature of the architecture makes it easy to do further experiments on this.

Memory module

The magic of memory network models lies in their formulation of the memory module, which performs a soft attention mechanism over the fact embeddings. Literature on memory networks and other attention-based models introduces many different types of attention mechanisms, but all of them hinge on the concept of an element-wise dot product followed by a summation between two vectors as an operation measuring semantic or syntactic similarity. We will call it the reduce-dot operation, which receives two vectors and results in a single number denoting a similarity score.

We have formulated our attention mechanism as follows:

1. The context vector is used to encode all the information required to produce an output and is initialized as the question vector
2. The reduce-dot operation between each of the fact vectors and the context vector gives us similarity scores for each of the fact vectors
3. We then take a softmax over these similarity scores to normalize these scores into probability values between 0 and 1
4. For each fact vector, we then multiply each element of the vector by the similarity probability value for that fact
5. Finally, we take an element-wise sum of these weighted fact vectors to get a context representation where certain facts have higher importance than others
6. The context vector is then updated by element-wise adding this context representation to it

7. The updated context vector is used to attend to the fact vectors and is subsequently updated further using multiple passes over the facts, termed **hops**

The steps can be understood through an expanded view of the memory module:

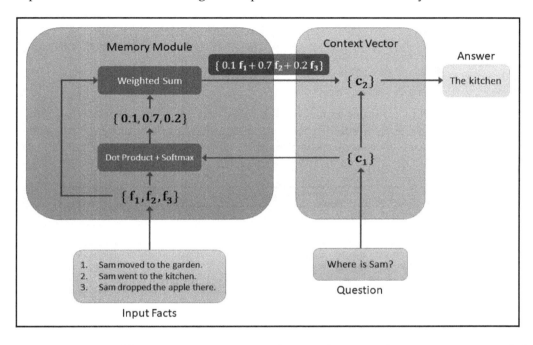

We must use NumPy-like atomic operations in TensorFlow to write our memory module, as there is no high-level wrapper in the API for performing reduce-dot operations:

```
def _memory_module(self, questions_emb, facts_emb):
    with tf.variable_scope("MemoryModule"):
        initial_context_vector = questions_emb
        context_vectors = [initial_context_vector]
        # Multi-hop attention over facts to update context vector
        for hop in range(self._hops):
            # Perform reduce_dot
            context_temp = tf.transpose(
                tf.expand_dims(context_vectors[-1], -1), [0, 2, 1])
            similarity_scores = tf.reduce_sum(
                facts_emb * context_temp, 2)
            # Calculate similarity probabilities
            probs = tf.nn.softmax(similarity_scores)
            # Perform attention multiplication
            probs_temp = tf.transpose(tf.expand_dims(probs, -1),
```

```
                                            [0, 2, 1])
            facts_temp = tf.transpose(facts_emb, [0, 2, 1])
            context_rep = tf.reduce_sum(facts_temp*probs_temp, 2)
            # Update context vector
            context_vector = tf.matmul(context_vectors[-1],
                                    self.transformation_matrix) \
                            + context_rep
            # Append to context vector list to use in next hop
            context_vectors.append(context_vector)
        # Return context vector for last hop
        return context_vector
```

Each hop may attend to different aspects of the facts, and using such a multi-hop attention mechanism leads to richer context vectors. The mechanism allows models to understand and reason over the facts in a step-by-step manner, as we can see by visualizing the values of the similarity probabilities at each hop:

Story (2: 2 supporting facts)	Hop 1	Hop 2	Hop 3
John dropped the milk.	0.06	0.00	0.00
John took the milk there.	0.88	1.00	0.00
Sandra went back to the bathroom.	0.00	0.00	0.00
John moved to the hallway.	0.00	0.00	1.00
Mary went back to the bedroom.	0.00	0.00	0.00
Where is the milk? Answer: hallway Prediction: hallway			

Output module

The output module usually depends on the task at hand. In this case, it is used to retrieve the most appropriate reply from a set of candidates. It does this by first converting each candidate into embeddings in the same way as the input and question modules did, and then taking dot products of each candidate embedding with the context vector from the memory module. For each candidate, we get a similarity or matching score with the context vector. For inference, we apply a softmax function over the similarity values for all the candidates to select the most appropriate one:

```
    def _output_module(self, context_vector):
        with tf.variable_scope("OuptutModule"):
            candidates_emb =
    tf.nn.embedding_lookup(self.output_word_emb_matrix,
                                        self._candidates_vec)
            candidates_emb_sum = tf.reduce_sum(candidates_emb, 1)
            return tf.matmul(context_vector,
    tf.transpose(candidates_emb_sum))
```

If the task required the generation of a response instead of retrieval, an RNN could have been used to generate the answer token-by-token in a fashion similar to machine translation tasks.

Putting it together

We can then write an `inference` method to bring together the various modules into a single pipeline for reading inputs and questions, obtaining context vectors, and producing an output:

```
def _inference(self, facts, questions):
    with tf.variable_scope("MemoryNetwork"):
        input_vectors = self._input_module(facts)
        question_vectors = self._question_module(questions)
        context_vectors = self._memory_module(question_vectors,
                                               input_vectors)
        output = self._output_module(context_vectors)
        return output
```

Lastly, we define the `fit` and `predict` functions, which can be used to train and make predictions using the memory network as part of a larger pipeline. We use a `feed_dict` to pass data into the operations that we had defined in the initialization code, which in turn will run the `_inference` function:

```
def fit(self, facts, questions, answers):
    feed_dict = {self._facts: facts,
                 self._questions: questions,
                 self._answers: answers}
    loss, _ = self._session.run([self.loss_op, self.train_op],
                                feed_dict=feed_dict)
    return loss

def predict(self, facts, questions):
    feed_dict = {self._facts: facts, self._questions: questions}
    return self._session.run(self.predict_op, feed_dict=feed_dict)
```

Extending memory networks for dialog modeling

We consider a dialog as a turn-based conversation between two participants (say A and B), where each turn of dialog involves an utterance by A followed by a response by B. We can then treat the production of a response at each turn as an NLU task where we must choose or generate an appropriate response for an incoming query based on the entire conversation history before the query.

We have already discussed how we can build a memory network-based QA model, which takes a question and some associated facts as input, and produces a response to the question by reasoning over the facts. To effectively model dialog as part of such a framework, the utterance at each turn of the conversation would be a question, and the entire dialog history would be the facts, based on which a memory network will produce the response:

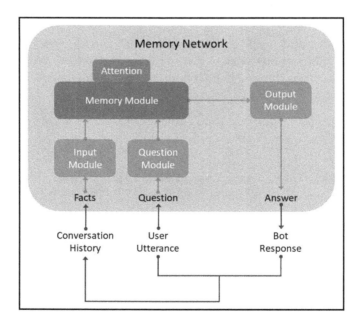

For dialog to continue at the next turn, the previous utterance and response pair will have to be appended to the conversation history. The model will then be used to process the next utterance and produce an appropriate response for it, till the end of the conversation.

Before we dive into the code behind a memory network chatbot, we will introduce a few dialog datasets, and talk about one in particular—the bAbI dialog dataset by Facebook AI research.

Dialog datasets

Dialog tasks are generally divided into two broad categories: open-ended conversation (also known as **chit-chat**) and goal-oriented systems.

Open-ended dialog systems generally deal with conversing on unrestricted subjects and are trained using large scale corpuses from Twitter conversations, reddit replies, or similar forum posts. Since most open-ended tasks require the generation of responses, most models use the seq2seq framework, similar to machine translation or text summarization, and are evaluated using a combination of translation metrics (such as BLEU score) and human evaluation.

The key challenges involved in building these neural conversational models besides language modelling and generation are the lack of consistent personality, as the models are trained on many dialogs with different speakers, and have the tendency to produce non-committal answers (such as I don't know) to every utterance.

Goal-oriented dialog systems, on the other hand, are designed for extremely specific interactions between users and bots, such as customer care services, restaurant reservations, movie bookings, or other concierge services. They are usually evaluated on their ability to predict the dialog state by slot filling or to select the most appropriate response at each turn of dialog.

The key challenge for goal-oriented systems is combining prior knowledge, conversation history, and context to meet the goals set for them. Hence, the most common architectures involve extending QA models to conduct dialogs, as discussed in the previous section.

The bAbI dialog dataset

The bAbI dialog dataset (introduced by Bordes et al. in 2016) is one of the simplest goal-oriented dialog datasets aimed at testing end-to-end trained systems in the domain of restaurant reservations. The dialog tasks are meant to complement the bAbI tasks for text understanding, which were described earlier.

Complete information about the creation and usage of the `bAbI dialog` dataset can be found in the paper *Learning End-to-End Goal-Oriented Dialog* by Antoine Bordes, Y-Lan Boureau, and Jason Weston at `http://arxiv.org/abs/1605.07683`. The data can be downloaded from the following URL: `https://research.fb.com/downloads/babi/`.

Set in the domain of restaurant reservation, this synthetically generated dataset breaks down a conversation between a bot and a user into five tasks to test some crucial capabilities that dialog systems should have. Given a **knowledge base** (**KB**) of restaurants and their properties (location, type of cuisine, and so on), the aim of the dialog is to book a restaurant for the user. Full dialogs are divided into various stages, each of which tests whether models can learn abilities, such as implicit dialog state tracking, using KB facts in dialog, and dealing with new entities that don't appear in dialogs from the training set.

The following figure will help you understand the tasks better:

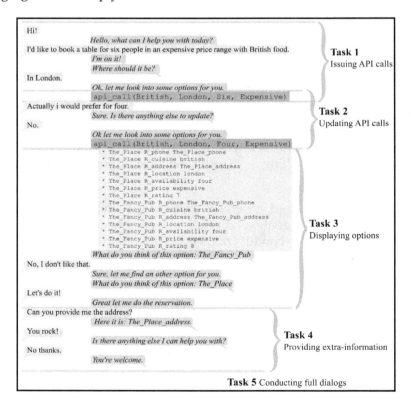

The conversations are generated by a simulator (in a fixed template format) based on an underlying KB containing all the restaurants and their properties. Each restaurant is defined by a type of cuisine (ten choices, for example, Italian, Indian), a location (ten choices, for example, London, Tokyo), a price range (cheap, moderate, or expensive), a party size (2, 4, 6, or 8 people), and a rating (from 1 to 8). Each restaurant also has an address and a phone number. Making an API call to the KB returns a list of facts related to all the restaurants that satisfy the four parameters: location, cuisine, price range, and party size. In addition to the user and bot utterances, dialogs in each task are comprised of API calls and the resulting facts. Conversations are generated using natural language patterns after randomly selecting each of the four required fields: location, cuisine, price range, and party size. There are 43 patterns for the user and 15 for the bot (the user can say something in up to four different ways, while the bot only has one).

Although the tasks were designed to be used as a framework to analyze the shortcomings of dialog systems in a goal-oriented setting, we will focus on the fifth task: conducting a full conversation. This task combines all aspects of the first four tasks into full dialog scripts and can be used to train a simple chatbot for restaurant reservations.

Raw data format

Each of the five tasks has 1,000 dialogues each for training, validation, and testing. The file format for each task is as follows:

```
ID user_utterance [tab] bot_response
...
```

The IDs for a given dialog start at 1 and increase. When the IDs in a file reset back to 1, the following sentences are the start of a new dialog. This is an example of a raw dialog:

```
1 hi          hello what can i help you with today
2 can you make a restaurant reservation with french cuisine for four
  people in an expensive price range        i'm on it
3 &lt;SILENCE&gt;        where should it be
4 tokyo please   ok let me look into some options for you
5 &lt;SILENCE&gt;         api_call french tokyo four expensive
```

The model must learn to predict the bot response for each user utterance. The response can be a sentence or an API call (starting with `api_call`).

Writing a chatbot in TensorFlow

In the following sections, we shall go through a pipeline for training and interacting with a memory network chatbot using the `bAbI dialog` dataset: we will load the data, process it to be compatible with the memory network framework, write a wrapper around the model described previously, and finally train our chatbot.

Loading dialog datasets in the QA format

As described in the previous section, we need to convert dialog data from line-by-line conversation turns into a (facts, question, answer) tuple format for each turn of the dialog. For this purpose, we need to write a method that will read lines from the raw dialog corpus and return the desired tuples for training in a memory network paradigm.

Since we will be using word vectors as inputs to our model, we first need to define a `tokenize` method which will be used for converting a sentence into a list of words (minus special symbols and common words):

```
def tokenize(sent):
    stop_words = {"a", "an", "the"}
    sent = sent.lower()
    if sent == '&lt;silence&gt;':
        return [sent]
    # Convert sentence to tokens
    result = [word.strip() for word in re.split('(\W+)?', sent)
                if word.strip() and word.strip() not in stop_words]
    # Cleanup
    if not result:
        result = ['&lt;silence&gt;']
    if result[-1]=='.' or result[-1]=='?' or result[-1]=='!':
        result = result[:-1]
    return result
```

Then, we can define a function to read the raw data files from the `bAbI dialog` dataset and process them. We parse the text in a file, line-by-line, and keep track of all possible (facts, question, answer) tuples in the data. We must keep updating the facts list in a dialog as we move from one line to the next, and reset the facts list when we encounter a blank line. We must also be careful about lines which do not contain an (utterance, response) pair:

```
def parse_dialogs_per_response(lines, candidates_to_idx):
    data = []
    facts_temp = []
    utterance_temp = None
    response_temp = None
```

```
# Parse line by line
for line in lines:
    line = line.strip()
    if line:
        id, line = line.split(' ', 1)
        if '\t' in line: # Has utterance and response
            utterance_temp, response_temp = line.split('\t')
            # Convert answer to integer index
            answer = candidates_to_idx[response_temp]
            # Tokenize sentences
            utterance_temp = tokenize(utterance_temp)
            response_temp = tokenize(response_temp)
            # Add (facts, question, answer) tuple to data
            data.append((facts_temp[:], utterance_temp[:], answer))
            # Add utterance/response encoding
            utterance_temp.append('$u')
            response_temp.append('$r')
            # Add turn count temporal encoding
            utterance_temp.append('#' + id)
            response_temp.append('#' + id)
            # Update facts
            facts_temp.append(utterance_temp)
            facts_temp.append(response_temp)
        else: # Has KB Fact
            response_temp = tokenize(line)
            response_temp.append('$r')
            response_temp.append('#' + id)
            facts_temp.append(response_temp)
    else: # Start of new dialog
        facts_temp = []
return data
```

An important nuance to note is that we have added two extra symbols (utterance/response encoding and turn count encoding) to the tokenized versions of all facts, questions, and responses in our data. This results in our model treating these encodings as words and building word vectors for them. The utterance/response encoding helps the model to differentiate between sentences spoken by the user and the bot, and the turn count encoding builds temporal understanding in the model.

Here, the candidates dictionary is a mapping of candidate answers to integer indices. We need to do such a conversion because our memory network will be performing a softmax over the candidates, dictionary integer entries, which can then point us to the chosen response. The candidates dictionary can be constructed directly from a file containing all possible response candidates line-by-line, along with tokenized versions of the response candidates themselves, as follows:

```
candidates = []
candidates_to_idx = {}
with open('dialog-babi/dialog-babi-candidates.txt') as f:
    for i, line in enumerate(f):
        candidates_to_idx[line.strip().split(' ', 1)[1]] = i
        line = tokenize(line.strip())[1:]
        candidates.append(line)
```

Next, we can use the `candidates` dictionary to load the training, validation, and testing dialogs in the QA format using the parsing method we just defined:

```
train_data = []
with open('dialog-babi/dialog-babi-task5-full-dialogs-trn.txt') as f:
    train_data = parse_dialogs_per_response(f.readlines(),
candidates_to_idx)

test_data = []
with open('dialog-babi/dialog-babi-task5-full-dialogs-tst.txt') as f:
    test_data = parse_dialogs_per_response(f.readlines(),
candidates_to_idx)

val_data = []
with open('dialog-babi/dialog-babi-task5-full-dialogs-dev.txt') as f:
    val_data = parse_dialogs_per_response(f.readlines(), candidates_to_idx)
```

Vectorizing the data

The final stage of preprocessing the data is to vectorize or quantize our dialogs and candidates. This entails converting each word or token into an integer value, which implies that any sequence of words is now transformed into a sequence of integers corresponding to each word.

We will first write a method to vectorize candidate texts. We also have to keep in mind a fixed word length (`sentence_size`) of each vectorized candidate. Hence, we need to pad (with 0s, which corresponds to empty words) those candidate vectors whose length is less than the required sentence size:

```
def vectorize_candidates(candidates, word_idx, sentence_size):
    # Determine shape of final vector
    shape = (len(candidates), sentence_size)
    candidates_vector = []
    for i, candidate in enumerate(candidates):
        # Determine zero padding
        zero_padding = max(0, sentence_size - len(candidate))
        # Append to final vector
```

```
candidates_vector.append(
    [word_idx[w] if w in word_idx else 0 for w in candidate]
    + [0] * zero_padding)
# Return as TensorFlow constant
return tf.constant(candidates_vector, shape=shape)
```

Next, we will write a method to vectorize our dialog data in a similar manner. Another important aspect we need to care about is to ensure that we pad the facts vector for each data sample with empty memories (vectors of 0s of sentence_size) to a fixed memory size:

```
def vectorize_data(data, word_idx, sentence_size, batch_size,
max_memory_size):
    facts_vector = []
    questions_vector = []
    answers_vector = []
    # Sort data in descending order by number of facts
    data.sort(key=lambda x: len(x[0]), reverse=True)
    for i, (fact, question, answer) in enumerate(data):
        # Find memory size
        if i % batch_size == 0:
            memory_size = max(1, min(max_memory_size, len(fact)))
        # Build fact vector
        fact_vector = []
        for i, sentence in enumerate(fact, 1):
            fact_padding = max(0, sentence_size - len(sentence))
            fact_vector.append(
                [word_idx[w] if w in word_idx else 0 for w in sentence]
                + [0] * fact_padding)
        # Keep the most recent sentences that fit in memory
        fact_vector = fact_vector[::-1][:memory_size][::-1]
        # Pad to memory_size
        memory_padding = max(0, memory_size - len(fact_vector))
        for _ in range(memory_padding):
            fact_vector.append([0] * sentence_size)
        # Build question vector
        question_padding = max(0, sentence_size - len(question))
        question_vector = [word_idx[w] if w in word_idx else 0
                           for w in question] \
                          + [0] * question_padding
        # Append to final vectors
        facts_vector.append(np.array(fact_vector))
        questions_vector.append(np.array(question_vector))
        # Answer is already an integer corresponding to a candidate
        answers_vector.append(np.array(answer))
    return facts_vector, questions_vector, answers_vector
```

We emphasize knowing these dimensions beforehand because we will be sending these vectors to the TensorFlow model, which needs to know the sizes of its input to construct the model graph.

Wrapping the memory network model in a chatbot class

We will be feeding data to a generic chatbot class and calling the vectorize methods inside it. We will use it as a wrapper for the memory network model we defined earlier. In theory, the model can be swapped out for any other QA-based model.

Class constructor

The class constructor lets us load the data and candidates, and then build a vocabulary and subsequently initialize our TensorFlow session and memory network object:

```
class ChatBotWrapper(object):
    def __init__(self, train_data, test_data, val_data,
                 candidates, candidates_to_idx,
                 memory_size, batch_size, learning_rate,
                 evaluation_interval, hops,
                 epochs, embedding_size):
        self.memory_size = memory_size
        self.batch_size = batch_size
        self.evaluation_interval = evaluation_interval
        self.epochs = epochs

        self.candidates = candidates
        self.candidates_to_idx = candidates_to_idx
        self.candidates_size = len(candidates)
        self.idx_to_candidates = dict((self.candidates_to_idx[key], key)
                                      for key in self.candidates_to_idx)
        # Initialize data and build vocabulary
        self.train_data = train_data
        self.test_data = test_data
        self.val_data = val_data
        self.build_vocab(train_data + test_data + val_data, candidates)
        # Vectorize candidates
        self.candidates_vec = vectorize_candidates(
            candidates, self.word_idx, self.candidate_sentence_size)
        # Initialize optimizer
        optimizer = tf.train.AdamOptimizer(learning_rate=learning_rate)
        # Initialize TensorFlow session and Memory Network model
        self.sess = tf.Session()
        self.model = MemoryNetwork(
                     self.sentence_size, self.vocab_size,
```

```
self.candidates_size, self.candidates_vec,
embedding_size, hops,
optimizer=optimizer, session=self.sess)
```

Building a vocabulary for word embedding lookup

We want to create word embeddings for each of the words in our `facts`, `candidates`, and `questions`. Hence, we need to read our data and candidates to calculate the number of words to create embeddings for, as well as maximum sentence lengths. This information is passed to the memory network model to initialize the embedding matrices and input placeholders:

```
def build_vocab(self, data, candidates):
    # Build word vocabulary set from all data and candidate words
    vocab = reduce(lambda x1, x2: x1 | x2,
        (set(list(chain.from_iterable(facts)) + questions)
            for facts, questions, answers in data))
    vocab |= reduce(lambda x1, x2: x1 | x2,
        (set(candidate) for candidate in candidates))
    vocab = sorted(vocab)
    # Assign integer indices to each word
    self.word_idx = dict((word, idx + 1) for idx, word in
enumerate(vocab))
    # Compute various data size numbers
    max_facts_size = max(map(len, (facts for facts, _, _ in data)))
    self.sentence_size = max(
        map(len, chain.from_iterable(facts for facts, _, _ in data)))
    self.candidate_sentence_size = max(map(len, candidates))
    question_size = max(map(len, (questions for _, questions, _ in
data)))
    self.memory_size = min(self.memory_size, max_facts_size)
    self.vocab_size = len(self.word_idx) + 1 # +1 for null word
    self.sentence_size = max(question_size, self.sentence_size)
```

Training the chatbot model

We can pass the vectorized training data (using the method we defined in the previous section) to our chatbot and call the memory network's `fit` method to train over mini-batches of the training data while evaluating our model's performance on the validation set at fixed intervals:

```
def predict_for_batch(self, facts, questions):
    preds = []
    # Iterate over mini-batches
    for start in range(0, len(facts), self.batch_size):
```

```
            end = start + self.batch_size
            facts_batch = facts[start:end]
            questions_batch = questions[start:end]
            # Predict per batch
            pred = self.model.predict(facts_batch, questions_batch)
            preds += list(pred)
        return preds

    def train(self):
        # Vectorize training and validation data
        train_facts, train_questions, train_answers = vectorize_data(
            self.train_data, self.word_idx, self.sentence_size,
            self.batch_size, self.memory_size)
        val_facts, val_questions, val_answers = vectorize_data(
            self.val_data, self.word_idx, self.sentence_size,
            self.batch_size, self.memory_size)
        # Chunk training data into batches
        batches = zip(range(0, len(train_facts) - self.batch_size,
                            self.batch_size),
                      range(self.batch_size, len(train_facts),
                            self.batch_size))
        batches = [(start, end) for start, end in batches]
        # Start training loop
        for epoch in range(1, self.epochs + 1):
            np.random.shuffle(batches)
            total_cost = 0.0
            for start, end in batches:
                facts = train_facts[start:end]
                questions = train_questions[start:end]
                answers = train_answers[start:end]
                # Train on batch
                batch_cost = self.model.fit(facts, questions, answers)
                total_cost += batch_cost
            if epoch % self.evaluation_interval == 0:
                # Compute accuracy over training and validation set
                train_preds = self.predict_for_batch(
                    train_facts, train_questions)
                val_preds = self.predict_for_batch(
                    val_facts, val_questions)
                train_acc = metrics.accuracy_score(
                    train_preds, train_answers)
                val_acc = metrics.accuracy_score(
                    val_preds, val_answers)
                print("Epoch: ", epoch)
                print("Total Cost: ", total_cost)
                print("Training Accuracy: ", train_acc)
                print("Validation Accuracy: ", val_acc)
                print("---")
```

Evaluating the chatbot on the testing set

We can then write a method to predict the responses for each of the dialogs in our testing dataset and obtain accuracy scores:

```
def test(self):
    # Compute accuracy over test set
    test_facts, test_questions, test_answers = vectorize_data(
        self.test_data, self.word_idx, self.sentence_size,
        self.batch_size, self.memory_size)
    test_preds = self.predict_for_batch(test_facts, test_questions)
    test_acc = metrics.accuracy_score(test_preds, test_answers)
    print("Testing Accuracy: ", test_acc)
```

Interacting with the chatbot

Finally, we can interact with our chatbot by following the framework described in the previous sections. After each user utterance, we ask the memory network to predict a response based on the conversation history and the utterance. Then, the utterance and response are appended to the conversation history and we can enter an utterance once again:

```
def interactive_mode(self):
    facts = []
    utterance = None
    response = None
    turn_count = 1
    while True:
        line = input("==&gt; ").strip().lower()
        if line == "exit":
            break
        if line == "restart":
            facts = []
            turn_count = 1
            print("Restarting dialog...\n")
            continue
        utterance = tokenize(line)
        data = [(facts, utterance, -1)]
        # Vectorize data and make prediction
        f, q, a = vectorize_data(data, self.word_idx,
            self.sentence_size, self.batch_size, self.memory_size)
        preds = self.model.predict(f, q)
        response = self.idx_to_candidates[preds[0]]
        # Print predicted response
        print(response)
        response = tokenize(response)
```

```
# Add turn count temporal encoding
utterance.append("$u")
response.append("$r")
# Add utterance/response encoding
utterance.append("#" + str(turn_count))
response.append("#" + str(turn_count))
# Update facts memory
facts.append(utterance)
facts.append(response)
turn_count += 1
```

Putting it all together

To run everything we have just coded, we will define our model hyperparameters and instantiate our chatbot model. We will then proceed to start training the model for 200 epochs, evaluating its performance on the validation set every 10 epochs. After training, we can test the model on the testing data as follows:

```
chatbot = ChatBotWrapper(train_data, test_data, val_data,
                         candidates, candidates_to_idx,
                         memory_size=50,
                         batch_size=32,
                         learning_rate=0.001,
                         evaluation_interval=10,
                         hops=3,
                         epochs=100,
                         embedding_size=50)
chatbot.train()
chatbot.test()
```

The following is the output:

```
Epoch: 10
Total Cost: 17703.9733608
Training Accuracy: 0.756870229008
Validation Accuracy: 0.729912770223
-------------------------------------------------
Epoch: 20
Total Cost: 7439.67566451
Training Accuracy: 0.903217011996
Validation Accuracy: 0.857127377147
-------------------------------------------------
Epoch: 30
Total Cost: 3179.78263753
Training Accuracy: 0.982769901854
Validation Accuracy: 0.939372595763
.
```

```
.
.
-------------------------------------------------
Epoch: 80
Total Cost: 1949.99280906
Training Accuracy: 0.980861504907
Validation Accuracy: 0.937747196186
-------------------------------------------------
Epoch: 90
Total Cost: 500.894205613
Training Accuracy: 0.995637949836
Validation Accuracy: 0.95400119196
-------------------------------------------------
Epoch: 100
Total Cost: 912.067172846
Training Accuracy: 0.995092693566
Validation Accuracy: 0.954813891748
-------------------------------------------------
Testing Accuracy:   0.958093271008
```

As we train our `chatbot`, we can evaluate its performance on the validation data and should see its loss decrease and accuracy increase. At the end of training, we end up having a model with decent performance on the test set, although it can be even better if we employ more rigorous regularization schemes, such as gradient clipping, L2 norm regularization, or dropout. Adding them is fairly straightforward using TensorFlow, and is left as an exercise to the reader.

Example of an interactive conversation

We can also run our trained chatbot in interactive mode to have a real-time conversation with it:

```
chatbot.interactive_mode()
```

We can interact with the chatbot by typing text whenever prompted by the ==> symbol:

```
==&gt; good morning
hello what can i help you with today
==&gt; i'd like to book a table for eight
i'm on it
==&gt;
any preference on a type of cuisine
==&gt; with italian cuisine
where should it be
==&gt; in bombay
which price range are looking for
```

```
==&gt; i am looking for a moderate restaurant
ok let me look into some options for you
==&gt;
api_call italian bombay eight moderate
==&gt; instead could it be in a cheap price range
sure is there anything else to update
==&gt; actually i would prefer in london
sure is there anything else to update
==&gt; no
ok let me look into some options for you
==&gt;
api_call italian london eight cheap
==&gt;
    .
    .
    .
```

As we try various types of interactions, we can see that our simple memory network has learned to produce an appropriate response to most of our questions, but may stumble when dealing with proper nouns or named entities, such as restaurants and the associated facts stored in the KB. Dealing with such entities can be considered a line of research in itself, and many subfields of NLP research need to come together to build chatbots for real-world deployment.

Literature on and related to memory networks

For more curious readers, here is a list of papers introducing new ideas and architectures related to or inspired by memory networks for natural language understanding:

Title	Description	ArXiv URL
Dynamic Memory Networks (DMNs) and **Dynamic Coattention Networks (DCNs)**	Introduced by Salesforce Research at around the same time as Facebook's memory networks, DMNs use more sophisticated RNNs for representation building and iterating over episodic memory. DCNs are Salesforce's latest iteration of attention-based reasoning models with a novel coattention mechanism.	https://arxiv.org/abs/1506.07285 https://arxiv.org/abs/1711.00106

Neural Turing Machines (NTMs) and Differentiable Neural Computer (DNC)	DeepMind's NTMs and DNC set themselves more enthusiastic goals: to make neural networks that can read and write to an external storage and execute any algorithms that computers can.	`https://arxiv.org/abs/1410.5401` `https://www.nature.com/articles/nature20101`
Seq2seq Memory Network	Microsoft Research introduced a seq2seq model for dialog generation, which they augmented with a memory module very similar to memory networks.	`https://arxiv.org/pdf/1702.01932.pdf`
Recurrent Entity Networks	Facebook's latest iteration of attention-based models, which can build memory and reason over it on the fly, as opposed to explicitly in the case of memory networks.	`https://arxiv.org/pdf/1612.03969.pdf`

Summary

We've taken a whirlwind tour of Question-Answering as a natural language understanding problem and learned how to build a generic memory network model for any QA task. We then investigated the problem of conversation modelling as a QA task, and extended the memory network to train a goal-oriented chatbot.

We built a simple retrieval-based chatbot to help users book restaurants according to their preferences. Some of the aspects that readers can explore further could be more sophisticated attention mechanisms, more powerful representation encoders for sentences, and using generative models instead of retrieval methods.

In the next chapter, we shall cover language translation using encoder-decoder models and introduce more complicated attention mechanisms for sequence alignment.

10
Machine Translation Using the Attention-Based Model

Machine translation systems convert text from one language to text in another language. One such example system is the Google Translate service (`https://translate.google.com/`). In this chapter, we will look into the architecture of these systems and how to build one. While the focus of this chapter will be on **neural machine translation** (**NMT**), we will briefly take a look at traditional approaches for understanding the challenges in machine translation. We will focus mainly on the following topics:

- A brief overview of machine translation
- An overview of neural machine translation
- Developing and training a neural machine translation model with an attention mechanism

Overview of machine translation

There are different types of machine translation methods that are in use, but for conciseness, we will look into two of the main approaches. One of them is **statistical machine translation** (**SMT**) and the other is **neural machine translation** (**NMT**), which is the topic of this chapter. We will briefly look at these two methods.

Statistical machine translation

Statistical machine translation combines a translation model with a target language model to convert sentences from the source text in one language to sentences in the target language. This is illustrated in the following diagram. The translation model maps words and phrases from the source language to the target language. The language model captures statistics of how likely words follow a specific sequence in the target language. SMT, therefore, tries to maximize the probability of choosing a target sentence that is the translation of the source sentence. These statistical models are derived from a large corpus of source-to-target language translations:

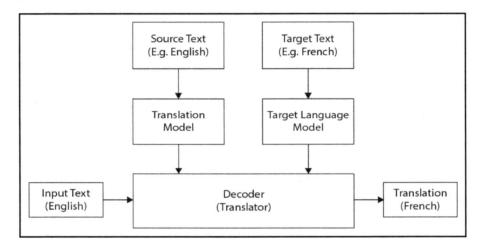

Prior to SMT, machine translation involved defining linguistic and syntactic rules by experts to make the translation work. SMT was a step forward in automatic machine translation where such rules are statistically learned from a large collection of bilingual data. One of the major difficulties with SMT is that it can only perform well when translating text similar to the training corpuses or domain. For new input text from a different domain, SMT may not translate well. Another disadvantage is that we need a large collection of bilingual training data, which may be difficult for rare language pairs. SMT also needs a separate specialized pipeline for each source and target language translation.

English to French using NLTK SMT models

We will now look into an example of statistical machine translation using NLTK. We will use translated TED Talks from `https://wit3.fbk.eu/mt.php?release=2015-01` as our training and test dataset. The data contains some of the TED Talks in French translated into English. The complete code and data for this example are available under the `Chapter10/` directory of this book's code repository. We will use the IBM lexical alignment models, which are simple statistical translation models. These models take a collection of alignment pairs between the source and target languages and compute probabilities of their associations or alignments. We will use the basic IBM Model 1, which performs a one-to-one alignment of the source and target sentences. Therefore, the model produces exactly one target word for each source word without considering any reordering or translation of one source word to multiple words or the dropping of words.

The `nltk.translate` package provides the implementation of the IBM alignment models. We will first import these and define a function to read English and corresponding French translated data:

```
from nltk.translate.ibm1 import IBMModel1
from nltk.translate.api import AlignedSent
import dill as pickle
import randomdef

read_sents(filename):
    sents = []
    c=0
    with open(filename,'r') as fi:
        for li in fi:
            sents.append(li.split())
    return sents
```

The `AlignedSent` class will be used to supply the French-English alignment data during training. `read_sents()` reads each line from the input file and converts it into a list of tokens for each sentence. We will now create the alignment data and train the model:

```
max_count=5000
eng_sents_all = read_sents('data/train_en_lines.txt')
fr_sents_all = read_sents('data/train_fr_lines.txt')
eng_sents = eng_sents_all[:max_count]
fr_sents = fr_sents_all[:max_count]
print("Size of english sentences: ", len(eng_sents))
print("Size of french sentences: ", len(fr_sents))
aligned_text = []
for i in range(len(eng_sents)):
    al_sent = AlignedSent(fr_sents[i],eng_sents[i])
```

```
    aligned_text.append(al_sent)
print("Training smt model")
ibm_model = IBMModel1(aligned_text,5)
print("Training complete")
```

We use about 5,000 sentences (`max_count`) as the training data for faster convergence, though you can change this to train on the complete data. We will then create the list of French-English sentence pairs with `AlignedSent` for model training. After the training, we will look at how the model performs in the translation task:

```
n_random = random.randint(0,max_count)
fr_sent = fr_sents_all[n_random]
eng_sent_actual_tr = eng_sents_all[n_random]
tr_sent = []
for w in fr_sent:
    probs = ibm_model.translation_table[w]
    if(len(probs)==0):
        continue
    sorted_words = sorted([(k,v) for k, v in probs.items()],key=lambda x:
x[1], reverse=True)
    top_word = sorted_words[1][0]
    if top_word is not None:
        tr_sent.append(top_word)
print("French sentence: ", " ".join(fr_sent))
print("Translated Eng sentence: ", " ".join(tr_sent))
print("Original translation: ", " ".join(eng_sent_actual_tr))
```

We can pick a random sentence from the list of French sentences and look up the corresponding English word using `translation_table`. This table stores the probabilities of an alignment between a given French word and the corresponding English words. We pick the English word that is more likely a translation of the given French word using these alignment probabilities. This lookup is done for all the French words in the original sentence to get the corresponding English phrase in `tr_sent`. Finally, we print the French sentence, the SMT translated sentence, and the correct translation:

```
French sentence:  On appelle ça l'accessibilité financière.
Translated Eng sentence:  suggests affordability. works. called called
Original translation:  And it's called affordability.
```

We can see that the SMT translation can get some of the words correct, such as the word `affordability`, but the translation is not meaningful compared to the original one. This can be improved by running the training on the whole dataset and increasing the iterations. But it should also be noted that we used a simple model that does not consider word order in the target language. The more complex IBM models, which are 3, 4, and 5, can capture word order as well as fertility (the source language word that does not always have a one-to-one mapping with the target language word). Model 5 uses a **Hidden Markov Model (HMM)** along with the alignments to provide better translations.

Neural machine translation

Neural machine translation (**NMT**) uses a neural network to learn to translate text from a source language into a target language. Unlike SMT, one key advantage of NMT is that it needs only one model to translate end-to-end from a source language into a target language. More importantly, NMT works on whole segments of the source text rather than chunks or phrases as in SMT. This is achieved by learning context through word embeddings. Therefore, NMT performs translation while preserving the context of the original text, as well. We will now look at some of the common deep learning architectures used in NMT.

Encoder-decoder network

The most common types of architectures are encoder-decoder networks. These are similar to the one we used in the chapter on text summarization. In fact, the model architecture is not much different from the one we used there. The source text phrase is first fed into the encoder, which transforms it into a thought vector that represents the meaning of the phrase. This dense representation is then fed into a decoder, along with the original translation in the target language during training. It serves as a preconditioning on the decoder, which learns the corresponding translation based on the original translation that's fed while training.

The following diagram shows the encoder-decoder network as described in the paper *Effective Approaches to Attention-Based Neural Machine Translation* by Luong et al.

In this diagram, the translation is from the source language text, which is English, into the target language text in French:

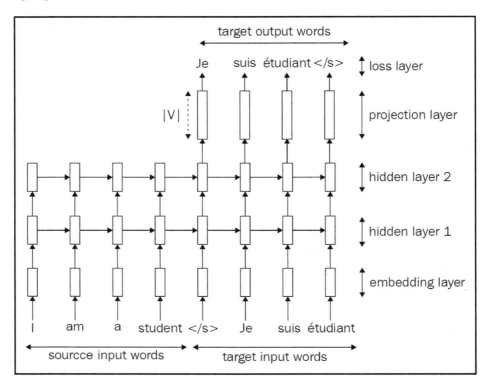

A common choice for both the encoder and decoder is the RNN due to the sequential nature of both the input and the output. An LSTM or GRU is usually used, which can capture the long-term associations in both the source and target texts. The encoder RNN reads the source language phrase word for word and generates a final state. This final state encapsulates the meaning of the phrase in the form of a compressed vector representation. By feeding this vector representation as the initial state of the decoder along with the target phrase, the decoder learns the translations.

During inference, the encoder outputs the phrase word by word in the target language using the compressed representation of the final state of the decoder obtained from the phrase in the source language. In the preceding diagram, the embedding layer converts the words into dense representations, which are then transformed into a projection of all the words in the target vocabulary by the decoder. The final translated words are picked from the projection based on the softmax probabilities.

Encoder-decoder with attention

The encoder-decoder architecture described in the previous section has one major shortcoming. As the final encoder state is of a fixed length, it can lead to loss of information. While this may not be a problem for short phrases, for longer source language inputs, the encoder may not be able to capture long-term dependencies. This leads to the decoder not being able to output good translations. To overcome this problem, the attention mechanism was introduced by Bahdanau et al. in their paper *Neural Machine Translation by Jointly Learning to Align and Translate*. The following diagram is an illustration of the architecture as taken from their paper:

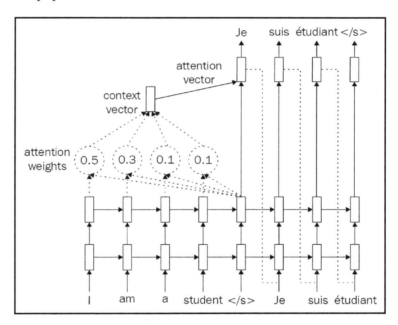

The main idea behind attention is to focus or pay attention to important parts of the input source text while learning to translate. The attention mechanism, in effect, builds shortcut connections between the input source text and target text through weights that are learned during training. These connections enhance the ability of the decoder to translate longer phrases in the input, thereby leading to more accurate translations.

NMT for French to English using attention

In this section, we will use the same dataset as the one we used in SMT. We will build the network based on the attention mechanism. You will also find that the network resembles the same architecture as described in the chapter on text summarization. The complete Python notebook for this example is found under `Chapter10/02_example.ipynb` in this book's code repository.

Data preparation

First, we will read the source text and the target text, which are in French and English, respectively:

```
frdata=[]
endata=[]
with open('data/train_fr_lines.txt') as frfile:
    for li in frfile:
        frdata.append(li)
with open('data/train_en_lines.txt') as enfile:
    for li in enfile:
        endata.append(li)
mtdata = pd.DataFrame({'FR':frdata,'EN':endata})
mtdata['FR_len'] = mtdata['FR'].apply(lambda x: len(x.split(' ')))
mtdata['EN_len'] = mtdata['EN'].apply(lambda x: len(x.split(' ')))
print(mtdata['FR'].head(2).values)
print(mtdata['EN'].head(2).values)
```

Output:

```
['Voici Bill Lange. Je suis Dave Gallo.\n'
 'Nous allons vous raconter quelques histoires de la mer en vidéo.\n']
["This is Bill Lange. I'm Dave Gallo.\n"
 "And we're going to tell you some stories from the sea here in video.\n"]
```

As we will be using pre-trained embedding vectors, we will first load them to create an index of, word to embeddings dictionary that will be used to prepare the input text data for training:

```
def build_word_vector_matrix(vector_file):
    embedding_index = {}
    with codecs.open(vector_file, 'r', 'utf-8') as f:
        for i, line in enumerate(f):
            sr = line.split()
    word = sr[0]
```

```
    embedding = np.asarray(sr[1:], dtype='float32')
    embedding_index[word] = embedding
    return embedding_index
embeddings_index = build_word_vector_matrix('glove.6B.50d.txt')
```

Since the encoder and decoder inputs are word identifiers, we will create both word to ID and ID to word mappings that will later be used during training and inference. During training, we will use the word to ID mapping. The ID to word mapping will be used to get the translated text back during inference:

```
def build_word2id_mapping(word_counts_dict):
    word2int = {}
    count_threshold = 20
    value = 0
    for word, count in word_counts_dict.items():
        if count &gt;= count_threshold or word in embeddings_index:
            word2int[word] = value
            value += 1
    special_codes = [TOKEN_UNK, TOKEN_PAD, TOKEN_EOS, TOKEN_GO]
    for code in special_codes:
        word2int[code] = len(word2int)
    int2word = {}
    for word, value in word2int.items():
        int2word[value] = word
    return word2int, int2word
```

This will transform both the input words and the special tokens, TOKEN_UNK, TOKEN_PAD, TOKEN_EOS, and TOKEN_GO, into corresponding numeric identifiers. These are defined as string UNK, PAD, EOS, and GO, respectively. We will apply the build_word2id_mapping() and build_embeddings() functions to both the English and French texts. Note that we only use words that occur with a frequency more than count_threshold, which is set as 20 in the preceding code:

```
fr_word2int, fr_int2word = build_word2id_mapping(word_counts_dict_fr)
en_word2int, en_int2word = build_word2id_mapping(word_counts_dict_en)
fr_embeddings_matrix = build_embeddings(fr_word2int)
en_embeddings_matrix = build_embeddings(en_word2int)
print("Length of french word embeddings: ", len(fr_embeddings_matrix))
print("Length of english word embeddings: ", len(en_embeddings_matrix))

Output:

Length of french word embeddings: 19708
Length of english word embeddings: 39614
```

Next, we will define a function to transform both the source and target phrases into numeric identifiers:

```
def convert_sentence_to_ids(text, word2int, eos=False):
    wordints = []
    word_count = 0
    for sentence in text:
        sentence2ints = []
        for word in sentence.split():
            word_count += 1
            if word in word2int:
                sentence2ints.append(word2int[word])
            else:
                sentence2ints.append(word2int[TOKEN_UNK])
        if eos:
            sentence2ints.append(word2int[TOKEN_EOS])
        wordints.append(sentence2ints)
    return wordints, word_count
```

As we did previously, we will apply the `convert_sentence_to_ids()` function to the source and target text:

```
id_fr, word_count_fr = convert_sentence_to_ids(mtdata_fr, fr_word2int)
id_en, word_count_en = convert_sentence_to_ids(mtdata_en, en_word2int,
eos=True)
```

Since sentences/phrases that have many unknown words or tokens are not useful for training, we will remove them from the set:

```
en_filtered = []
fr_filtered = []
max_en_length = int(mtdata.EN_len.max())
max_fr_length = int(mtdata.FR_len.max())
min_length = 4
unknown_token_en_limit = 10
unknown_token_fr_limit = 10
for count,text in enumerate(id_en):
    unknown_token_en = unknown_tokens(id_en[count],en_word2int)
    unknown_token_fr = unknown_tokens(id_fr[count],fr_word2int)
    en_len = len(id_en[count])
    fr_len = len(id_fr[count])
    if( (unknown_token_en&gt;unknown_token_en_limit) or
(unknown_token_fr&gt;unknown_token_fr_limit) or
        (en_len&lt;min_length) or (fr_len&lt;min_length) ):
        continue
    fr_filtered.append(id_fr[count])
    en_filtered.append(id_en[count])
```

```
print("Length of filtered french/english sentences: ", len(fr_filtered),
len(en_filtered) )
```

Output:

Length of filtered french/english sentences: 200404 200404

Note that we remove sentences that have unknown tokens exceeding
`unknown_token_en_limit` or `unknown_token_fr_limit`, which is set as 10 in the code.
Similarly, we remove sentences that are shorter than 4 words.

Encoder network

We will now build the encoder network with a slight modification to the original
architecture that was described in the overview section. We will use a bidirectional RNN in
place of a unidirectional one, thereby capturing both forward and backward dependencies
in the input:

```
def get_rnn_cell(rnn_cell_size,dropout_prob):
    rnn_c = GRUCell(rnn_cell_size)
    rnn_c = DropoutWrapper(rnn_c, input_keep_prob = dropout_prob)
    return rnn_c

def encoding_layer(rnn_cell_size, sequence_len, n_layers, rnn_inputs,
dropout_prob):
    for l in range(n_layers):
        with tf.variable_scope('encoding_l_{}'.format(l)):
            rnn_fw = get_rnn_cell(rnn_cell_size,dropout_prob)
            rnn_bw = get_rnn_cell(rnn_cell_size,dropout_prob)
    encoding_output, encoding_state =
tf.nn.bidirectional_dynamic_rnn(rnn_fw,  rnn_bw, rnn_inputs,
                                       sequence_len,dtype=tf.float32)
    encoding_output = tf.concat(encoding_output,2)
    return encoding_output, encoding_state
```

We used a GRU as the recurrent cell of the RNN. The input to the `rnn_inputs` encoder will
be the embeddings of the input sentence. The other arguments to the `encoding_layer`
function are the cell size, sequence length, and the dropout probability. We will later set the
sequence length to be equal to the maximum length of the French text.

Note that we have concatenated the encoding output of both the forward
and backward RNN. We also used `DropoutWrapper` to incorporate
dropout in the encoding layer.

Decoder network

The decoder network is also created with **Gated Recurrent Unit** (GRU) cells. The `decoding_layer` function takes the output of the encoder and the word embeddings of the English text as input. It produces an output projection vector of a size equal to the vocabulary size of the English text:

```
def decoding_layer(decoding_embed_inp, embeddings, encoding_op,
encoding_st, v_size, fr_len,          en_len,max_en_len, rnn_cell_size,
word2int, dropout_prob, batch_size, n_layers):
    for l in range(n_layers):
        with tf.variable_scope('dec_rnn_layer_{}'.format(l)):
            gru = tf.contrib.rnn.GRUCell(rnn_len)
            decoding_cell =
tf.contrib.rnn.DropoutWrapper(gru,input_keep_prob = dropout_prob)
    out_l = Dense(v_size, kernel_initializer =
tf.truncated_normal_initializer(mean = 0.0,
            stddev=0.1))
    attention = BahdanauAttention(rnn_cell_size, encoding_op,fr_len,
normalize=False,
name='BahdanauAttention')
    decoding_cell = AttentionWrapper(decoding_cell,attention,rnn_len)
    attention_zero_state = decoding_cell.zero_state(batch_size , tf.float32
)
    attention_zero_state = attention_zero_state.clone(cell_state =
encoding_st[0])
    with tf.variable_scope("decoding_layer"):
        logits_tr = training_decoding_layer(decoding_embed_inp, en_len,
decoding_cell,
attention_zero_state,out_l,v_size, max_en_len)
    with tf.variable_scope("decoding_layer", reuse=True):
        logits_inf = inference_decoding_layer(embeddings,
word2int[TOKEN_GO],word2int[TOKEN_EOS],
                       decoding_cell, attention_zero_state,
out_l,max_en_len,batch_size)
    return logits_tr, logits_inf
```

We also include dropout in the decoder using `DropoutWrapper`. The `Dense` layer incorporates the projection vector, and `BahdanauAttention` together with `AttentionWrapper` capture the attention between the encoder output and the decoder. Note that we also use different decoding mechanisms for training and inference:

```
def training_decoding_layer(decoding_embed_input, en_len, decoding_cell,
    initial_state, op_layer,          v_size, max_en_len):
    helper =
TrainingHelper(inputs=decoding_embed_input,sequence_length=en_len,time_majo
r=False)
```

```
    dec = BasicDecoder(decoding_cell,helper,initial_state,op_layer)
    logits, _, _ =
dynamic_decode(dec,output_time_major=False,impute_finished=True,
    maximum_iterations=max_en_len)
    return logits
```

During training, we use the normal `TrainingHelper` from the TensorFlow `seq2seq`
package, whereas we utilize `GreedyEmbeddingHelper` during inference:

```
def inference_decoding_layer(embeddings, start_token, end_token,
decoding_cell,
        initial_state, op_layer,max_en_len, batch_size):
    start_tokens = tf.tile(tf.constant([start_token], dtype=tf.int32,
                    [batch_size],name='start_tokens')
    inf_helper = GreedyEmbeddingHelper(embeddings,start_tokens,end_token)
    inf_decoder =
BasicDecoder(decoding_cell,inf_helper,initial_state,op_layer)
    inf_logits, _, _ =
dynamic_decode(inf_decoder,output_time_major=False,impute_finished=True,
                    maximum_iterations=max_en_len)
    return inf_logits
```

`GreedyEmbeddingHelper` selects the words with the maximum probabilities in the
projection vector output by the encoder.

Sequence-to-sequence model

We will now combine the encoder and decoder to create the sequence-to-sequence model:

```
def seq2seq_model(input_data, target_en_data, dropout_prob, fr_len, en_len,
max_en_len,
            v_size, rnn_cell_size, n_layers, word2int_en, batch_size):
    input_word_embeddings = tf.Variable(fr_embeddings_matrix,
name="input_word_embeddings")
    encoding_embed_input = tf.nn.embedding_lookup(input_word_embeddings,
input_data)
    encoding_op, encoding_st = encoding_layer(rnn_cell_size, fr_len,
                            n_layers, encoding_embed_input,
dropout_prob)
    decoding_input = process_encoding_input(target_en_data, word2int_en,
batch_size)
    decoding_embed_input = tf.nn.embedding_lookup(en_embeddings_matrix,
decoding_input)
    tr_logits, inf_logits = decoding_layer(decoding_embed_input,
en_embeddings_matrix,
                        encoding_op,encoding_st, v_size,
                        fr_len, en_len, max_en_len,
```

```
                           rnn_cell_size, word2int_en,
                           dropout_prob, batch_size,n_layers)
      return tr_logits, inf_logits
```

The `seq2seq_model` function combines the source text embeddings, encoder, and decoder and outputs the logits. The input is the French text embeddings, `fr_embeddings_matrix`. The encoder and decoder layers are created using the functions defined earlier.

Building the graph

We will now combine all of the individual components created earlier to build the complete graph:

```
train_graph = tf.Graph()
with train_graph.as_default():
    input_data, targets, learning_rate, dropout_probs,
                          en_len, max_en_len, fr_len =model_inputs()
logits_tr, logits_inf = seq2seq_model(tf.reverse(input_data, [-1]),
targets, dropout_probs,
                       fr_len,en_len,max_en_len,
                       len(en_word2int)+1,rnn_len, n_layers,
                       en_word2int,batch_size)
logits_tr = tf.identity(logits_tr.rnn_output, 'logits_tr')
logits_inf = tf.identity(logits_inf.sample_id, name='predictions')
seq_masks = tf.sequence_mask(en_len, max_en_len, dtype=tf.float32,
name='masks')
with tf.name_scope("optimizer"):
    tr_cost = sequence_loss(logits_tr,targets,seq_masks)
    optimizer = tf.train.AdamOptimizer(learning_rate)
    gradients = optimizer.compute_gradients(tr_cost)
    capped_gradients = [(tf.clip_by_value(gradient, -5., 5.), var) for
gradient, var in gradients
                        if gradient is not None]
train_op = optimizer.apply_gradients(capped_gradients)
tf.summary.scalar("cost", tr_cost)
print("Graph created.")
```

We first use the `seq2seq_model` function to create the encoder-decoder network with attention. We compute the loss using the `sequence_loss` function of the `seq2seq` TensorFlow library with the output logits values. We also mask out the padding in the loss calculation. Finally, we use `AdamOptimizer` as our optimizer on the loss.

Training

We will now train our network on the French sentence and the corresponding English translation. Before that, we will look into the function that outputs the training batches:

```
def get_batches(en_text, fr_text, batch_size):
    for batch_idx in range(0, len(fr_text)//batch_size):
        start_idx = batch_idx * batch_size
        en_batch = en_text[start_idx:start_idx + batch_size]
        fr_batch = fr_text[start_idx:start_idx + batch_size]
        pad_en_batch = np.array(pad_sentences(en_batch, en_word2int))
        pad_fr_batch = np.array(pad_sentences(fr_batch,fr_word2int))
        pad_en_lens = []
        for en_b in pad_en_batch:
            pad_en_lens.append(len(en_b))
        pad_fr_lens = []
        for fr_b in pad_fr_batch:
            pad_fr_lens.append(len(fr_b))
        yield pad_en_batch, pad_fr_batch, pad_en_lens, pad_fr_lens
```

The `get_batches` function returns the French and English sentence batches of the size, `batch_size`. It also pads the sentences with the padding token. This makes all sentences of an equal length to the maximum length in the batch. We will now look at the training loop:

```
min_learning_rate = 0.0006
display_step = 20
stop_early_count = 0
stop_early_max_count = 3
per_epoch = 3
update_loss = 0
batch_loss = 0
summary_update_loss = []
en_train = en_filtered[0:30000]
fr_train = fr_filtered[0:30000]

update_check = (len(fr_train)//batch_size//per_epoch)-1
checkpoint = logs_path + 'best_so_far_model.ckpt'
with tf.Session(graph=train_graph) as sess:
    tf_summary_writer = tf.summary.FileWriter(logs_path, graph=train_graph)
    merged_summary_op = tf.summary.merge_all()
    sess.run(tf.global_variables_initializer())
    for epoch_i in range(1, epochs+1):
        update_loss = 0
        batch_loss = 0
        for batch_i, (en_batch, fr_batch, en_text_len, fr_text_len) in
enumerate(
```

```
            get_batches(en_train, fr_train, batch_size)):
        before = time.time()
        _,loss,summary = sess.run([train_op,
tr_cost,merged_summary_op],
                        {input_data: fr_batch,
                        targets: en_batch,learning_rate: lr,
                        en_len: en_text_len,fr_len:
fr_text_len,dropout_probs: dr_prob})
        batch_loss += loss
        update_loss += loss
        after = time.time()
        batch_time = after - before
        tf_summary_writer.add_summary(summary, epoch_i * batch_size +
batch_i)
        if batch_i % display_step == 0 and batch_i > 0:
            print('** Epoch {:>3}/{} Batch {:>4}/{} -
            Batch Loss: {:>6.3f}, seconds:
{:>4.2f}'.format(epoch_i,epochs, batch_i,
                len(fr_filtered) // batch_size, batch_loss /
display_step,
                batch_time*display_step))
            batch_loss = 0
        if batch_i % update_check == 0 and batch_i > 0:
            print("Average loss:", round(update_loss/update_check,3))
            summary_update_loss.append(update_loss)
            if update_loss <= min(summary_update_loss):
                print('Saving model')
                stop_early_count = 0
                saver = tf.train.Saver()
                saver.save(sess, checkpoint)
            else:
                print("No Improvement.")
                stop_early_count += 1
                if stop_early_count == stop_early_max_count:
                    break
            update_loss = 0
    if stop_early_count == stop_early_max_count:
        print("Stopping Training.")
        break

Output :

** Epoch   5/20 Batch   440/3131 - Batch Loss:  1.038, seconds: 170.97
** Epoch   5/20 Batch   460/3131 - Batch Loss:  1.154, seconds: 147.05
Average loss: 1.139
Saving model
```

The main part of the code is the training loop, where we fetch the batches and feed them to the network, keep track of the loss, and save the model if there is an improvement in the loss. If there is no improvement in the loss for `stop_early_max_count`, the training terminates. We find that the average loss reduces to around `1.139` from `6.49`.

> Note that this value may change for each run. Refer to the notebook for the complete output.

Inference

We will load the model from the checkpoint file and test the translation on the set of sample data:

```
with tf.Session(graph=loaded_graph) as sess:
    loader = tf.train.import_meta_graph(checkpoint + '.meta')
    loader.restore(sess, checkpoint)
    input_data = loaded_graph.get_tensor_by_name('input_data:0')
    logits = loaded_graph.get_tensor_by_name('predictions:0')
    fr_length = loaded_graph.get_tensor_by_name('fr_len:0')
    en_length = loaded_graph.get_tensor_by_name('en_len:0')
    dropout_prob = loaded_graph.get_tensor_by_name('dropout_probs:0')
    result_logits = sess.run(logits, {input_data: [fr_text]*batch_size,
                en_length: [len(fr_text)],
                fr_length: [len(fr_text)]*batch_size,
                dropout_prob: 1.0})[0]

pad = en_word2int[TOKEN_PAD]
print('\nFrench Text')
print(' Word Ids: {}'.format([i for i in fr_text]))
print(' Input Words: {}'.format(" ".join( [fr_int2word[i] for i in fr_text
] )))
print('\nEnglish Text')
print(' Word Ids: {}'.format([i for i in result_logits if i != pad]))
print(' Response Words: {}'.format(" ".join( [en_int2word[i]for i in
result_logits if i!=pad] )))
print(' Ground Truth: {}'.format(" ".join( [en_int2word[i] for i in
en_filtered[random]] )))
```

We will load the input and output prediction tensors to run the graph on the test data. The following are some of the translations that are given as output by our model:

```
Unseen Test Data

French Text
Word Ids: [119, 67, 1003, 699, 11, 192, 13740]
Input Words: C'est environ 100 millions de ces planètes.
English Text
Word Ids: [119, 61, 1004, 2467, 21, 193, 17860]
Response Words: It's about 100 million of these planets.
Ground Truth: It's about 100 million such planets. &lt;EOS&gt;


French Text
Word Ids: [1255, 34, 21, 1263, 147, 1591, 609, 111, 1466, 3388, 21, 12253,
21, 22, 1673, 816]
Input Words: Qu'est-ce que les gens ont voulu donner au premier groupe, les
20% les plus pauvres ?
English Text
Word Ids: [320, 227, 227, 1511, 8, 636, 77, 14, 257, 2010, 14, 5433, 21,
14, 5433, 39610]
Response Words: What guys guys wanted to give at the first group, the
poorest of the poorest &lt;UNK&gt;
Ground Truth: What did people want to give to the first group, the bottom
20 &lt;UNK&gt; &lt;EOS&gt;INFO:tensorflow:Restoring parameters from
/tmp/models/best_so_far_model.ckpt


French Text
Word Ids: [31, 14982, 972, 33, 1043, 111, 2822, 131, 162, 4136, 11, 388,
94, 34, 7, 7499, 119, 413, 2973]
Input Words: La 2e étape est d'apprendre au chien à avoir envie de faire ce
que vous voulez. C'est très simple.
English Text
Word Ids: [34, 1560, 989, 1, 793, 8, 96, 8, 391, 8, 391, 99, 132, 128,
2938, 39612]
Response Words: The second step is learning to have to do to do what you're
familiar simple. &lt;EOS&gt;
Ground Truth: So the second stage in training is to teach the dog to want
to do what we want him to do, and this is very easy. &lt;EOS&gt;


French Text
Word Ids: [722, 4957, 873, 974, 6186, 24, 718, 816, 19704, 125, 1001, 375,
977]
Input Words: J'ai répondu : « Bien, et pourquoi ? &lt;UNK&gt; un peu plus. »
English Text
```

```
Word Ids: [52, 153, 2773, 29, 744, 897, 1609, 136, 215, 3141, 1111, 1124,
39610]
Response Words: I said, "Well, and why what? let's a little bit more more.
&lt;UNK&gt;
Ground Truth: And I said, "Well, why? Tell me a little bit about it."
&lt;EOS&gt;
```

We can observe that some of the translations are very close to the first example phrase, though it's not seen by the network during training. We will also test some of the training data:

```
Training Data

French Text
Word Ids: [422, 53, 1668, 277, 29, 378, 19704, 131, 1937, 4373, 4374, 218,
369, 538, 204, 157, 396, 704, 1791, 817, 34, 129, 87, 2172, 704, 1791, 87,
2172, 704, 3681]
Input Words: Donc pour moi, c'est une chose &lt;UNK&gt; à faire, d'essayer
d'atteindre l'autre côté avant qu'il ne soit trop tard, parce que quand il
sera trop tard, il sera trop tard.
English Text
Word Ids: [420, 57, 1323, 83, 1, 136, 464, 39610, 8, 391, 678, 8, 566, 225,
223, 564, 564, 118, 563, 737, 4316, 178, 131, 118, 565, 737, 4317, 39612]
Response Words: So for me, this is a thing &lt;UNK&gt; to do try to start
other side before before it doesn't too late, because when it will too
late. &lt;EOS&gt;
Ground Truth: So to me, this is the courageous thing to do, to try to reach
the other side before it's too late, because when it's going to be too
late, it's going to be too late. &lt;EOS&gt;

French Text
Word Ids: [1029, 33, 94, 625, 19704, 11, 3404, 735, 11, 19704, 131, 12,
5973, 816]
Input Words: Quel est ce besoin &lt;UNK&gt; de l'argent, puis de
&lt;UNK&gt; à la philanthropie ?
English Text
Word Ids: [2168, 83, 657, 21, 2853, 29, 319, 39610, 39610, 39612]
Response Words: What's this need of money, and then &lt;UNK&gt; &lt;UNK&gt;
&lt;EOS&gt;
Ground Truth: Why the need for accumulating money, then doing &lt;UNK&gt;
&lt;EOS&gt;
```

The quality of the translations are not that different from the test data. Note that, in spite of having used only 50% of the data for training, we can get decent translations. You may train on the whole data to get even better results on the translations.

TensorBoard visualization

We will now briefly look at the graph and loss of the network during training in TensorBoard:

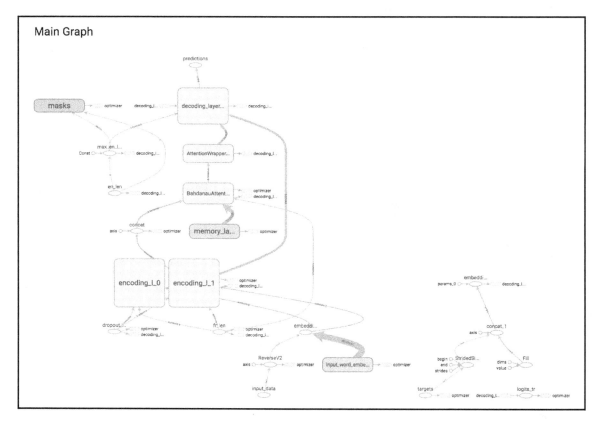

Graph and loss of network during training

We can see that the encoding and decoding layer is fed with the corresponding word embeddings of the source and target text. The attention mechanism couples the encoder output and the decoder through the memory layer weights. You can click on the respective components in TensorBoard to understand the details of the connections and tensor dimensions. We will now take a look at the plot of the cost function during training:

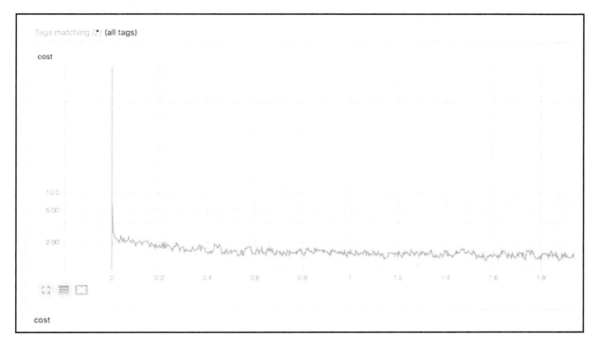

Cost functioning plot

Summary

In this chapter, we described the different commonly used machine translation methods with particular focus on neural machine translation. We briefly described classic statistical machine translation in the context of lexical alignment models. We showed a simple example for building an SMT alignment model using NLTK. SMT can be used when we have a large corpus of bilingual data.

The main shortcoming of such models is that they do not generalize well to domains (or contexts) other than the one in which they were trained. Recently, deep neural networks have become the popular approach to machine translation, mainly because of their effectiveness in producing close to human-level translations. We described in detail how to build an NMT model using RNNs with attention. We trained the model to translate French phrases into English from a real-world dataset of TED Talks. You can use a similar model for your own machine translation problems other than French-English translation. You can also improve on the model we developed by using a different attention mechanism or a deeper encoder/decoder network.

11
Speech Recognition Using DeepSpeech

Speech recognition is the task in which a machine or computer transforms spoken language into text. A good example is the voice typing feature in Google Docs which converts speech to text as you speak. In this chapter, we will look into how to build such systems using deep learning models. In particular, we will focus on using **recurrent neural network (RNNs)** models as these are found to be effective in practice for speech recognition. This is because RNNs can capture temporal dependencies in the speech data that is important in the task of converting it into text.

The following is an overview of the topics that will be covered in this chapter:

- Overview of speech recognition
- RNN models for isolated spoken word recognition
- Speech recognition using the DeepSpeech model for continuous speech

Overview of speech recognition

Speech recognition is a complex task as it has to consider several sources of variation in the data. Some of these are variations in the speaker, the size of the vocabulary, ambient noise, accent, speaker characteristics, and so on. For example, one person would be saying a word like *apple* very fast compared to another who might be saying it more slowly like *app........le*. In both cases, the speech recognition system should produce the word *apple*. The most common approach to speech recognition uses **Hidden Markov Models (HMMs)** since speech data can be considered as a stochastic or probabilistic process, and for a short time, slices can be considered to be independent of time. The HMM model can be trained on short slices of the speech data that represents a phoneme or word. It can then predict the next phoneme or word that can be combined together to form the speech text.

Speech recognition can further be classified as isolated word recognition and continuous speech recognition. Isolated word recognition refers to transcribing individual words spoken with a clear delineation. On the other hand, continuous speech recognition refers to the way we normally speak as continuous words. It is clear that the former is an easier task compared to the latter. While isolated words are often spoken with a clear pronunciation and it's easier to identify the boundaries, continuous speech can have lots of variations in pronunciations, gaps, and interword dependencies. HMMs have been used for both these type of tasks for a while. HMM models assume a specific structure in the speech data and can be trained on less data. Recent models using BiLSTMs can perform end to end speech recognition without any assumption of structure in the data. The network can learn both the features in the data and capture temporal dependencies. One simple rule is that if we have more data, then using a neural network model over an HMM might give better results. Next, we will look at building simple models for isolated word recognition.

Building an RNN model for speech recognition

We will be using the free-spoken digits audio dataset from `https://github.com/Jakobovski/free-spoken-digit-dataset/tree/master/recordings` for our basic model. Download the data to any directory on your system. In the example code, replace the path referring to the `.wav` file with the path you have copied the data to.

 Note that we have split the data into training data which includes 1,470 files and 30 for the test set.

Before we get into the details of the model itself, we will look at how to prepare it for the training. The most common preprocessing step used in practice is to transform the raw audio data into its frequency spectrum. The frequency spectrum or power spectrum is like a fingerprint for the data in which the raw audio is broken into constituent parts or frequencies. This representation helps in identifying which frequencies (high or low pitch) dominate (in power or energy) in the signal compared to others. We will now look at how to extract this frequency or power spectrum representation.

Audio signal representation

Let's now look at how to extract the frequency spectrum from the spoken digits dataset. This dataset contains the recording of the digits spoken in the form of a `.wav` file. We will utilize the `librosa` library which is commonly used for audio data analysis. First, we need to install the package using the following command:

```
pip install librosa
```

For other methods of installing this library, you can look at `https://github.com/librosa/librosa`. We will use the MFCC, or **Mel frequency cepstral coefficient feature**, of the audio signal. MFCC is a kind of power spectrum that is obtained from short time frames of the signal. The main assumption is that for short durations of the order of 20 ms to 40 ms, the frequency spectrum does not change much. Therefore, the signal is sliced into these short time periods and the spectrum is computed for each slice. Fortunately, we do not have to worry about these details as the `librosa` library can do this for us. We utilize the following function to extract the MFCC feature:

```
def get_mfcc_features(fpath):
    raw_w,sampling_rate = librosa.load(fpath,mono=True)
    mfcc_features = librosa.feature.mfcc(raw_w,sampling_rate)
    if(mfcc_features.shape[1]>utterance_length):
        mfcc_features = mfcc_features[:,0:utterance_length]
    else:
        mfcc_features=np.pad(mfcc_features,((0,0),(0,utterance_length-
mfcc_features.shape[1])),
                            mode='constant', constant_values=0)
    return mfcc_features
```

The `librosa.load` function loads the `.wav` file outputting the raw wav data `raw_w` and the sampling rate `sampling_rate`. The MFCC features are obtained by calling the `librosa.feature.mfcc` function on the raw data. Note that we also truncate the feature size to the `utterance_length` which is set to 35 in the code. This was set based on the average length of the utterance in the digit dataset. You can experiment with a higher value if required. For further details, you can take a look at the Jupyter Notebook under `Chapter11/01_example.ipynb` in this book's code repository. We will now print the shape of the feature and plot it to see what the power spectrum looks like:

```
import matplotlib.pyplot as plt
import librosa.display
%matplotlib inline
mfcc_features =
get_mfcc_features('../../speech_dset/recordings/train/5_theo_45.wav')
plt.figure(figsize=(10, 6))
```

```
plt.subplot(2, 1, 1)
librosa.display.specshow(mfcc_features, x_axis='time')
print("Feature shape: ", mfcc_features.shape)
print("Features: ", mfcc_features[:,0])
```

```
Output:
Feature shape: (20, 35)
Features:[-5.16464322e+02 2.18720111e+02 -9.43628435e+01 1.63510496e+01
   2.09937445e+01 -4.38791200e+01 1.94267052e+01 -9.41531735e-02
  -2.99960992e+01 1.39727129e+01 6.60561909e-01 -1.14758965e+01
   3.13688180e+00 -1.34556070e+01 -1.43686686e+00 1.17119580e+01
  -1.54499037e+01 -1.13105764e+01 2.53027299e+00 -1.35725427e+01]
```

We can see that the spectrum (for spoken digit five here) consists of 20 features (the
`librosa` default) for the 35 time slices of the audio signal. We can also see the MFCC
feature values of the first time slice. We will now visualize the MFCC feature:

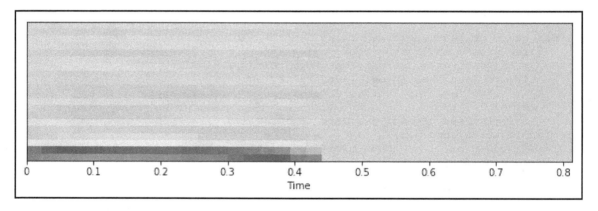

The regions toward the red (dark gray) color in the preceding figure indicates a large value
of the MFCC coefficients while those toward the blue (light gray) indicates smaller values.
Now, we will build a simple model for recognizing the digits in our audio data.

LSTM model for spoken digit recognition

For this example, we will use the `tflearn` package for simplicity. The `tflearn` package
can be installed using the following command:

```
pip install tflearn
```

We will define the function to read the `.wav` files and prepare it for batch training:

```
def get_batch_mfcc(fpath,batch_size=256):
    ft_batch = []
    labels_batch = []
    files = os.listdir(fpath)
    while True:
        print("Total %d files" % len(files))
        random.shuffle(files)
        for fname in files:
            if not fname.endswith(".wav"):
                continue
    mfcc_features = get_mfcc_features(fpath+fname)
    label = np.eye(10)[int(fname[0])]
    labels_batch.append(label)
    ft_batch.append(mfcc_features)
    if len(ft_batch) >= batch_size:
        yield ft_batch, labels_batch
    ft_batch = []
    labels_batch = []
```

In the `get_batch_mfcc` function, we read the `.wav` files and use the `get_mfcc_features` function defined earlier to extract the MFCC features. The `label` is one-hot encoded for the 10 digits from zero to nine. The function then returns the data in batches of 256 by default. Next, we will define the **Long Short-Term Memory (LSTM)** model:

```
train_batch = get_batch_mfcc('../../speech_dset/recordings/train/')
sp_network = tflearn.input_data([None, audio_features, utterance_length])
sp_network = tflearn.lstm(sp_network, 128*4, dropout=0.5)
sp_network = tflearn.fully_connected(sp_network, ndigits,
activation='softmax')
sp_network = tflearn.regression(sp_network, optimizer='adam',
learning_rate=lr, loss='categorical_crossentropy')
sp_model = tflearn.DNN(sp_network, tensorboard_verbose=0)
while iterations_train > 0:
    X_tr, y_tr = next(train_batch)
    X_test, y_test = next(train_batch)
    sp_model.fit(X_tr, y_tr, n_epoch=10, validation_set=(X_test, y_test),
show_metric=True, batch_size=bsize)
    iterations_train-=1
sp_model.save("/tmp/speech_recognition.lstm")
```

The model basically consists of an LSTM layer followed by a fully connected layer. We use the categorical cross-entropy as the `loss` function with the Adam optimization. The model is trained on the batch inputs from the `get_batch_mfcc` function. We get the following output after 300 epochs:

```
Training Step: 1199  | total loss: 0.45749 | time: 0.617s
| Adam | epoch: 300  | loss: 0.45749 - acc: 0.8975 -- iter: 192/256
```

Now, we will make a prediction on the audio file from the test set. The test audio is for the spoken digit 4:

```
sp_model.load('/tmp/speech_recognition.lstm')
mfcc_features =
get_mfcc_features('../../speech_dset/recordings/test/4_jackson_40.wav')
mfcc_features =
mfcc_features.reshape((1,mfcc_features.shape[0],mfcc_features.shape[1]))
prediction_digit = sp_model.predict(mfcc_features)
print(prediction_digit)
print("Digit predicted: ", np.argmax(prediction_digit))
```

```
Output:
INFO:tensorflow:Restoring parameters from /tmp/speech_recognition.lstm
[[2.3709694e-03 5.1581711e-03 7.8898791e-04 1.9530311e-03 9.8459840e-01
  1.1394228e-03 3.0317350e-04 1.8992715e-03 1.6027489e-03 1.8592674e-
  04]]
Digit predicted: 4
```

We load the trained model and get the features for the test audio file. As seen from the output, the model was able to predict the correct digit. We can also see the predicted probabilities for the 10 digits. Next, we will look at model visualization in TensorBoard.

TensorBoard visualization

We will first look at the accuracy and loss during the training. Start TensorBoard, pointing to the log directory `/tmp/tflearn_logs` (default for tflearn):

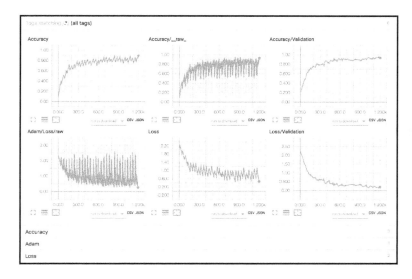

We find that both the validation and training loss decrease with the time steps. Note that the validation set we used was the same as from training, which was just a quick hack. You can set aside a separate validation set from the original data like we did for the test set. Next, we will look at the graph of the model in TensorBoard, as shown in the following screenshot:

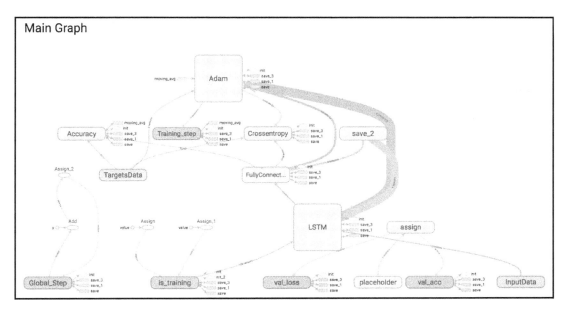

Graph of model in TensorBoard

As explained previously, we have an input layer that feeds the MFCC audio features tensor to the LSTM layer. The output of the LSTM is then fed to a fully connected layer that outputs the predictions. Next, we will look at creating a speech to text model using the DeepSpeech architecture.

Speech to text using the DeepSpeech architecture

DeepSpeech is an end-to-end architecture where deep learning replaces traditional hand engineered speech to text algorithms. The model performs well, independent of speaker adaptation as it directly learns from data. We will take a brief look at the model architecture of DeepSpeech.

Overview of the DeepSpeech model

The model consists of a stack of fully connected hidden layers followed by a bidirectional RNN and with additional hidden layers at the output. The first three nonrecurrent layers act like a preprocessing step to the RNN layer. One addition is the use of clipped **rectified linear units (ReLUs)** to prevent the activations from exploding. The input audio feature is the Mel cepstrum coefficients that the nonrecurrent layers see in time slices of spectrograms. In addition to the usual time slices, the spectrum data is preprocessed to include past and future contexts. The fourth layer is the RNN layer which has both a forward recurrence and a backward recurrence. The fifth layer takes the concatenated outputs of the forward and backward recurrence and produces an output that is fed to a final softmax layer that predicts the character probabilities. The following diagram shows the architecture of the model from the original paper. For more details on the architecture, you can take a look at `https://arxiv.org/abs/1412.5567`. The following diagram shows the hidden layers and the bidirectional recurrent layer denoted by the blue and red arrows:

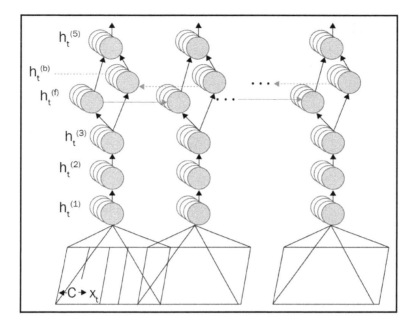

The audio input with the context is also shown in the preceding diagram along with the time sliced MFCC features. We will now look at how to implement this model in TensorFlow. The complete Jupyter Notebook can be found under `Chapter11/02_example.ipynb` in this book's code repository. Before that, we will briefly take a look at the data we will be using for our model training.

Speech recordings dataset

We will be utilizing the speech recordings of the **Linguistic Data Consortium** (**LDC**), which is available from Kaggle. You can download the dataset from `https://www.kaggle.com/nltkdata/timitcorpus` with an account in Kaggle. The data consists of free speech recordings of different speakers. While the original dataset is quite huge (several gigabytes), the data from Kaggle is a small subset that we can use for training within a reasonable time. Note that speech to text requires a large amount of transcribed audio data that may take several hours or days to train to get a model with good, meaningful transcriptions. You can use the same model we build here on a larger data to achieve better speech to text accuracy. For the complete code in this section, you can refer to the Jupyter Notebook that can be found under `Chapter11/02_example.ipynb` of this book's code repository.

Preprocessing the audio data

The MFCC features are extracted from the audio data just like in our previous example. In addition to that, we also add the context that was used in the original paper:

```
def audiofile_to_vector(audio_fname, n_mfcc_features, nctx):
    sampling_rate, raw_w = wavfile.read(audio_fname)
    mfcc_ft = mfcc(raw_w, samplerate=sampling_rate, numcep=n_mfcc_features)
    mfcc_ft = mfcc_ft[::2]
    n_strides = len(mfcc_ft)
    dummy_ctx = np.zeros((nctx, n_mfcc_features), dtype=mfcc_ft.dtype)
    mfcc_ft = np.concatenate((dummy_ctx, mfcc_ft, dummy_ctx))
    w_size = 2*nctx+1
    input_vector = np.lib.stride_tricks.as_strided(mfcc_ft,(n_strides, w_size,
                       n_mfcc_features,(mfcc_ft.strides[0],
mfcc_ft.strides[0], mfcc_ft.strides[1]),
                       writeable=False)
    input_vector = np.reshape(input_vector, [n_strides, -1])
    input_vector = np.copy(input_vector)
    input_vector = (input_vector -
np.mean(input_vector))/np.std(input_vector)
    return input_vector
```

We first read the `.wav` file and extract the MFCC features `mfcc_ft`. A dummy context is added to the front and back of each time slice using the NumPy `as_strided` function. The `audiofile_to_vector` functions finally returns the MFCC features with the past and future context. Next, we will look at how we extract the source and transcribed text from the dataset for our batch training:

```
def get_wav_trans(fpath,X, y):
    files = os.listdir(fpath)
    for fname in files:
        next_path = fpath + "/" + fname
        if os.path.isdir(next_path):
            get_wav_trans(next_path,X,y)
        else:
            if fname.endswith('wav'):
                fname_without_ext = fname.split(".")[0]
                trans_fname = fname_without_ext + ".txt"
                trans_fname_path = fpath + "/" + trans_fname
                if os.path.isfile(trans_fname_path):
                    mfcc_ft = audiofile_to_vector(next_path,n_inp,n_ctx)
                    with open(trans_fname_path,'r') as content:
                        transcript = content.read()
                        transcript = re.sub(regexp_alphabets, ' ',
transcript).strip().lower()
```

```
        trans_lbl = get_string2label(transcript)
    X.append(mfcc_ft)
    y.append(trans_lbl)
```

We recurse through the provided path, `fpath`, to extract the MFCC features of all the `wav` files. The function described before `audio_file_to_vector` extracts the MFCC features of each `wav` file we find and the corresponding transcribed text is read from the text file. The regular expression `regexp_alphabets` removes non-alphabetic characters from the transcribed text. The raw text `transcript` is passed to the `get_string2label` function that converts the text to integer labels that we use as target labels for the model training:

```
regexp_alphabets = "[^a-zA-Z']+"
cnt=0
def get_label(ch):
    global cnt
    label = cnt
    cnt+=1
    return label
chr2lbl = {c:get_label(c) for c in list(chars)}
lbl2chr = {chr2lbl[c]:c for c in list(chars)}
def get_string2label(strval):
    strval = strval.lower()
    idlist = []
    for c in list(strval):
        if c in chr2lbl:
            idlist.append(chr2lbl[c])
    return np.array(idlist)

def get_label2string(lblarr):
    strval = []
    for idv in lblarr:
        strval.append(lbl2chr[idv])
    return ''.join(strval)
```

The `get_string2label` basically converts a string to a list of integer labels that are obtained with the `chr2lbl` dictionary, which maps characters from a–z (additionally with a space and an apostrophe) to integer values. Similarly, we use the `get_label2string` function to convert the list of labels (with the reverse mapping `lbl2chr`) to the original string. Next, we will look at creating the DeepSpeech model.

Creating the model

We will replicate the exact model as described in the original DeepSpeech paper. As explained earlier, the model consists of both recurrent and nonrecurrent layers. We will now look at the `get_layers` function in the code:

```
with tf.name_scope('Lyr1'):
    B1 = tf.get_variable(name='B1', shape=[n_h],
    initializer=tf.random_normal_initializer(stddev=0.046875))
    H1 = tf.get_variable(name='H1', shape=[n_inp + 2*n_inp*n_ctx, n_h],
    initializer=tf.contrib.layers.xavier_initializer(uniform=False))
    logits1 = tf.add(tf.matmul(X_batch, H1), B1)
    relu1 = tf.nn.relu(logits1)
    clipped_relu1 = tf.minimum(relu1,20.0)
    Lyr1 = tf.nn.dropout(clipped_relu1, 0.5)

with tf.name_scope('Lyr2'):
    B2 = tf.get_variable(name='B2', shape=[n_h],
    initializer=tf.random_normal_initializer(stddev=0.046875))
    H2 = tf.get_variable(name='H2', shape=[n_h,n_h],
    initializer=tf.random_normal_initializer(stddev=0.046875))
    logits2 = tf.add(tf.matmul(Lyr1, H2), B2)
    relu2 = tf.nn.relu(logits2)
    clipped_relu2 = tf.minimum(relu2,20.0)
    Lyr2 = tf.nn.dropout(clipped_relu2, 0.5)

with tf.name_scope('Lyr3'):
    B3 = tf.get_variable(name='B3', shape=[2*n_h],
    initializer=tf.random_normal_initializer(stddev=0.046875))
    H3 = tf.get_variable(name='H3', shape=[n_h,2*n_h],
    initializer=tf.random_normal_initializer(stddev=0.046875))
    logits3 = tf.add(tf.matmul(Lyr2, H3), B3)
    relu3 = tf.nn.relu(logits3)
    clipped_relu3 = tf.minimum(relu3,20.0)
    Lyr3 = tf.nn.dropout(clipped_relu3, 0.5)
```

The first three hidden layers are nonrecurrent. The parameters H1, H2, H3, and B1, B2, B3 are the weights and biases of the layers, respectively. The outputs of the layers pass through a clipped ReLU function to avoid exploding activations. We also have dropout for all of the first three hidden layers. Note that the first hidden layer weights have shape $[n\_inp + 2*n\_ip*n\_ctx, n\_h]$, which is the same as the MFCC input with context. In the following code, we have set the number of hidden units n_h as 1024, MFCC features n_inp as 26 and context n_ctx as 9. Afterwards, we will look at the recurrent layer:

```
with tf.name_scope('RNN_Lyr'):
    fw_c = tf.contrib.rnn.BasicLSTMCell(n_h, forget_bias=1.0,
```

```
state_is_tuple=True,
    reuse=tf.get_variable_scope().reuse)
    fw_c = tf.contrib.rnn.DropoutWrapper(fw_c, input_keep_prob=0.7,
            output_keep_prob=0.7,seed=123)
    bw_c = tf.contrib.rnn.BasicLSTMCell(n_h, forget_bias=1.0,
state_is_tuple=True,
    reuse=tf.get_variable_scope().reuse)
    bw_c = tf.contrib.rnn.DropoutWrapper(bw_c,input_keep_prob=0.7,
            output_keep_prob=0.7, seed=123)
    Lyr3 = tf.reshape(Lyr3, [-1, X_batch_shape[0], 2*n_h])
    outs, out_states = tf.nn.bidirectional_dynamic_rnn(cell_fw=fw_c,
            cell_bw=bw_c,inputs=Lyr3,dtype=tf.float32,time_major=True,
            sequence_length=seq_len)
    outs = tf.concat(outs, 2)
    outs = tf.reshape(outs, [-1, 2 * n_h])
```

As described previously, the recurrent layer is a bidirectional LSTM with dropout. The concatenated output of the forward and backward LSTM are input to the next hidden layer. Now, we will look at the last two hidden layers at the output:

```
with tf.name_scope('Lyr4'):
    B4 = tf.get_variable(name='B4', shape=[n_h],
    initializer=tf.random_normal_initializer(stddev=0.046875))
    H4 = tf.get_variable(name='H4', shape=[(2 * n_h), n_h],
    initializer=tf.random_normal_initializer(stddev=0.046875))
    logits4 = tf.add(tf.matmul(outs, H4), B4)
    relu4 = tf.nn.relu(logits4)
    clipped_relu4 = tf.minimum(relu4,20.0)
    Lyr4 = tf.nn.dropout(clipped_relu4, 0.5)

with tf.name_scope('Lyr5'):
    B5 = tf.get_variable(name='B5', shape=[n_h],
    initializer=tf.random_normal_initializer(stddev=0.046875))
    H5 = tf.get_variable(name='H5', shape=[n_h, n_chars],
    initializer=tf.random_normal_initializer(stddev=0.046875))
    Lyr5 = tf.add(tf.matmul(Lyr4, H5), B5)
    Lyr5 = tf.reshape(Lyr5, [-1, X_batch_shape[0], n_chars])
```

Like the hidden layers in the input, the final two hidden layers have weights and biases H4, H5 and B4, B5, respectively. Layer four has the output ReLU activations clipped with dropout. Layer five output finally outputs the probabilities for n_chars (number of alphabets plus blank), one character at a time. Afterwards, we will look at the definition of the loss function and the optimizer:

```
def get_cost(tgts,logits,len_seq):
    loss_t = ops.ctc_ops.ctc_loss(tgts, logits, len_seq)
    loss_avg = tf.reduce_mean(loss_t)
```

```
            return loss_avg

def get_optimizer(logits,len_seq,loss_avg):
    adm_opt =
tf.train.AdamOptimizer(learning_rate=plr,beta1=pb1,beta2=pb2,epsilon=peps)
    adm_opt = adm_opt.minimize(loss_avg)
    dec, prob_log = ops.ctc_ops.ctc_beam_search_decoder(logits, len_seq,
merge_repeated=False)
    return adm_opt,dec
```

We will be using the **Connectionist Temporal Classification** (**CTC**) loss function, which is available in TensorFlow tensorflow.python.ctc_ops.ctc_loss. It takes the logits and the target variables as inputs and computes the loss. From this, the average loss is computed by the get_costs function. This average loss is minimized using the AdamOptimizer in the get_optimizer function. We will now look at the batch data feeder for training our model:

```
class Batch:
    def __init__(self):
        self.start_idx = 0
        self.batch_size = 10
        self.audio = []
        self.transcript = []
get_wav_trans("../../speech_dset/timit/",self.audio,self.transcript)

    def pad_seq(self,seqs):
        seq_lens = np.asarray([len(st) for st in seqs], dtype=np.int64)
        n_s = len(seqs)
        max_seq_len = np.max(seq_lens)
        s_shape = tuple()
        for s in seqs:
            if len(s) > 0:
                s_shape = np.asarray(s).shape[1:]
                break
        seqs_trc = (np.ones((n_s, max_seq_len) + s_shape) *
0.).astype(np.float32)
        for ix, s in enumerate(seqs):
            if len(s) == 0:
                continue
        trc = s[:max_seq_len]
        trc = np.asarray(trc, dtype=np.int64)
        if trc.shape[1:] != s_shape:
            raise ValueError("ERROR in truncation shape")
        seqs_trc[ix, :len(trc)] = trc
      return seqs_trc, seq_lens

    def get_sp_tuple(self,seqs):
```

```
            ixs = []
            vals = []
            for n, s in enumerate(seqs):
                ixs.extend(zip([n] * len(s), range(len(s))))
                vals.extend(s)
                ixs = np.asarray(ixs, dtype=np.int64)
                vals = np.asarray(vals, dtype=np.int32)
                shape = np.asarray([len(seqs), ixs.max(0)[1] + 1],
dtype=np.int64)
            return ixs, vals, shape

    def get_next_batch(self):
        src = self.audio[self.start_idx:self.start_idx+self.batch_size]
        tgt =
self.transcript[self.start_idx:self.start_idx+self.batch_size]
        self.start_idx += self.batch_size
        if(self.start_idx>len(self.audio)):
            self.start_idx=0
            src,src_len = self.pad_seq(src)
            sp_lbls = self.get_sp_tuple(tgt)
        return src, src_len, sp_lbls
```

We utilize the `get_wav_trans` to get all the audio (MFCC features) and the
text `transcript` from the `.wav` and `.txt` files. The `get_next_batch` function returns the
source (audio) and target (transcript) in the size of `batch_size`. The `pad_seq` function
pads the MFCC sequence to a maximum length of the sequence within a specific batch.
Similarly, the `get_sp_tuple` obtains a sparse representation of the target labels. Now, we
will look at the training setup:

```
def get_model():
    input_t = tf.placeholder(tf.float32, [None, None, n_inp + (2 * n_inp *
n_ctx)], name='inp')
    tgts = tf.sparse_placeholder(tf.int32, name='tgts')
    len_seq = tf.placeholder(tf.int32, [None], name='len_seq')
    logits = get_logits(input_t,tf.to_int64(len_seq))
    return input_t, tgts, len_seq, logits
```

The `get_model` function creates the input placeholder tensors for the source (MFCC
features), target (transcribed text labels), and sequence lengths. Then, it calls the
`get_logits` function, which in turn calls the `get_layers` described earlier. This function
thereby creates the model. Now, we will look at the model training loop:

```
gr = tf.Graph()
with gr.as_default():
    input_t,tgts,len_seq,logits = get_model()
    loss_avg = get_cost(tgts,logits,len_seq)
```

```
    adm_opt, dec = get_optimizer(logits,len_seq,loss_avg)
    error_rate = get_error_rates(dec,tgts)
    sess = tf.Session()
    writer = tf.summary.FileWriter('/tmp/models/', graph=sess.graph)
    loss_summary = tf.summary.scalar("loss_avg", loss_avg)
    sum_op = tf.summary.merge_all()
    init_op = tf.global_variables_initializer()
    sess.run(init_op)
    for ep in range(epochs):
        train_cost = 0
        label_err_rate = 0
        batch_feeder = Batch()
        n_batches =
np.ceil(len(batch_feeder.audio)/batch_feeder.batch_size)
        n_batches = int(n_batches)
        st = time.time()
        for batch in range(n_batches):
            src,len_src,labels_src = batch_feeder.get_next_batch()
            data_dict = {input_t: src, tgts: labels_src,len_seq:len_src}
            batch_cost, _,summ = sess.run([loss_avg, adm_opt,sum_op],
data_dict)
            train_cost += batch_cost * batch_feeder.batch_size
            print("Batch cost: {0}, Train cost:
{1}".format(batch_cost,train_cost))
            label_err_rate += sess.run(error_rate, feed_dict=data_dict) *
batch_feeder.batch_size
            print('Label error: {}'.format(label_err_rate))
            writer.add_summary(summ, ep*batch_feeder.batch_size+batch)
            saver = tf.train.Saver()
            saver.save(sess, '/tmp/models/speech2txt.ckpt')
        decoded_val = sess.run(dec[0], feed_dict=data_dict)
        d_decoded_val = tf.sparse_tensor_to_dense(decoded_val,
                    default_value=-1).eval(session=sess)
        d_lbl = decoded_val_to_text(labels_src)
        cnt = 0
        cnt_max = 4
        if cnt < cnt_max:
            for actual_val, decoded_val in zip(d_lbl, d_decoded_val):
                d_str = array2txt(decoded_val)
                print('Batch {}'.format(batch))
                print('Actual: {}'.format(actual_val))
                print('Predicted: {}'.format(d_str))
                cnt += 1
        time_taken = time.time() - st
        log = 'Epoch {}/{}, training_cost: {:.3f}, error_rate: {:.3f},
time: {:.2f} sec'
        print(log.format(ep,epochs,train_cost/len(batch_feeder.audio),
            (label_err_rate/len(batch_feeder.audio)), time_taken))
```

We first set up the graph and training by calling `get_model`, `get_cost`, `get_optimizer`, and `get_error_rates` to create the graph, loss function, optimizer, and to calculate error rates, respectively. We initialize the `batch_feeder` to get the training data in batches. The `feed` dictionary is populated with the source `src`, target `labels_src`, and source length `src_len`. After completion of each batch, we print the batch error, label error rate, and save the model. We also print the example predicted text after each completion of an epoch.

TensorBoard visualization

We will now look at the graph and loss function using TensorBoard. Start TensorBoard and point to the log directory `/tmp/models` defined in the code or any other path that you have set for saving the TensorFlow logs. The following is the visualization of the graph:

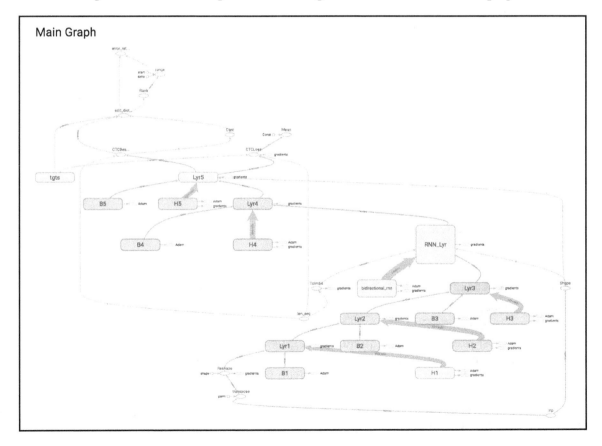

Visualization of the graph on TensorBoard

We can quickly find the resemblance between this model and the model architecture of the original DeepSpeech paper. We have the input nonrecurrent layers, followed by the RNN layer and the output hidden layers. We will now look at how the average CTC loss varies with the training:

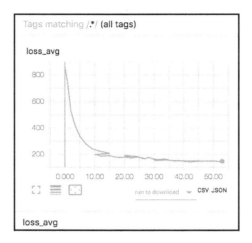

The CTC loss can be seen to steadily decrease with the training steps. Though our model replicates the architecture of DeepSpeech, we only trained on a small dataset. To achieve good transcription accuracy (word error rate, CRT loss, and so on, which is speaker agnostic), we may need to train it on a large dataset. For further details, you may also look at another DeepSpeech implementation that can be found at `https://github.com/mozilla/DeepSpeech`. There, they use datasets of several 10's of Gigabytes and utilize distributed training on multiple GPUs. The purpose of the implementation we showed here is to quickly come up with a simple model and training.

State-of-the-art in speech recognition

The original DeepSpeech architecture uses a language model to correct some errors in the character sequences. It combines both the output of the RNN and a language model to arrive at the most probable text sequence for a given speech recording. As attention-based methods are getting popular due to their effectiveness on improving accuracies over non-attention-based systems, it has been adopted even for speech. The paper *Listen, Attend, and Spell: A Neural Network for Large Vocabulary Conversational Speech Recognition* (`https://ai.google/research/pubs/pub44926`) from Google incorporates an attention mechanism to transcribe speech recordings.

The main advantage of this system is that it uses an attention-based model and does not assume character independence in the sequence. The CTC-based methods, including DeepSpeech, assume independence in the probability distributions between subsequent characters in the sequence. Let's take a brief look at the architecture shown in the following figure:

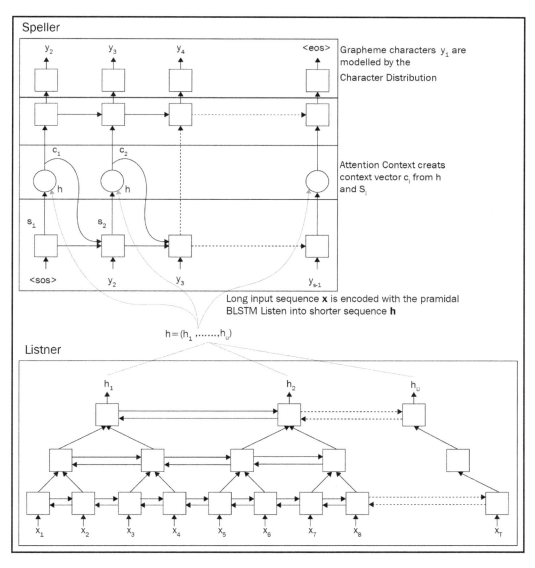

The figure shows the main components of the model which are the **Listener** and the **Speller**. The Listener encodes the input audio spectrum **x** into a high-level feature representation **h**. The main difference between a normal BiLSTM and the Listener architecture is that it uses a pyramidal structure. The pyramidal structure reduces the time resolution of very large input audio sequences at each level of the pyramid. This, in effect, reduces the amount of useful audio information that the Speller has to attend to produce the transcription. The speller uses the final high-level representation output by the listener to compute the attention context vector. At every time step, the speller will then compute the probabilities of the next character based on all the important characters seen before using the attention vector. The authors have reported good accuracy in terms of **word error rates** (**WER**) compared to the neural network and HMM-based state-of-art models.

Summary

In this chapter, we described deep learning methods in speech recognition. We looked at an overview of speech recognition software currently used in practice. We showed that traditional HMM-based methods might need to incorporate specific language models, whereas neural network-based methods can learn end to end speech transcription entirely from data. This is one main advantage of neural network models over HMM models. We developed a basic spoken digits recognition model using TensorFlow. We then used the open spoken digits dataset to train and make predictions on a test set. This example provided the background of the tasks involved in a speech recognition system like extraction of the frequency spectrum like MFCC features from the raw audio data and converting the text transcripts to labels. We then introduced the DeepSpeech architecture from Baidu, which is one of the most recent popular models in transcribing speech. We then explained a complete implementation of the DeepSpeech model in TensorFlow and trained it on a subset of the LDC dataset. To explore further, the reader can tweak the model parameters and train it on a larger dataset.

We then briefly looked at the state-of-the-art in speech recognition, mainly on attention-based models. We looked at the attention-based model described in the Listen, Attend, and Spell (LAS) paper. While CTC-based models assume character independence, the LAS model does not make such assumptions. This was one of the main advantages of LAS over DeepSpeech-like models, as described by the authors. The interested reader may take a look at the PyTorch implementation of this model at `https://github.com/XenderLiu/Listen-Attend-and-Spell-Pytorch`.

In the next chapter, we will look at the reverse task of speech recognition, which is text to speech.

Text-to-Speech Using Tacotron **12**

Text-to-speech (**TTS**) is the act of converting text into intelligible and natural speech. Before we delve into deep learning approaches to handle TTS, we should ask ourselves the following questions: what are TTS systems for? And why do we need them in the first place?

Well, there are many use cases for TTS. One of the most obvious is that it allows blind people to listen to written content. Indeed, Braille-based books, devices, or signs are not always available, and blind people can't always have someone read to them. In the near future, there might be smart glasses that can describe the surrounding environment and read urban signs and text-based indications to their users.

Many people struggle from childhood with learning disabilities like dyslexia. Robust TTS systems can help them on a daily basis, increasing their productivity at school or work, for instance.

Also, related to the area of learning, it is commonly proposed that different individuals have different preferred styles of absorbing knowledge. For instance, there are those that have great visual memory, those that more easily retain information they have heard, and those that rely more on their kinesthetic memory (memory associated with physical movements). TTS systems can help auditory learners take advantage of that particular way of learning.

In our increasingly fast-paced world, multitasking often becomes a necessity. It is not rare to see a person walking in the street and reading some content displayed on their smartphone at the same time. Someone might also be cooking and following recipe instructions on a touchscreen device. But what if the lack of visual attention leads to an accident (in the first scenario), and what if dirty and sticky fingers prevent an aspiring chef from scrolling down to read the rest of the recipe (in the second scenario)? Again, TTS is a natural solution to avoid these inconveniences.

As you can see, TTS applications have the potential to enhance many aspects of our everyday lives.

In this chapter, we will cover the following topics:

- A quick overview of the field
- A few recent deep learning approaches for TTS
- A step-by-step implementation of Tacotron—an end-to-end deep learning model

Overview of text to speech

Here, we will give some general information about TTS algorithms. It is not our ambition to thoroughly tackle the different components of the field, which is quite a complex task and requires cross-domain knowledge in areas like linguistic or signal processing.

We will stick to the following high-level questions: what makes a TTS system good or bad? How is it evaluated? What are some traditional techniques, and why does the field need to move toward deep learning? We will also prepare for the next sections by giving a few basic pieces of information on spectrograms.

Naturalness versus intelligibility

The quality of a TTS system is traditionally assessed through two criteria: **naturalness** and **intelligibility**. This is motivated by the fact that people are not only sensitive to what the audio content is, but also to how that content is delivered. Basically, we want a TTS system that can produce clear audio content in a human-like way. More precisely, intelligibility is about the audio *quality* or *cleanness*, and naturalness is about communicating the message with the proper pronunciation, timing, and range of emotions.

With a highly intelligible system, it is effortless for the user to distinguish between different words. On the other hand, when intelligibility is low, some words might be confused with others or difficult to identify, and the separation between words might be unclear. In most scenarios, intelligibility is the more important parameter of the two. That is because conveying a clear and unambiguous message to the user is often the priority, whether it sounds natural or not. If a user can't understand the generated audio, it is a failure. Therefore, it is necessary to have a minimum level of intelligibility, before we try to optimize the naturalness of the generated speech.

When a TTS algorithm has a high-level of naturalness, the produced content is so smooth that the user feels like another human being is talking to them. It is hardly possible to tell that the speech was artificially created. On the other hand, a discontinuous, monotonous, and lifeless intonation is typical of unnatural speech.

Note that these are relatively subjective criteria. Therefore, they are not measured with objective metrics. Indeed, because of the nature of the problem, a TTS system can only be evaluated by humans.

How is the performance of a TTS system evaluated?

A subjective measure of sound quality, the **mean opinion score** (**MOS**), is one of the most commonly used tests for assessing the performance of a TTS algorithm. Usually, several native speakers are asked to give a score of naturalness, from 1 (bad quality) to 5 (excellent quality), and the mean of those scores is the MOS. Audio samples recorded by professionals typically have an MOS of around 4.55, as shown in the *WaveNet: A Generative Model for Raw Audio* paper that will be presented later in this chapter (`https://arxiv.org/abs/1609.03499`).

This way of benchmarking TTS algorithms is not entirely satisfactory, however. For instance, it does not allow for a rigorous comparison of different algorithms presented in different papers. Indeed, algorithm A is not necessarily evaluated by the same sample of listeners as algorithm B. Since different individuals are likely to have different standards, more or less, regarding what a natural sound is, if A has an MOS score of 4.2 and B has an MOS score of 4.1, it does not necessarily mean that A is better than B (unless they are evaluated within the same study, by the same group of individuals). Besides, the sample size as well as the population from which the sample of listeners is selected are difficult to standardize, and might make a difference.

Traditional techniques – concatenative and parametric models

Before the rise of deep learning in TTS tasks, either concatenative or parametric models where used.

To create concatenative models, one needs to record high quality-audio content, split it into small chunks, and then recombine these chunks to form new speech. With parametric models, we have to create the features with signal processing techniques, which requires some extra domain knowledge.

Concatenative models tend to be intelligible, but lack naturalness. They require a huge dataset that takes into account as many human-generated audio units as possible. Therefore, they usually take a long time to develop.

In general, parametric models perform worse than concatenative models. They may lack intelligibility, and do not sound particularly natural, either. This is due to the fact that the feature generation process is based on how we humans think speech works. The way we model speech is probably biased and restrictive. However, with a deep learning approach, there are very few preconceptions about what speech is. The model learns features that are inherent to the data. That is where the potential of deep learning lies.

A few reminders on spectrograms and the mel scale

As we will see in the next sections, some efficient techniques used in state-of-the-art TTS systems (deep learning-based, or otherwise) rely on tricks that come from the signal processing world. For instance, generating a spectrogram instead of a waveform of a signal, and then applying a conversion algorithm, is often preferred over directly predicting a waveform. This can provide better results in a faster way. This section is a quick recap on spectrograms, and it will help you to understand many ideas that will be presented later in the chapter.

Essentially, a spectrogram is a way to represent the strength of an audio signal. It can be shown on a two-dimensional graph, where the x axis is the time and the y axis is the frequency of the signal. A third dimension is represented by a heatmap, which tells us what is the importance of each frequency at a particular time. Usually, cold colors are used for smaller amplitudes and hot colors are used for larger amplitudes.

To compute the spectrogram of a given digital signal, one needs to first use the **short-time Fourier transform** (**STFT**). We can get the STFT by calculating the Fourier transform for consecutive frames in the signal:

$$STFT(m, w) = \sum_{n=-\infty}^{\infty} x[n]w[n - m]e^{-jwn}, j^2 = -1$$

In the preceding formula, w is the chosen sliding window.

We can then obtain the spectrogram:

$$SPECTRO(m, w) = |STFT(m, w)|^2$$

In practice, the non-squared magnitude of the STFT is used.

In order to exploit a representation that is closer to the way human beings perceive sounds, a mel scaled spectrogram is sometimes favored. The mel scale is designed so that consecutive mel-frequencies are perceived (by listeners) to be equally spaced. Its definition was established based on subjective experiments, involving people listening to sounds with different frequencies and then estimating the distances between those sounds, based on how they perceived pitches. Different experiments lead to the definitions of different conversion formulas. One of the most popular (and the one that we will use) is the following:

$$Mel(f) = 2595 \times log10(1 + \frac{f}{700})$$

For those who prefer to visualize functions, the following is the graph associated with this formula, where the x axis represents frequencies and the y axis represents mel-frequencies:

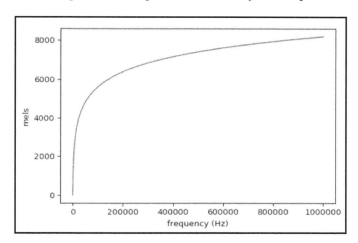

Basically, the frequency component of the spectrogram is transformed into a mel component through the aforementioned formula. This conversion is done together with a **binning** operation, where a triangular filter bank, with k filters spaced according to the mel scale, is applied on the spectrogram, so that a limited number of mel-frequency bands are extracted.

The following is an example of such a filter bank, with *k=20* triangular filters:

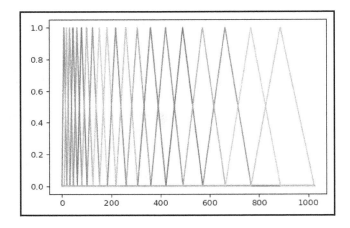

Additionally, we prefer to use the decibel scale for both the spectrogram and the mel-spectrogram, because the amplitude of a sound is also perceived by human beings in a logarithmic way:

$$SPECTRO_{db}(m, w) = 20 \times log10(SPECTRO(m, w))$$

We can illustrate these notions with the following audio signal (with a sampling rate of 22,050 Hz):

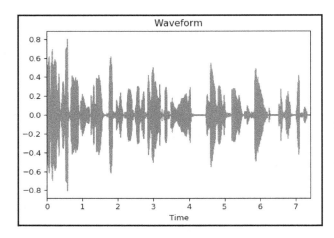

When we look at its spectrogram (the magnitude of its STFT computed with 2,048 points), we can barely distinguish the parts where the amplitude is the most important, because of its logarithmic nature. That is why we use the decibel scale:

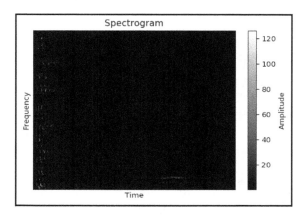

When we use the decibel scale, the visualization is neater. It becomes easy to see which frequencies have the biggest amplitude across time:

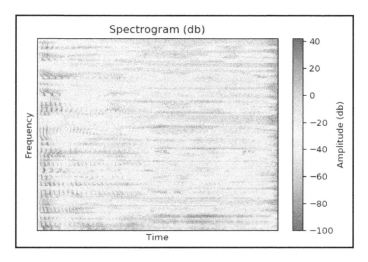

Applying the mel scale on the frequency, along with an 80-band filterbank, allows us to obtain a more condensed representation of the spectrogram, which has the advantage of reducing the size of the spectrogram matrix and decreasing the number of operations in any next processing steps:

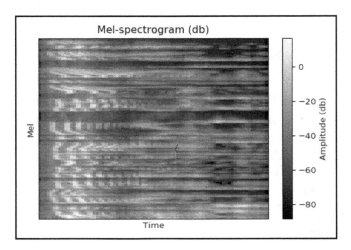

We are now better equipped to tackle the next sections.

TTS in deep learning

Over the last few years, the field of TTS has been shaken by several deep learning-based breakthroughs. Here, we will present two of them: WaveNet (probably the most notorious one) and Tacotron (which has the advantage of being an end-to-end approach).

WaveNet, in brief

The WaveNet paper was presented in 2016, and it showed results that outperformed the classical TTS approaches. Basically, WaveNet is an audio generative model. It takes a sequence of audio samples as input and predicts the most likely following audio sample. By adding an extra input, it can be conditioned to accomplish more tasks. For instance, if the audio transcript is additionally provided during training, WaveNet can turn it into a TTS system.

WaveNet uses many interesting ideas to train very deep neural networks. The main concept involves dilated causal convolutions (check out the paper to learn more about them).

In the paper, TTS is tackled, among other tasks, and the model is not directly fed with raw text, but with engineered linguistic features that require extra domain knowledge. Thus, WaveNet is not an end-to-end TTS model. Besides, the architecture is quiet complex, and it requires a lot of tuning as well as a tremendous amount of computational power to get decent results in a decent amount of time.

WaveNet is evaluated on both a North American English and a Mandarin Chinese dataset. The MOS is given and compared with a concatenative (HMM-based) and a parametric (LSTM-based) system:

	North American English MOS	Mandarin Chinese MOS
WaveNet	4.21 ± 0.081	4.08 ± 0.085
Parametric	3.67 ± 0.098	3.79 ± 0.084
Concatenative	3.86 ± 0.137	3.47 ± 0.108

Since we are more interested in end-to-end models for TTS, we will focus on one of the most popular ones: Tacotron.

Tacotron

Tacotron (https://arxiv.org/abs/1703.10135) was one of the first end-to-end TTS deep learning models. Basically, it is a complex encoder-decoder model that uses an attention mechanism for alignment between the text and audio. The decoder produces the spectrogram of the audio, which is then converted into the corresponding waveform by a technique called the **Griffin-Lim algorithm**.

The following is a representation of the entire architecture. We will present it in detail in the following paragraphs:

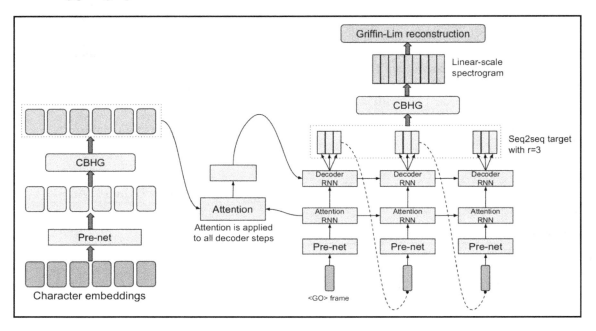

The encoder

The encoder takes a sequence of characters as input, where each character is represented by a one-hot vector. An embedder is then used to project the input into a continuous space. Remember that, because of their high-dimensionality and their sparsity, one-hot encoded vectors can lead to computational inefficiency, if they are not used with techniques that exploit these characteristics. An embedder allows for significantly reducing the size of the representation space. Besides, using an embedder allows us to learn about the relationships between the different characters of our vocabulary.

The embedding layer is then followed by a pre-net, which is a set of non-linear transformations. Basically, it is comprised of two consecutive, fully-connected layers, with **rectified linear unit (ReLU)** activation and dropout. Dropout (http://jmlr.org/papers/v15/srivastava14a.html) is a regularization technique that ignores some randomly selected units (or neurons) during training, in order to avoid overfitting. Indeed, during training, some neurons can develop a relationship of codependency that can result in overfitting. With dropout, the neural network tends to learn more robust features.

The second FC layer has two times fewer units than the first one. It is a **bottleneck** layer that helps with convergence and improves generalization.

The Tacotron team uses a module called **CBHG** on top of the pre-net. The name of this module comes from its building blocks: a 1-D **convolution bank** (**CB**), followed by a **highway network** (**H**) and a **bidirectional GRU** (**G**).

K layers of 1-D convolutional filters are used to form the convolution bank. The layer of index, K, contains C_k filters of the width k ($k = 1, 2, ..., K$). With this structure, we should be able to model unigrams, bigrams, and so on.

Max pooling is used right after the convolution bank. It is a down-sampling technique that is commonly applied in **Convolutional Neural Networks** (**CNNs**). It has the advantage of making the learned features locally invariant. Here, it is used with a stride of 1, in order to maintain the time resolution.

Batch Normalization: Accelerating Deep Network Training by Reducing Internal Covariate Shift (https://arxiv.org/abs/1502.03167) is utilized by all of the convolutional layers in the CBHG. It improves the performance as well as the stability of neural networks. It modifies the input of a layer, so that the output given by the activation has a mean of zero and a standard deviation of one. It is known to help the network converge faster, to allow for higher learning rates (thus, making bigger steps toward a good minimum) in deep networks, alleviating the sensitivity of the network to weight initialization and to add extra regularization by providing some noise.

Following the max pooling layer, two supplementary 1-D convolutional layers are used (with ReLU and linear activations, respectively). A residual connection (https://arxiv.org/abs/1512.03385) binds the initial input with the output of the second convolutional layer. Deep networks allow for capturing more complexity in the data, and have the potential to perform better than shallower networks on a given task. But, in general, the gradient tends to vanish with very deep networks. Residual connections allow for a better propagation of the gradient.

Thus, they significantly improve the training of deep models:

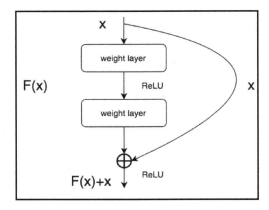

The next block of the CBHG module, a highway network (https://arxiv.org/abs/1505.00387), has a similar role.

To finalize the CBHG module, as well as the encoder, a bidirectional GRU is used to learn the long-term dependencies in the sequence, from both the forward and the backward context. The encoder output will then be used by the attention layer:

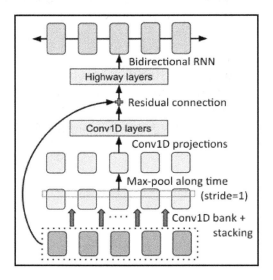

The attention-based decoder

Here, the decoder uses an attention mechanism on the encoder's output, to produce mel-spectrogram frames.

For each mini-batch, the decoder is given a **GO** frame, which contains only zeros as input. Then, for every time-step, the previously predicted mel-spectrogram frame is used as input. This input fuels a pre-net that has the exact same architecture as the encoder's pre-net.

The pre-net is followed by a one-layer GRU, whose output is concatenated with the encoder's output to produce the context vector through the attention mechanism. This GRU output is then concatenated with the context vector, to produce the input of the decoder RNN block.

The decoder RNN is a two-layer residual GRU that uses vertical residual connections, as shown by Wu et al. (`https://arxiv.org/abs/1609.08144`). In their paper, they use a type of residual connection that is a bit more complicated than what we presented a few paragraphs ago. Indeed, instead of just adding the output of the last layer to the initial input, at each layer, we add the layer's output to the layer's input, and we use the result of the addition as the input for the following layer:

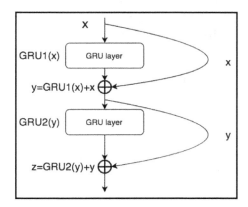

The decoder RNN module produces r mel-spectrogram frames, and only the last one is used by the pre-net during the next time-step. The choice of generating r frames, instead of one at each time-step, is motivated by the fact that one character in the encoder input usually corresponds to multiple frames. Therefore, by outputting one frame, we force the model to attend to the same input element for multiple time-steps, thus slowing down attention during training. Values of $r = 2$ and $r = 3$ are mentioned in the paper. Increasing r also reduces the model size and decreases the inference time.

The Griffin-Lim-based postprocessing module

The purpose of the postprocessing block is to convert the predicted mel-spectrogram frame into the corresponding waveform.

A CBHG module is used, right on top of the predicted mel-spectrogram frame, to extract both backward and forward features (thanks to the bidirectional GRU at the end), as well as to correct errors in the predicted frame. Thus, the raw spectrogram is predicted.

Even if a spectrogram is a good way to represent speech, it lacks information about the phase. Luckily, we have signal-processing algorithms such as Griffin-Lim (`https://ieeexplore.ieee.org/document/1164317/`), which can infer the likely speech waveform by estimating the phase from the spectrogram. It iteratively attempts to find the waveform whose STFT magnitude is closest to the generated spectrogram.

Details of the architecture

The Adam optimizer (`https://arxiv.org/abs/1412.6980`) is used with a particular learning rate schedule. Indeed, the learning rate is initialized at 0.001, and is then reduced to 0.0005, 0.0003, and 0.0001, after 500,000, 1 million, and 2 million global steps. A step is one gradient update. It shouldn't be confused with an epoch, which is a full cycle of gradient updates across the entire training dataset.

L1 loss is used for both the encoder-decoder that predicts the mel-spectrograms and the postprocessing block that predicts the spectrograms.

Limitations

The main contribution of Tacotron is undoubtedly the provision of an end-to-end deep learning-based TTS system that is intelligible and decently natural. Indeed, Tacotron's naturalness is assessed through the MOS, and is compared with a state-of-the-art parametric system and a state-of-the-art concatenative system (the same as in the WaveNet paper). Even though it remains less natural than the latter, it beats the former. Note that the MOS was assessed on a North American English dataset:

	North American English MOS
Tacotron	3.82 ± 0.085
Parametric	3.69 ± 0.109
Concatenative	4.09 ± 0.119

However, it is important to keep in mind that Tacotron is characterized by many simplistic design choices. For instance, the Griffin-Lim reconstruction algorithm is light and straightforward, but it is also known to cause artifacts that can negatively impact naturalness. Replacing this block of the pipeline with a more powerful technique could potentially further increase the MOS. Many other parts can be tuned and improved: the model's hyperparameters, the attention mechanism, the learning rate schedule, the loss functions, and more.

Now that we have a strong understanding of how Tacotron works, it is time to get our hands dirty and implement it.

Implementation of Tacotron with Keras

In this section, we will present an implementation of Tacotron by using Keras on top of TensorFlow. The advantage of Keras over vanilla TensorFlow is that it allows for faster prototyping. This is permitted by its high modularity. However, in terms of flexibility, TensorFlow has an edge over Keras, even if it requires more effort to master it. At the moment, TensorFlow also offers more built-in functionalities (for example, attention mechanisms), some of which will have to be re-implemented here.

We will use Keras 2.1.5 with TensorFlow 1.6.0 as a backend.

The code base is organized as follows:

- The /data folder is meant to contain the raw dataset, and will be enhanced through several processing steps.
- The /model folder contains the following:
    - building_blocks.py, which defines all of the essential units of the Tacotron model
    - tacotron_model.py, where the creation of the Tacotron model occurs
- The /processing folder contains the following:
    - proc_audio.py, which provides the audio processing functions, allowing us to transform the waveforms into spectrograms
    - proc_text.py, which allows for the transformation of the raw transcripts into a more suitable format for deep learning
- The /results folder will contain trained models, with their recorded losses.
- 1_create_audio_dataset.py generates the training and testing audio data (model target).

- `2_create_text_dataset.py` generates the training and testing text data (model input).
- `3_train.py` trains a model by using the training data, and saves it as well as its recorded loss history.
- `4_test.py` tests the last trained model on a chosen item of the testing dataset.
- `constants.py` contains all of the necessary constants.

The following are the most important Python modules used in this project. We haven't mentioned the different dependencies, since they should be automatically installed when `pip install` is triggered:

Module Name	Description
pandas	Used for data reading, processing, and analysis
NumPy	Provides data structures and methods for scientific computing
Scikit-learn	Contains many machine learning related processing methods
TensorFlow	Deep learning framework used as backend for Keras in this chapter
Keras	A simple and modular high-level API for the design of neural networks
Librosa	Gives processing functions for audio analysis
tqdm	Allows for the display of a progress bar to track the evolution of for - loops
Matplotlib	Can be used to visualize estimated and ground truth spectrograms and waveforms

The dataset

We will use the LJ Speech dataset for this task (`https://keithito.com/LJ-Speech-Dataset/`). It contains 13,100 `.wav` recordings with their corresponding transcripts. The transcripts are available in both their raw and normalized formats. In the normalized version of a transcript, numbers are written in full words.

The recordings were produced with the same voice. The total length of the audio content is roughly 24 hours, with samples that can last from 1 to 7 seconds. This dataset is in the public domain, and there are no restrictions on its use.

 Note that the dataset will occupy roughly 3.8 GB on your hard disk after the extraction of the ZIP file, downloadable from the aforementioned link.

The dataset folder contains a CSV file named `metadata.csv`, a README file, and a folder, `/wavs`, that contains the `.wav` audio files. `metadata.csv` is comprised of three columns, and each row corresponds to one of the 13,100 recordings. The first column gives the name of the corresponding `.wav` file, and the other two columns give the raw and normalized transcripts, respectively:

	0	1	2
0	LJ001-0001	Printing, in the only sense with which we are ...	Printing, in the only sense with which we are ...
1	LJ001-0002	in being comparatively modern.	in being comparatively modern.
2	LJ001-0003	For although the Chinese took impressions from...	For although the Chinese took impressions from...

Once downloaded, the ZIP file containing the data should be extracted in the `/data` folder.

Data preparation

To be able to train Tacotron, we need to apply several preprocessing steps on this dataset. We have to prepare the normalized text data in `metadata.csv`, so that it has the proper shape to be used as the input of the encoder. Also, we should extract the mel and magnitude spectrograms that will be output by the decoder and the postprocessing CBHG module, respectively.

The data can be loaded with the `read_csv` pandas. We need to take into account the fact that the CSV file does not contain any header, uses the pipe character to separate the columns, and contains quotation marks that are not always closed (the transcripts are not always full sentences):

```
metadata = pd.read_csv('data/LJSpeech-1.1/metadata.csv',
                       dtype='object', quoting=3, sep='|',
                       header=None)
```

We decided to use 90% of the data (11,790 million items) for training, and keep the remaining 10% for testing (1,310 items). This is an arbitrary choice, and we will define a variable, `TRAIN_SET_RATIO`, that can be tuned by the reader:

```
TRAIN_SET_RATIO = 0.9
```

Preparation of text data

As is typical in NLP tasks, all strings are converted into lowercase. Since the model will be considering sequences of characters (and not sequences of words), we obtain the training vocabulary as the set of unique characters used in the dataset. We add a character, P, that corresponds to padding, since we will need to define a fixed input length, NB_CHARS_MAX, and pad strings that are smaller than that:

```
list_of_existing_chars = list(set(texts.str.cat(sep=' ')))
vocabulary = ''.join(list_of_existing_chars)
vocabulary += 'P' # add padding character
```

Each character is then associated with an integer that will represent it:

```
# Create association between vocabulary and id
vocabulary_id = {}
i = 0
for char in list(vocabulary):
    vocabulary_id[char] = i
    i += 1
```

We are now ready to transform the text data. We define a function, `transform_text_for_ml`, which takes a list of strings, `list_of_strings`, where each string is a transcript; a dictionary, `vocabulary_ids`, which maps the characters in the vocabulary to integers; and the maximum number of characters per transcripts, `max_length`. Basically, this function transforms each transcript into a list of its characters (in their order of appearance, obviously) and adds as many padding characters as necessary (so that there are `max_length` characters):

```
def transform_text_for_ml(list_of_strings, vocabulary_ids, max_length):
    transformed_data = []

    for string in tqdm(list_of_strings):
        list_of_char = list(string)
        list_of_char_id = [vocabulary_ids[char] for char in list_of_char]

        nb_char = len(list_of_char_id)

        # padding for fixed input length
        if nb_char < max_length:
            for i in range(max_length - nb_char):
                list_of_char_id.append(vocabulary_ids['P'])
```

```
        transformed_data.append(list_of_char_id)

    ml_input_training = np.array(transformed_data)

    return ml_input_training
```

We can now apply this processing function:

```
text_input_ml = transform_text_for_ml(texts.values,
                                      vocabulary_id,
                                      NB_CHARS_MAX)
```

The Python script, `2_create_text_dataset.py`, loads the text data, processes it (as shown previously), divides the results into training and testing, and dumps both the training and testing sets as pickle files. The vocabulary dictionary that maps the characters with their associated integers is also saved:

```
# split into training and testing
len_train = int(TRAIN_SET_RATIO * len(metadata))
text_input_ml_training = text_input_ml[:len_train]
text_input_ml_testing = text_input_ml[len_train:]

# save data
joblib.dump(text_input_ml_training, 'data/text_input_ml_training.pkl')
joblib.dump(text_input_ml_testing, 'data/text_input_ml_testing.pkl')

joblib.dump(vocabulary_id, 'data/vocabulary.pkl')
```

Preparation of audio data

In this section, many terms from the signal processing world will be used. We will explain some of them, and we don't expect the reader to know about the others. This book is about deep learning per se, and we encourage curious readers to perform their own research on the signal processing notions that are not thoroughly explained.

We will use the following parameters (they are obtained from the paper) for the spectral analysis and processing of the `.wav` files:

Variable Name	Description	Value
N_FFT	Number of Fourier transform points	1024
PREEMPHASIS	Parameter of the pre-emphasis technique that gives more importance to high frequencies in the signal	0.97
SAMPLING_RATE	Sampling rate	16000

WINDOW_TYPE	Type of window used to compute the Fourier transform	'hann'
FRAME_LENGTH	Length of the window	50 ms
FRAME_SHIFT	Temporal shift	12.5 ms
N_melS	Number of mel bands	80
r	Reduction factor	5

 Even though the native sampling rate of the audio signals is 22.05 kHz, we have decided to use 16 kHz, to reduce the number of computational operations. Besides, the suggested number of Fourier transform points in the paper is 2,048. Here, we use 1,024 points, to make the task even lighter less burdensome.

The Tacotron model optimizes two objective functions: one for the mel-spectrogram output that comes out of the decoder RNN, and the other for the spectrogram output that is given by the postprocessing CBHG applied on the mel-spectrogram. Therefore, we need to prepare these two types of output.

First, from the file path of a `.wav` file, we return both the spectrogram and the mel-spectrogram of the signal:

```python
def get_spectros(filepath, preemphasis, n_fft,
                 hop_length, win_length,
                 sampling_rate, n_mel,
                 ref_db, max_db):
    waveform, sampling_rate = librosa.load(filepath,
                                           sr=sampling_rate)

    waveform, _ = librosa.effects.trim(waveform)

    # use pre-emphasis to filter out lower frequencies
    waveform = np.append(waveform[0],
                waveform[1:] - preemphasis * waveform[:-1])

    # compute the stft
    stft_matrix = librosa.stft(y=waveform,
                               n_fft=n_fft,
                               hop_length=hop_length,
                               win_length=win_length)

    # compute magnitude and mel spectrograms
    spectro = np.abs(stft_matrix)

    mel_transform_matrix = librosa.filters.mel(sampling_rate,
                                               n_fft,
                                               n_mel,
```

```
                                            htk=True)
    mel_spectro = np.dot(mel_transform_matrix,
                        spectro)

    # Use the decidel scale
    mel_spectro = 20 * np.log10(np.maximum(1e-5, mel_spectro))
    spectro = 20 * np.log10(np.maximum(1e-5, spectro))

    # Normalise the spectrograms
    mel_spectro = np.clip((mel_spectro - ref_db + max_db) / max_db, 1e-8,
1)
    spectro = np.clip((spectro - ref_db + max_db) / max_db, 1e-8, 1)

    # Transpose the spectrograms to have the time as first dimension
    # and the frequency as second dimension
    mel_spectro = mel_spectro.T.astype(np.float32)
    spectro = spectro.T.astype(np.float32)

    return mel_spectro, spectro
```

Then, we pad the time dimension of the spectrogram if its total length is not a multiple of r, so that it becomes a multiple of r:

```
def get_padded_spectros(filepath):
    filename = os.path.basename(filepath)
    mel_spectro, spectro = get_spectros(filepath)
    t = mel_spectro.shape[0]
    nb_paddings = r - (t % r) if t % r != 0 else 0 # for reduction
    mel_spectro = np.pad(mel_spectro,
                        [[0, nb_paddings], [0, 0]],
                        mode="constant")
    spectro = np.pad(spectro,
                    [[0, nb_paddings], [0, 0]],
                    mode="constant")
    return filename, mel_spectro.reshape((-1, N_mel * r)), spectro
```

get_padded_spectros is applied to all of the .wav files of the dataset through the 1_create_audio_dataset.py script. It then generates all of the spectrograms and mel-spectrograms as arrays, as well as the decoder's input. The three arrays are then split into training and testing datasets, in the same method used for the processed text data.

Note that running the script can take quite a long time (up to a few hours). That is why the resulting data is also pickled, so that we don't need to reprocess the files every single time we want to train a model.

Implementation of the architecture

Now that the data is ready, we can build the model. We will start by implementing the building blocks of the network, and we will then combine them. All of this is done in /model.

Pre-net

We will implement the pre-net block, which is being used in both the encoder and the decoder, as it is described in the paper. The simplicity and modularity of Keras make this part quite straightforward:

```
def get_pre_net(input_data):
    prenet=Dense(256)(input_data)
    prenet=Activation('relu')(prenet)
    prenet=Dropout(0.5)(prenet)
    prenet=Dense(128)(prenet)
    prenet=Activation('relu')(prenet)
    prenet=Dropout(0.5)(prenet)
    return prenet
```

Encoder and postprocessing CBHG

To prepare the code for the CBHG module, we first implement two of its major elementary units—the 1-D convolution bank and the highway network:

```
def get_conv1dbank(K_, input_data):
    conv=Conv1D(filters=128, kernel_size=1,
                strides=1,padding='same')(input_data)
    conv=BatchNormalization()(conv)
    conv=Activation('relu')(conv)

    for k_ in range(2,K_+1):
        conv=Conv1D(filters=128, kernel_size=k_,
                    strides=1,padding='same')(conv)
        conv=BatchNormalization()(conv)
        conv=Activation('relu')(conv)

    return conv
```

With Keras 2, the development team of Keras decided to remove highway networks, probably because they were rarely used, and also because they are quite easy to implement. Since we are using Keras 2, we need to explicitly write our own highway layer. We define the `get_highway_output` function, based on the highway network paper referenced previously. Given an input tensor, `highway_input`, it returns the output of a highway network defined by the `nb_layers` layers; an activation function, `activation`; and `initial_bias` (typically –1 or –3, according to the highway network paper):

```
def get_highway_output(highway_input, nb_layers, activation="relu",
bias=-3):
    dim = K.int_shape(highway_input)[-1] # dimension must be the same
    initial_bias = k_init.Constant(bias)
    for n in range(nb_layers):
        H = Dense(units=dim, bias_initializer=initial_bias)(highway_input)
        H = Activation("sigmoid")(H)
        carry_gate = Lambda(lambda x: 1.0 - x,
                            output_shape=(dim,))(H)
        transform_gate = Dense(units=dim)(highway_input)
        transform_gate = Activation(activation)(transform_gate)
        transformed = Multiply()([H, transform_gate])
        carried = Multiply()([carry_gate, highway_input])
        highway_output = Add()([transformed, carried])
    return highway_output
```

We are now ready for the implementation of the CBHG modules. The encoder and postprocessing CBHG differ slightly in their architectures. Even though we could have written only one function with extra input parameters, we decided to write two different functions, for more readability:

```
def get_CBHG_encoder(input_data, K_CBHG):
    conv1dbank = get_conv1dbank(K_CBHG, input_data)
    conv1dbank = MaxPooling1D(pool_size=2, strides=1,
                              padding='same')(conv1dbank)
    conv1dbank = Conv1D(filters=128, kernel_size=3,
                        strides=1, padding='same')(conv1dbank)
    conv1dbank = BatchNormalization()(conv1dbank)
    conv1dbank = Activation('relu')(conv1dbank)
    conv1dbank = Conv1D(filters=128, kernel_size=3,
                        strides=1, padding='same')(conv1dbank)
    conv1dbank = BatchNormalization()(conv1dbank)

    residual = Add()([input_data, conv1dbank])

    highway_net = get_highway_output(residual, 4, activation='relu')

    CBHG_encoder = Bidirectional(GRU(128,
```

```
        return_sequences=True))(highway_net)

    return CBHG_encoder

def get_CBHG_post_process(input_data, K_CBHG):
    conv1dbank = get_conv1dbank(K_CBHG, input_data)
    conv1dbank = MaxPooling1D(pool_size=2, strides=1,
                                padding='same')(conv1dbank)
    conv1dbank = Conv1D(filters=256, kernel_size=3,
                        strides=1, padding='same')(conv1dbank)
    conv1dbank = BatchNormalization()(conv1dbank)
    conv1dbank = Activation('relu')(conv1dbank)
    conv1dbank = Conv1D(filters=80, kernel_size=3,
                        strides=1, padding='same')(conv1dbank)
    conv1dbank = BatchNormalization()(conv1dbank)

    residual = Add()([input_data, conv1dbank])

    highway_net = get_highway_output(residual, 4, activation='relu')

    CBHG_post_proc = Bidirectional(GRU(128))(highway_net)

    return CBHG_post_proc
```

Attention RNN

As described previously, the attention RNN is a simple, 1-layer GRU. It contains 256 units, as defined in the paper. Defining a function for it looks like overkill, but it allows for better readability, especially since we have already described the architecture with the terminology used in the paper:

```
def get_attention_RNN():
    return GRU(256)
```

Decoder RNN

The decoder RNN is a 2-layer GRU with vertical residual connections (as explained previously):

```
def get_decoder_RNN_output(input_data):
    rnn1 = GRU(256, return_sequences=True)(input_data)

    inp2 = Add()([input_data, rnn1])
    rnn2 = GRU(256)(inp2)
```

```
decoder_rnn = Add()([inp2, rnn2])

return decoder_rnn
```

 Note that we have to use return_sequences=True when we define the first GRU layer. That way, for each input timestep, an output will be returned, so that, given a sequence as input, a sequence is output by the first GRU. If we don't do so, the first GRU returns only one output for the entire input sequence, while the second GRU expects a sequence as input.

The attention mechanism

The attention context is obtained by first concatenating the output vector generated by the bidirectional GRU layer of the CBHG-based encoder with the output of the attention RNN. Then, the resulting vector feeds a `tanh` activated dense layer, followed by another dense layer. A softmax layer allows for getting the activation weights that give the attention context, through a dot product with the encoder output vector:

```
def get_attention_context(encoder_output,attention_rnn_output):
    attention_input=Concatenate(axis=-1)([encoder_output,
                                          attention_rnn_output])
    e=Dense(10, activation = "tanh")(attention_input)
    energies=Dense(1, activation = "relu")(e)
    attention_weights=Activation('softmax')(energies)
    context=Dot(axes = 1)([attention_weights,
                          encoder_output])
    return context
```

Full architecture, with attention

Now, let's combine the previously defined functions to form the full Tacotron model.

But first, let's define some extra parameters that characterize the network:

```
NB_CHARS_MAX = 200 # maximum length of the input text
EMBEDDING_SIZE = 256

K1 = 16 # number of 1-D convolution blocks in the encoder CBHGH
K2 = 8 # number of 1-D convolution blocks in the postprocessing CBHG

BATCH_SIZE = 32
```

Note that the model is defined by two input objects and two output objects.

The two input objects correspond to the encoder input and the decoder input. The former is expected to be the input text. The latter should be the last mel-spectrogram frame, among the *r* frames predicted by the decoder before the postprocessing CBHG. The first frame of the decoder input is full of zeros, as shown in the paper.

The output corresponds to the mel-scaled spectrogram predicted by the decoder RNN, and the spectrogram predicted by the postprocessing CBHG module:

```
def get_tacotron_model(n_mels, r, k1, k2, nb_char_max,
                       embedding_size, mel_time_length,
                       mag_time_length, n_fft,
                       vocabulary):
    # Encoder:
    input_encoder = Input(shape=(nb_char_max,))

    embedded = Embedding(input_dim=len(vocabulary),
                         output_dim=embedding_size,
                         input_length=nb_char_max)(input_encoder)
    prenet_encoding = get_pre_net(embedded)

    cbhg_encoding = get_CBHG_encoder(prenet_encoding,
                                     k1)

    # Decoder-part1-Prenet:
    input_decoder = Input(shape=(None, n_mels))
    prenet_decoding = get_pre_net(input_decoder)
    attention_rnn_output = get_attention_RNN()(prenet_decoding)

    # Attention
    attention_rnn_output_repeated = RepeatVector(
        nb_char_max)(attention_rnn_output)

    attention_context = get_attention_context(cbhg_encoding,
attention_rnn_output_repeated)

    context_shape1 = int(attention_context.shape[1])
    context_shape2 = int(attention_context.shape[2])
    attention_rnn_output_reshaped = Reshape((context_shape1,
context_shape2))(attention_rnn_output)

    # Decoder-part2:
```

```
input_of_decoder_rnn = concatenate(
    [attention_context, attention_rnn_output_reshaped])
input_of_decoder_rnn_projected = Dense(256)(input_of_decoder_rnn)

output_of_decoder_rnn = get_decoder_RNN_output(
    input_of_decoder_rnn_projected)

# mel_hat=TimeDistributed(Dense(n_mels*r))(output_of_decoder_rnn)
mel_hat = Dense(mel_time_length * n_mels * r)(output_of_decoder_rnn)
mel_hat_ = Reshape((mel_time_length, n_mels * r))(mel_hat)

def slice(x):
    return x[:, :, -n_mels:]

mel_hat_last_frame = Lambda(slice)(mel_hat_)
post_process_output = get_CBHG_post_process(mel_hat_last_frame,
                                            k2)

z_hat = Dense(mag_time_length * (1 + n_fft // 2))(post_process_output)
z_hat_ = Reshape((mag_time_length, (1 + n_fft // 2)))(z_hat)

model = Model(inputs=[input_encoder, input_decoder],
              outputs=[mel_hat_, z_hat_])
return model
```

We can then compile the model. Since two output objects are defined, we need two loss functions. In the paper, two *l1* losses are picked, with equal weights. We have decided to do the same. Besides, Adam is used as an optimizer, with its parameters, by default. We decided to not follow the learning rate schedule used in the paper, to keep things simple. We encourage the reader to try more advanced settings:

```
opt = Adam()
model.compile(optimizer=opt,
              loss=['mean_absolute_error','mean_absolute_error'])
```

Training and testing

After the previous steps, training and testing can be achieved through 3_train.py and 4_test.py.

The first script trains a Tacotron model on the prepared training set across the NB_EPOCHS epochs, and then saves the model in the /results folder.

The second script allows the user to apply the previously saved model on any transcript of testing dataset. The selection of the audio to predict is done through a variable, `item_index`, which should contain the index (in the testing dataset) of the wanted item.

The estimated spectrogram is then converted to a waveform through the Griffin-Lim algorithm. The conversion function, `from_spectro_to_waveform`, is defined in the `/processing/proc_audio.py` file.

We strongly encourage the reader to change the default settings of the code base and to play around with more advanced approaches, in order to improve the quality of the generated waveform or the convergence speed of the model.

Summary

In this chapter, we provided an overview of the TTS field. We explained the criteria that a good TTS system should follow. We explored the tip of the iceberg in traditional TTS methods.

Then, we presented a state-of-the-art, end-to-end deep learning approach, Tacotron. Its implementation concluded the chapter, with instructions to experiment with the model on an open source dataset adapted to the problem.

In the third part of the chapter, we saw how Keras simplifies the process of building seemingly complex neural networks. However, making a prototype is one thing; scaling up is another thing. Indeed, even if a proof of concept runs smoothly on your computer, managing to make it functional for a large amount of users on different platforms (web and mobile) can be challenging, for many reasons (such as throughput). The next chapter will tackle the problem of shipping deep learning models to production environments.

Deploying Trained Models 13

In this chapter, you will learn how to deploy trained deep learning models to production environments on various platforms, such as cloud and mobile. For cloud deployment, the latency and throughput are important. The latency has to be at a minimum, and the throughput has to be high. The performance largely depends on the model and hardware. There are several optimizations available for CPU and GPU. For mobile platforms, speed, and energy consumption are important.

In this chapter, you will learn techniques to meet your deployment goals through the following topics:

- Increasing performance by changing models
- Using the TensorFlow serving tool
- Deploying to cloud services, such as AWS, GCP, and Azure
- Deploying to mobile devices, such as iPhone, Android, and Tegra
- The impact of hardware on performance

Increasing performance

Inference time depends on the **Floating-Point Operations Per Second (FLOPS)** required to run a model with hardware. The FLOPS is influenced by the number of model parameters and floating-point operations involved. The floating-point operations are mostly matrix operations, such as addition, products, and division. For example, a convolution operation has a few parameters representing the kernel, but takes longer to compute, as the operation has to be performed across the input matrix. In the case of a fully connected layer, the parameters are huge, but run quickly.

The weights of the model are usually double or high precision floating-point values, and an arithmetic operation on such numbers is more expensive than performing an operation on quantized values. In the next section, we will illustrate how quantizing the weights affects the model's performance.

Quantizing the weights

Quantizing the weights of a model reduces its floating-point precision. The weights of the model can perform with a reasonable accuracy metric, despite this reduction in the precision. Modern hardware can perform operations with less precision and with a lower computation time.

MobileNets

Howard et al. proposed a solution for faster inference with a learning paradigm. The following is an illustration of the use of mobile inference for various models. The models generated with this technique can be used to serve from the cloud, as well:

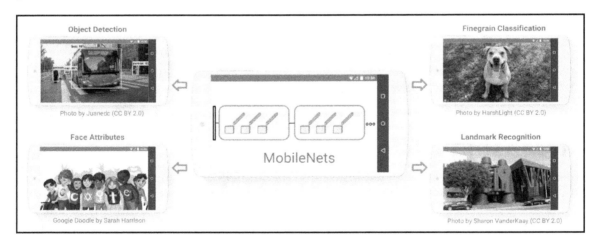

Reproduced from Howard et al.- Use of mobile inference for various models

There are three ways to apply convolution, as shown in the following diagram:

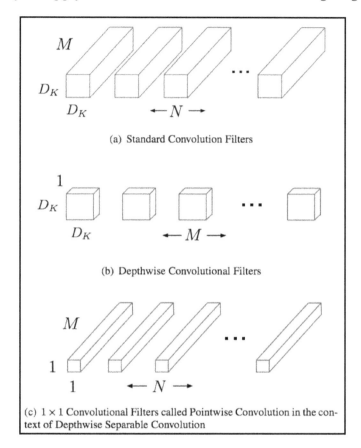

(a) Standard Convolution Filters

(b) Depthwise Convolutional Filters

(c) 1 × 1 Convolutional Filters called Pointwise Convolution in the context of Depthwise Separable Convolution

Reproduced from Howard, et al.

A normal convolution can be replaced with depthwise convolution, as follows:

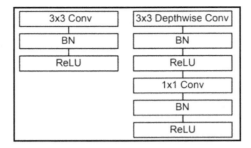

Reproduced from Howard, et al.

The following is a graph that represents the linear dependence of accuracy, with respect to the number of operations performed:

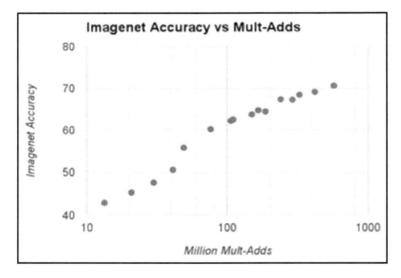

Reproduced from Howard, et al.

The following is a graph representing the accuracy dependence on the number of parameters. The parameters are plotted in a logarithmic scale:

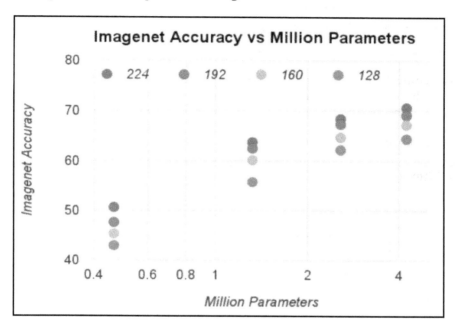

Reproduced from Howard, et al.

From the preceding discussion, it is clear that quantization gives a performance boost to the inference of models. In the next section, we will see how TensorFlow Serving can be used to serve models in production.

TensorFlow Serving

TensorFlow Serving is a project by Google that deploys models to production environments. TensorFlow Serving offers the following advantages:

- High speed of inference with good latency
- Concurrency, providing good throughput
- Model version management, so models can be swapped without a downtime in production

These advantages make TensorFlow Serving a great tool for deployment to the cloud. TensorFlow is served by a `gRPC` server. `gRPC` is a remote procedure call system from Google. Since most of the production environments run on Ubuntu, the easiest way to install TensorFlow Serving is by using `apt-get`, as follows:

```
sudo apt-get install tensorflow-model-serving
```

It can also be compiled from a source in other environments. Due to the prevalence of using Docker for deployment, it's easier to build it as an Ubuntu image. For installation-related guidance, please visit `https://www.tensorflow.org/serving/setup`.

The following figure shows the architectural diagram of TensorFlow Serving:

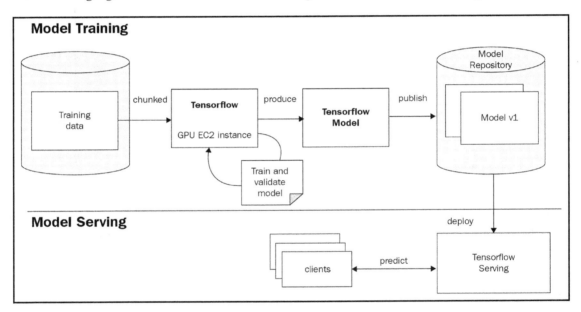

Once the model has been trained and validated, it can be pushed to the model repository. Based on the version number, TensorFlow Serving will start serving the model. A client can query the server using the TensorFlow Serving client. To use the client from Python, install the TensorFlow Serving API, as follows:

```
sudo pip3 install tensorflow-serving-api
```

The preceding command installs the client component of TensorFlow Serving. This can then be used to make inference calls to the server.

Exporting the trained model

The trained model can be saved by
using `tf.saved_model.builder.SavedModelBuilder` as a protocol buffer object. First,
we create the builder, input, and output tensor. The pseudocode that follows is to illustrate
the procedure. You have to replace the corresponding variables enclosed by <> with the
respective variables:

```
bldr = tf.saved_model.builder.SavedModelBuilder(<directory_to_export>)
tensor_inputs = tf.saved_model.utils.build_tensor_info(<inputs>)
tensor_outputs = tf.saved_model.utils.build_tensor_info(<outputs>)
```

The TensorFlow `utils.build_tensor_info` utility function helps us to create the
necessary input and output protocol buffers. Next, we will create the signature for the
inference protocol buffer:

```
inference_signature = (
tf.saved_model.signature_def_utils.build_signature_def(inputs={'inputs':
tensor_inputs},
    outputs={'predictions': tensor_outputs},
    method_name= tf.saved_model.signature_constants.PREDICT_METHOD_NAME)
```

The TensorFlow `signature_def_utils.build_signature_def` function can be used to
create the signature definition protocol buffer. After creating the inference signature, we
will export it and save it by using the `add_meta_graph_and_variables` function of the
model builder:

```
bldr.add_meta_graph_and_variables(tflow_s, [tf.saved_model.tag_constants.SER
VING],
    signature_def_map={ 'inference_results': inference_signature},
    legacy_init_op=<op_init>)
bldr.save()
```

This will save the model as a protocol buffer in the `export` directory.

Serving the exported model

Once the model has been exported, it can be started or served by
using `tensorflow_model_server`, with a command such as the following:

```
tensorflow_model_server --port=9000 --model_name=<modelname> --
model_base_path=<modelpath>
```

You can replace the <> with the corresponding model name and path where the model is exported.

Deploying in the cloud

There are many cloud vendors that can be used for deploying trained models. In this section, we will see the steps to use **Amazon Web Services (AWS)** and **Google Cloud Platform (GCP)**.

Amazon Web Services

AWS offers a number of products and solutions to support **machine learning (ML)**. First, let's look at how to use AWS to launch a simple machine, following these steps:

1. After logging into AWS, you will see the following screen:

Build a solution

Get started with simple wizards and automated workflows.

Launch a virtual machine
With EC2 or Lightsail
~1-2 minutes

Build a web app
With Elastic Beanstalk
~6 minutes

Host a static website
With S3, CloudFront, Route 53
~5 minutes

Connect an IoT device
With AWS IoT
~5 minutes

Start a development project
With CodeStar
~5 minutes

Register a domain
With Route 53
~3 minutes

2. Select the **Launch a virtual machine** option. Next, you will see the following screen:

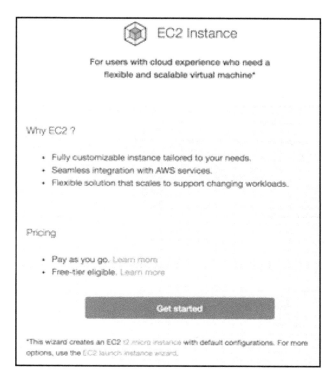

Getting started AWS screen

3. Click on **Get started** to go to the next screen, as follows:

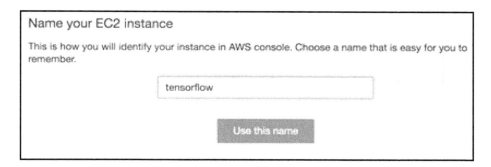

Entering your instance identity name

4. Enter a name (probably your own name) to go to the next screen:

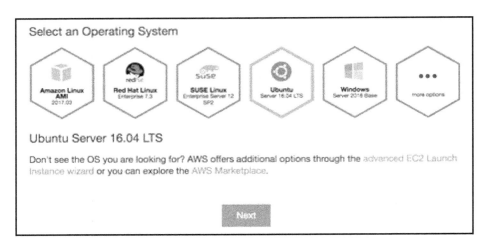

Selecting the operating system

5. Select the operating system for deployment. Ubuntu is a good choice:

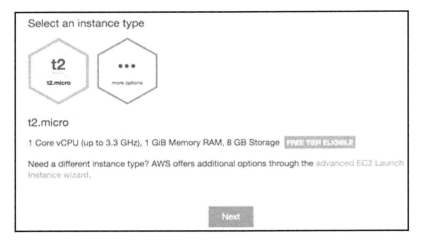

Selecting Ubuntu for deployment

6. Select the type of instance, based on the hardware requirements:

Create a key pair

Amazon EC2 secures your instance using a key pair. In this step you will download the private key to your computer.

Save it in a safe place and use it when you connect to your instance.

tensorflow

7. In order to log in to the machine, a key pair has to be created for security. Provide a name for the file:

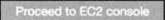

tensorflow
Status: Completed!

Verifying the machine name

8. You should see a status of **Completed,** as the preceding screenshot shows. Now, you can switch to the EC2 console by clicking on the following button:

Proceed to EC2 console

9. There will be a short pause, to launch the instance. Once the instance is created, an IP will appear for logging:

Launch Instance ▼ | Connect | Actions ⌄

Q Name : tensorflow   Add filter

	Name	⌄	Instance ID	⌃	Instance Type
▪	tensorflow		i-073f5797e4bcbb9e9		t2.micro

10. By clicking on the **Actions** button and choosing the **Terminate** button, one can terminate the instance, whenever required:

By following the preceding steps, one can create an instance with the required hardware and deploy TensorFlow Serving for inference to be queried by the client.

Google Cloud Platform

In GCP, one can create instances (like in AWS) and use them to serve models. One can log in by using Gmail; go to `https://cloud.google.com/`:

1. Click on the following button to go to the console:

2. All options are available to start the required instance. Choose **VM instances**, under **Computer Engine**:

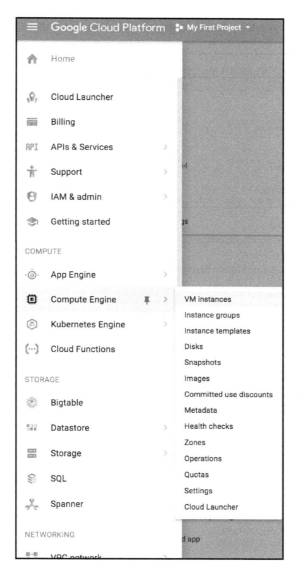

Selecting VM instance on the console

3. Then, click on **Create Instance**:

CREATE INSTANCE

4. Now, you can specify the number of cores and CPU required:

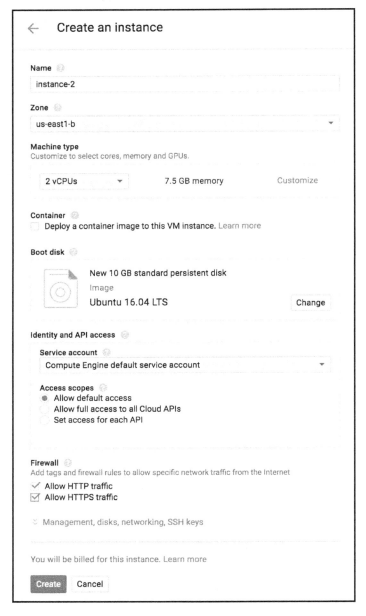

Selecting the requirement of cores, memory and GPUs

5. After some time, the instance will be available:

The instance can be accessed through a browser or SSH client, and can be used for serving models.

Deploying on mobile devices

Deploying models in a mobile environment has varying advantages, such as privacy and zero latency, as compared to the cloud. Famous mobile platforms, such as iPhone and Android, provide a lot of APIs that facilitate the deployment of models to mobile environments.

iPhone

Apple has introduced CoreML2 for ML-related apps. More details can be found at `https://developer.apple.com/machine-learning/`. There is a specific framework for **natural language processing** (**NLP**). There are pre-built APIs for tokenization, identifying a language, **parts of speech** (**POS**), named entity recognition, and so on. Custom models can be trained with as well. The use of CoreML models is fast in Apple devices. The data need not leave the device for inference. Most of the TensorFlow models can be converted to CoreML models.

Android

Android apps can use TensorFlow models directly without a lot of modification. Models can be exported (similar to exportation in TensorFlow Serving) and used in the apps. In order to increase the efficiency of the model, there is a set of instructions available with the Graph Transform tool. This can be used to remove the parts of the model that are used for training, thereby decreasing the size.

Summary

In this chapter, we looked at the various ways to deploy a trained model for NLP tasks. First, we learned about improving the performance of models by quantization, and we learned faster inference methods. Following that, we saw how TensorFlow Serving can be used to deploy models for faster and scalable inference. Finally, cloud deployment through AWS and GCP was explained. We concluded with a brief overview of deployment in some mobile platforms.

In this final chapter, we gave an overview of deploying trained models and serving them in the cloud. Equipped with this knowledge, you can further explore how to deploy your own models to production environments.

Other Books You May Enjoy

If you enjoyed this book, you may be interested in these other books by Packt:

Natural Language Processing with TensorFlow
Thushan Ganegedara

ISBN: 9781788478311

- Core concepts of NLP and various approaches to natural language processing
- How to solve NLP tasks by applying TensorFlow functions to create neural networks
- Strategies to process large amounts of data into word representations that can be used by deep learning applications
- Techniques for performing sentence classification and language generation using CNNs and RNNs
- About employing state-of-the art advanced RNNs, like long short-term memory, to solve complex text generation tasks
- How to write automatic translation programs and implement an actual neural machine translator from scratch
- The trends and innovations that are paving the future in NLP

Mastering Natural Language Processing with Python
Deepti Chopra

ISBN: 9781783989041

- Implement string matching algorithms and normalization techniques
- Implement statistical language modeling techniques
- Get an insight into developing a stemmer, lemmatizer, morphological analyzer, and morphological generator
- Develop a search engine and implement POS tagging concepts and statistical modeling concepts involving the n gram approach
- Familiarize yourself with concepts such as the Treebank construct, CFG construction, the CYK Chart Parsing algorithm, and the Earley Chart Parsing algorithm
- Develop an NER-based system and understand and apply the concepts of sentiment analysis
- Understand and implement the concepts of Information Retrieval and text summarization
- Develop a Discourse Analysis System and Anaphora Resolution based system

Leave a review - let other readers know what you think

Please share your thoughts on this book with others by leaving a review on the site that you bought it from. If you purchased the book from Amazon, please leave us an honest review on this book's Amazon page. This is vital so that other potential readers can see and use your unbiased opinion to make purchasing decisions, we can understand what our customers think about our products, and our authors can see your feedback on the title that they have worked with Packt to create. It will only take a few minutes of your time, but is valuable to other potential customers, our authors, and Packt. Thank you!

Index

placeholder, Tensorflow 134
Porter stemmer 33
POS tagger
  training 41, 43, 45
POS tagging
  about 38, 39
  applications 40
pretrained word embeddings, Named Entity
    Recognition (NER)
  effects 136
  neural network, architecture 138, 139
  predictions, decoding 140, 141
  training 141, 142, 146, 147

Q

Question-Answer (QA)
  about 175
  datasets 176
  memory networks for 176
  task 175
Quora 118

R

Rectified Linear Unit (ReLU) 54, 56, 230, 252
recurrent neural network (RNN)
  about 64, 91, 130, 149, 180, 223
  Long Short-Term Memory (LSTM) 65
  used, for generating text 149
regularization
  about 61
  batch normalization 62
  dropout 62
  L1 and L2 normalization 62
relation extraction 18
RNN model
  building, for speech recognition 224
  used, for identifying spam in YouTube video
    comments 98, 101, 103

S

semantic parsing 18
Semantic Role Labeling (SRL)
  reference link 17
sentence2vec 84, 85

sentiment classifier
  training, for movie reviews 45, 46, 47, 49
sentiment
  analyzing 12
short-time Fourier transform (STFT) 246, 256
sigmoid 55
skip-gram model
  about 73, 75
  building 76, 77, 78, 79
  comparing, with CBOW model 75
  word embeddings, visualization 79, 80, 82, 83
spam
  identifying, in YouTube video comments with
    RNN model 98, 101, 103
speaker identification
  reference link 26
speech recognition
  about 223
  RNN model, building for 224
  state-of-the-art, using 240
speech to text
  with DeepSpeech architecture 230
spoken dialog systems 27
spoken digit recognition
  LSTM model, using 226, 228
state-of-the-art
  used, in abstractive text summarization 170,
    171, 172
  used, in speech recognition 240
statistical machine translation (SMT)
  about 201, 202
  NLTK used 203, 205
stemming 33
stochastic gradient descent 61
stop words
  about 34
  removing 34
summarization
  with gensim 157
Support Vector Machines (SVMs) 130

T

Tacotron, architecture
  attention mechanism 267
  attention RNN 266

WordNet 29

Y

YouTube video comments
    spam, identifying with RNN model 98, 101, 103